1982

THE OVERREACHER

A Study of Christopher Marlowe

THE OVERREACHER

A Study of

Christopher Marlowe

by Harry Levin

GLOUCESTER, MASS.

PETER SMITH

1974

First published as a Beacon Paperback in 1964 by arrangement
with the Harvard University Press

Reprinted, 1974, by Permission of
Harvard University Press

ISBN: 0-8446-2458-6

To the memory
of DAVID PRALL

PREFACE

Marlowe's name is the one that comes after Shakespeare's in any discussion of English tragedy. The distance between the two is less than it might otherwise seem, when we recall that they were exact contemporaries, and that Marlowe made his contribution while Shakespeare was still emerging from his apprenticeship. This priority and ascendancy are duly registered in the histories and anthologies, which confirm the general tendency to consider Marlowe's work less for its own sake than as a landmark upon the way to Shakespeare's. What more difficult fate could there be for another writer, and what more critical test, than to have his name perennially bracketed with that of the greatest writer who ever lived? To have independently survived, and to have maintained an especially vital appeal for other writers, under the circumstances, count for much. But it must be admitted that lesser playwrights have managed to figure more frequently in the dramatic repertory, and that lesser poets have been made more available through the continued processes of evaluation and interpretation. Those mighty lines and purple passages could not easily have been forgotten; but, while they subsisted as fragments, they tended to obscure the seriousness of Marlowe's thought and to distort the integrity of his craftsmanship. As a pre-Shakespearean primitive, he held no position in English literature during its classical period. The appreciation he garnered, with the nineteenth century, came from such professional enthusiasts as Lamb and Swinburne. That professional cynic, Bernard Shaw, when he reviewed William Poel's revival of *Doctor Faustus* in 1896, dismissed the author as a "blank-verse beast."

During the two generations between the end of the nineteenth century and the middle of the twentieth, we have again learned to welcome poetry in the theater, as well as to contemplate violence in the world. Later revivals — Granville-Barker's *Edward II*, Orson Welles's *Doctor Faustus*, the Old Vic's recent production of *Tamburlaine* — have demonstrated Marlowe's stamina as an actor's dramatist. His direct assault on the ear recommends itself, at a time when the art of rhetoric is stimulated anew by the radio. His timeliness, on a more fundamental plane, is stressed in a current Italian study by Nicola D'Agostino, who finds a prognosis of modern disquietude in the "spiritual elephantiasis" of Marlowe's heroes. Marlowe was already, to Swinburne, the "soul nearest ours of all, that [was] most far." At this point, we may well find his remoteness quite as impressive as his proximity. It may be that today he seems more of a modernist than some of our men of letters, notably T. S. Eliot.

Yet there has been no more discerning critique than Mr. Eliot's, as set forth in his brief essay on Marlowe's verse and in succinct remarks elsewhere. George Santayana and William Empson have also contributed penetrating insights, which we could wish had been elaborated into essays on Marlowe. Beyond these very notable exceptions and a few others, it cannot be said that twentieth-century criticism has yet made its revaluation; nor has it attempted a reinterpretation on a scale commensurate with the interest of the theme — or, for that matter, with the effort that has been centered upon the comparable figure of John Donne.

Meanwhile scholarship, on the other hand, has documented Marlowe's life, and especially his death, with ingenuity and industry. The trend of biographical investigation, which reached its highly spectacular climax with Leslie Hotson's *Death of Christopher Marlowe*, has its rather perfunctory compendium in John Bakeless' *Tragicall History of Christopher Marlowe*. The record, though necessarily far from complete, is very much fuller now than it was a generation ago. Without ceasing to hope for unpredictable discoveries, we ought perhaps to admit that the inquest is over, that the likelier fields of documentation have been well gleaned, and that the latest findings confirm impressions which — as a matter of fact — have come down the centuries through rumor and surmise. With due gratitude to the investigators, we must not lose sight of the reasons that make the object worthy of their curiosity. When F. S. Boas, who has so helpfully elucidated many problems connected with it, undertook an interpretative synthesis, his large book faithfully mirrored the state of Marlovian studies: the chapter devoted to one of the dubious characters who happened to be present when Marlowe was killed is actually longer than the chapter on *Hero and Leander*. A subsequent volume by Michel Poirier succeeds in sustaining the French equilibrium between "the man" and "his work"; but the promised "esthetic evaluation" is neutralized by a so-called "psychological portrait"; and, rather too often, the mean that deftly yokes them together turns out to be moral judgment.

Biography proffers its handful of salient details, which help to triangulate Marlowe's artistic achievement. History offers more, since it views him as the most eloquent spokesman in England for the complex of attitudes and the sequence of undertakings that we vaguely term the Renaissance. The extent to which he was a man of his epoch, however, depends on the view that historians take of that epoch; and, since the days of that impassioned Marlovian, J. A. Symonds, their emphasis has shifted decidedly. The shift, in its turn, betrays the faltering allegiance of our own age to those ideals of worldly enlightenment which the sixteenth century put into operation. The renascence, as a rebirth of culture, was premised upon the notion of the Dark Ages; hence the advance of knowledge that retrospectively brightened the medieval picture has, by inevitable comparison, had a darkening effect on our approach to the ensuing period. Then, too, we have learned to differentiate England from the Continent in the arts and the classics, religion and education, science and trade. E. M. W. Tillyard has recently pushed these related questions to extremes by entitling a series of lectures *The English Renaissance: Fact or Fiction?* Though Dr. Tillyard gradually arrives at reassuring conclusions, and does not leave England — like Spain — in feudal darkness, he reveals a scholarly preference for stressing continuities at the expense of novelties. Had he selected his instances from the drama rather than from the lyric and the epic, he might have observed as swift and graphic a course of development as that which first led the chroniclers of Italian painting to formulate the conception of the Renaissance.

"Its great achievements," so the late Ernst Cassirer wisely summarized the controversy over the Renaissance, "lay much less in the new *content* it created — although that too is infinitely rich — than in the new *energies* it awakened and in the intensity with which these energies acted." This could also serve as an apt description of what might be called the Marlovian impetus. The doubts and aspirations that Marlowe voiced, the esthetic impulses and scientific curiosities, may be less typical of their time and place than has been commonly supposed; but to that extent he is the more original, and plays an even more strategic role than has been previously recognized. His combination of sensuous perception and speculative intelligence is not to be valued less because it is rare. Civilization is shaped and changed by genius and not by mediocrity — a consideration which intellectual historians, in their preoccupation with norms and survivals and backgrounds, sometimes neglect. The light that the history of ideas can throw upon Marlowe, and vice versa, is reflected in Paul H. Kocher's judicious monograph. The limitations of sheer historicism may be evinced by Dr. Kocher's failure, among less relevant names, to mention Goethe. Goethe could not have possibly influenced Marlowe, it might be retorted; and the retort would constitute an admission that the method was essentially genetic rather than philosophic. German scholars, on their side of the Faustian relationship, have done little except defend their poet against the imputation of foreign borrowing; while both sides have ignored the illuminating commentary that the situation holds for the drama of ideas.

The hazard of extracting ideas from the drama, of codifying incidental allusions into dogmatic professions, is exemplified in Roy W. Battenhouse's doctrinaire study of *Tamburlaine*. It should be added, in mitigation, that Marlowe is more expressly concerned with doctrine than most other playwrights. But his primary concern is the theater, and we shall not understand him without assimilating the Elizabethan theatrical conventions that he did so much to establish. Shakespeare was to modify and complicate Marlowe's stylization of experience; possibly for that very reason, Marlowe affords a sharper object lesson; with him the style is the man himself, to a degree which can seldom have been paralleled. We are interested in his "poetic" if not in his "practical" personality, to employ a Crocean distinction; and here the characteristics of an unusual mind have incisively molded a promising medium to their purposes. The result is not altogether bereft of parallels, and part of the present endeavor is to indicate some of them in classical and continental literature. Tradition, once it is pointed out, can only serve to emphasize Marlowe's originality. The most immediate manifestation is language, more particularly language projected from the stage. Therefore, with as much precision as we can bring to bear, we must explicate his poetry and his dramaturgy. We must try to bear in mind the idea that underlies the image, the gesture that accompanies the word. What David Masson — in connection with Shakespeare — termed "fervors" and "recurrences" should help us to retrace this configuration in Marlowe's own terms. The concept of hyperbole, which most of his critics have mentioned and none has defined, will provide a unifying key.

The very element of exaggeration that characterizes Marlowe's technique and outlook lends his writing its exemplary quality. We are fortunate in being able to keep the examples close at hand, since the one-volume Oxford edition of C. F. Tucker Brooke is readily procurable, and should indeed be reread in connection with the following chapters. Cross-reference from them to Brooke's text should be facilitated by the parenthetical line numbers; while further parentheses, enclosing in each case the standard numerical citation, refer to such other classics as are cited. Footnotes are thus dispensed with, and the modicum of secondary quotations and acknowledgments is dealt with alphabetically, chapter by chapter, under the title of "Authorities." To preserve the uniformity — or rather, to preserve the irregularity — of Elizabethan spelling, contemporary texts have been utilized, notably the First Folio of Shakespeare. A number of points, which must in passing be taken for granted, are amplified or illustrated by the Appendices. Still others probably need more qualification than the conditions of nontechnical discourse have allowed. Fortunately, the canon of Marlowe's works is more or less determined, and roughly coincides with the contents of Brooke's edition: specific queries can be met where they occur. The order is a more debatable matter, for Marlowe's productive career can hardly have lasted much longer than six years; none of his productions, with the exception of the anonymous *Tamburlaine*, was published during his lifetime, and most of them were maltreated by the printers. Yet, from one work to another, there seems to be a clearly discernible growth; and this evolution is not incompatible with the dates set by more external criteria. Individual debts can be acknowledged in context; a broad indebtedness to previous studies may be subsumed by referring the reader to Samuel A. Tannenbaum's bibliography.

This may be the occasion to correct a small mistake in Tannenbaum's supplement. There an apocryphal item, "Marlowe's Hyperbole," is listed under my name and the date 1940. In that year Professor H. N. Hillebrand, as chairman of the section on English drama, kindly invited me to read a paper at the meeting of the Modern Language Association. A change of plans intervened; the paper was neither read nor written; but the assiduous bibliographer picked up the title I tentatively proposed. I now feel that I am keeping a kind of engagement — or, at any rate, that this study is not gratuitously intruding into a closed subject. When the Trustee of the Lowell Institute extended a gracious invitation to me, I felt that the lecture hall — as middle ground between the stage and the library — might be the place for such a reconsideration as, I have long been convinced, Marlowe deserves from an educated public. These lectures are printed, with some addenda, substantially as delivered. They owe much to the facilities of the Houghton and Widener Libraries, and to the privilege I have enjoyed of discussing Elizabethan drama with graduate students at Harvard University and Radcliffe College during the past twelve years. In particular, I am indebted to John R. Moore for his help in gathering statistics. Among my colleagues, who have as always been stimulating and patient, I am particularly grateful to Perry Miller and John L. Sweeney for improving my manuscript with their suggestions. I am grateful to Edmund Wilson not only for encouraging conversations, but for letting me use his books at a time when I had access to no others.

I must thank the Liveright Publishing Corporation for permission to quote four lines from *The Collected Poems of Hart Crane*, copyright 1933 by Liveright, Inc. The problems of publication have been eased, at every stage, by the thoughtfulness of Thomas J. Wilson. The burdens of preparation have been lightened by the helpfulness of Eleanor Towle. My deepest obligation is one which I am enjoined from expressing.

HARRY LEVIN

Cambridge, Massachusetts
January 21, 1952

Contents

Chapter **I**

THE END OF SCHOLARISM

For a brief moment again a few years ago, Christopher Marlowe became what he had often been to his contemporaries: a subject of public inquiry. Somehow his name got enunciated before a Congressional hearing, whereupon an honorable gentleman raised the routine question: "Is he a Communist?" The witness, Mrs. Hallie Flanagan Davis, vindicating the admirable record of the Federal Theater Project, was able to submit a historical alibi. Yet the allegation was no farther fetched than many that have been finding their way to those quarters, and inquisitorial instinct is true to itself in sniffing the effluvia of brimstone across a distance of three and a half centuries. English poetry has its radical affiliations, which range back through Shelley and Blake toward Milton and Langland, not to mention the subsiding ardors of Wordsworth or Auden. But no other poet has been, so fully as Marlowe, a fellow-traveler with the subversive currents of his age. The witch-hunters of his age — an age which really believed in witches and all too literally burned them, along with persons suspected of heresy, of sodomy, and other dangerous thoughts or peculiar actions — counterattacked subversion just as loosely and just as vituperatively as some of our publicists have been doing lately. But, being Elizabethans, they had the advantage of a richer and more colorful vocabulary. Though they could hardly have accused Marlowe of Communism, they had other charges to fling. They called him an Atheist, a Machiavellian, an Epicurean.

History shows us, however, that yesterday's revolutions settle down into today's assumptions; and, when we reconsider the terms of this threefold indictment, we find it hard to be shocked. What is shocking, indeed, is how men's careers — and sometimes their lives — can hinge on vague epithets; how the Socinians, to cite an instance close to our subject, could go to the stake for professing a modification of Christian doctrine which nowadays would pass for respectable Unitarianism. We shall recognize, in Marlowe's so-called Atheism, a point of view which can be broadly designated as natural religion. Nor should we flinch at avowals of Machiavellianism, having survived the abandonment of so many political ideals to acknowledge *Realpolitik* as the virtual law of nations. As for Epicureanism, we cannot but consider it a soft impeachment; such a fondness for the good things of life, conceived as esthetic tastes rather than moral values, we like to think we inherited from the

Elizabethans. They sang, as we like to remember, about eating, drinking, and making merry; they also sermonized, less memorably but more extensively, about pestilence, sin, and death. They voiced their disapproval of libertines by calling them "merry Greeks," and Greece itself commanded no widespread approval among a people who claimed descent from the Trojans. Nor was the road from Italy as open as it may seem when retrospectively viewing the Renaissance. Englishmen condemned it as a continuous source of popery, poison, and plotting, all of which were incarnate in the sinister caricature of the Florentine politico who shared his nickname with the devil.

Looking northward toward the Reformation was no less unsettling; for "Divisions in Religion" were, as Bacon pointed out, the first cause of disbelief; and when Protestants divided from Catholics, or Puritans from Anglicans, they devoted much of their zeal to controverting each other's doctrines. This stimulated more curious minds to look beyond the orbit of Christianity itself. Echoing the pagan rationalism of Lucretius, Marlowe is reported to have said: "That the first beginning of Religioun was only to keep men in awe." But Lucretius, though he rejected deities, had invoked Venus and Mars to personify the forces of creation and destruction that moved his restless universe, the interplay between desire and conflict, organic growth and elemental strife. Following Epicurus himself, the Greek philosopher who had proved his worthiness to be numbered among the gods by having dispelled them, the Roman poet had proceeded logically from a materialistic system of metaphysics toward a hedonistic code of ethics. Between the sphere of nature and that of the individual, between Atheism and Epicureanism as thereby defined, lay that middle domain of society which can appropriately be delimited by the realism of Machiavelli. Thus the Marlovian trinity was based on positive, if heretical, premises; and its three articles of belief were closely related, if not interchangeable. In the same breath, which was all but his dying breath, Robert Greene could warn Marlowe against both "Machiuilian pollicy" and "Diabolicall Atheisme." And after Marlowe's even more notorious death, a contemporary preacher could point the moral in a chapter entitled "Of Epicures and Atheists."

Thanks partly to recent research and partly to Marlowe's habit of getting into trouble with the authorities, his escapades and blasphemies can be documented by a substantial body of external evidence. If — as the accusations run — he composed irreligious tracts, these have not been handed on to us. But it is well attested that he preached irreligion wherever he went, telling men not to be afraid of "bugbeares and hobgoblins." He seems to have made one convert whose testimony links Marlowe's skepticism with Sir Walter Ralegh's. Ralegh, who might almost have served as a living model for Marlowe's theatrical heroes, also came under investigation for allegedly sponsoring an atheistic school, where disciples were taught to smoke tobacco, scoff at the Bible, and spell the name of God backwards. A more authentic link between the two men was their friend, Thomas Harriot, the scientist whose pioneering experimentation seemed more impressive to Marlowe than Biblical miracles. Those had been nothing but juggler's tricks — or so it is recorded, along with a flow of ribaldries calculated to scandalize Marlowe's hearers, and commentaries revealing a serious interest in higher criticism. His Atheism is more explicit than his Machiavellianism, since the latter sets deeds above words by definition. Yet there too records exist to show, at first hand, an unhealthily circumstantial and ultimately fatal acquaintance with intrigue and violence. Whether he was more spied against than spying is arguable, entangled as he seems to have been in a network of counterespionage. On one suspicion and another, he began and ended his career under the ever-watchful eyes of the Privy Council. He was arrested for street fighting on at least two occasions, one of which involved his companion in homicide and Marlowe in a fortnight's imprisonment.

The sudden end of all this, the catastrophe, was uniquely edifying to moralists who bespoke poetic justice from the human drama. For Marlowe to have been killed in a tavern brawl which he provoked — to have been stabbed at Deptford, as it turned out, by his own dagger — was to have been outdone at his own game by the very hand of Providence. It was, with a vengeance, the Atheist's tragedy. The company, a trio of secret agents, was distinctly Machiavellian. The setting was Epicurean: that unhallowed place where prodigals were tempted in the morality plays, where Falstaff would stage his apology for the fleshpots, where the wandering clerks of the Middle Ages had proposed to die — *in taberna mori*. Elsewhere the witnesses testify to Marlowe's preoccupation with

THE OVERREACHER

forbidden pleasures, as instanced by his gibe: "That all they that loue not Tobacco & Boies were fooles." We should pay little attention to such hearsay if it did not underline tendencies which, we shall notice, are writ large throughout his work. All that we know about his character supports the impression of meteoric precocity, flamboyant brilliance, intellectual recklessness. Thomas Kyd, among those who bore witness against his "monstruous opinions," characterized him as "intemperate & of a cruel hart." It was precisely to characters like himself, "stiffe-necked and high minded," that the story of Dr. Faustus, the ultimate spokesman for his Atheism, had first been addressed. In short, it was an incendiary genius that crackled beneath the smoke of his reputation. And, though he had already been dead six years, it is fitting that his *Elegies* should have been cast into the Bishops' bonfire of 1599.

But we must oppose the iconoclast to his idols. When we recall that he was born in the cathedral town of Canterbury and that his family was connected with the gentle craft of shoemakers, Marlowe's iconoclasm stands out against the most solid traditions of church and guild. Under a scholarship from the humanistic archbishop, the late Matthew Parker, he was enrolled at Cambridge in 1581 at the age of seventeen. The rest of his life consists of two six-year periods, one at the university and the other in London. As a student, to judge from the archives of Corpus Christi College, he was less and less regularly in attendance. Having taken his bachelor's and master's degrees, a young man in his circumstances was then expected to take orders, to qualify himself as a minister or schoolmaster. To take, instead, the highroad to the metropolis was the apostasy of Marlowe's generation. That this was no primrose path is made fiercely explicit by his fellow Cantabrigian, Thomas Nashe, in the epistle prefacing Greene's *Menaphon*, "To the Gentlemen Students of both Universities." Greene, who prided himself upon being a master of arts from both universities, who barely managed to maintain a Bohemian existence by practicing all the available sorts of hack-writing, was to find his graceless vocation in journalistic exposures of the underworld. Nashe lamented the plight of the scholar-poet, wavering between the cloister and the printshop, vainly seeking patronage or preferment, and finally straying into the purlieus of the theater. This last resort was so dissolute and desperate that it inspired a punning sneer at the capers of Kyd, the townsman whose popularizations of Senecan tragedy were leading the scholarly flock astray.

Humanistic studies at Oxford and Cambridge, which had burgeoned in the epoch of Erasmus, declined somewhat in the second half of the sixteenth century. We can explain the decline by the very advance of creative literature for which they had opened the way, and by the displacement of talent when gentlemen-students doffed their gowns. But to an elder academic contemporary, like Gabriel Harvey, this movement was a treason of the clerks, a great betrayal. His controversy with Nashe was not less vociferous because Nashe might have become a bookish don and Harvey a literary free-lance. Clinging to the bosom of Alma Mater, Harvey speculated about the world; along the margins of his folios, he scribbled his yearnings for success and fame, his admiration of Alexander and Cæsar. Conscientiously, and a little wistfully, he noted disparities between theory and experience. Like a good scholar, he endeavored to learn all the worldly knowledge that books could teach him. Hence he made a special point of studying Machiavelli and took a sly satisfaction in the uncloistered hyperboles of Aretino:

> Mach: & Aretine knew y^r lessons by hart & were not to seeke howe to vse ye wicked world, ye flesh, & ye Diuel. They had lernid cunning enowgh: and had seen fasshions enowgh: and cowld & woold vse both, with aduantage enowgh. Two curtisan politiques.
>
> Schollars, & common youthes, euen amongst ye lustiest, & brauist courtiers; ar yet to lerne y^r lesson in ye world.
>
> Vita, militia: uel Togata, uel Armata.

Whether one wore the scholar's gown or the soldier's armor, life could be a battle. If it were so for the pedantic Harvey, how could it be otherwise for younger intellectuals, soldiers of fortune who — preferring action to contemplation — rejected the life of wisdom to live by their wits? The concept of wit itself depreciated, as they learned their lesson in the world. To the humanists it had been *Euphues*, a synonym for intelligence and imagination. Now it became *savoir-faire* or cunning, and pecuniary need was the whetstone that sharpened it. Still later, when Pope was playing upon its accumulated meanings, the word would be used to label a man about town. But here, where we encounter the University Wits, we are watching the transition from a monastic culture to a popular art.

That art, the drama, was originally rooted in religious observ-

THE OVERREACHER

ance; but over the preceding century it had been secularized. Interludes, supplanting the mysteries and moralities, were acted by troops of professional entertainers rather than by the amateurs of the medieval guilds. Meanwhile the revival of the classics had prompted schools and colleges to revive, perform, and imitate the tragedies and comedies of the ancients. Then, with the coronation of Elizabeth, the scene was set for a national pageant in which the actual theater was to present a play-within-the-play. The performance started slowly during the 1560's at the Inns of Court, on strategic ground between the academies and the court itself, with a series of experiments devised to reconcile classical form with native material. The peregrinations of strolling players, from village green to innyard, reached a congenial haven when playhouses were erected during the seventies. Thespis has inhabited many mansions, differing as widely as the orchestra of the Greeks differed from the modern proscenium. In this development from the horizontal to the vertical and from stylized presentation to naturalistic representation, the Elizabethan playhouse incorporated advantages from both: its centralized stage was nearly surrounded by spectators, yet backed by a tiring house which not only sheltered the actors but provided them with curtains, balconies, and scenic contrivances. We may doubt whether any arrangement has ever been better adapted to meet the basic problem of staging, as Goethe put it in the prologue of his *Faust*: to bring about the whole cycle of creation, quickly shifting from heaven through earth to hell, within a cramped house of boards.

With theaters built and companies trained and audiences gathering, what the mid-eighties needed most was a group of gifted writers who were rash enough to attempt playwriting as a profession. This was the cue for the University Wits. There was considerable variance among their gifts, which were not equally suited to the new medium. John Lyly deftly cultivated the witty conceits and artificial mazes of courtly comedy. George Peele would have been an exquisite lyrist, had the theatrical trend not forced him to strain his note. Greene, with his transmutations from Euphuism to muckraking, proved to be a literary chameleon; while Nashe and Thomas Lodge were more at home in argumentative prose. "If ever there was a born poet, Marlowe was one," declared a later and lesser poet, Leigh Hunt. What was even more to the purpose, in a period which already boasted its Sidney and Spenser but had still to achieve its preëminence in dramatic poetry, Marlowe was a born playwright. It was for him to discover that dominant mode, to explore and chart and extend its potentialities. It is not surprising that the stage historian, in quest of conventions, is balked by his plays and more easily rewarded by the work of less original minds. Many of their conventions were Marlowe's innovations. Yet, despite his conspicuous leadership, his career of high thinking and low living was even shorter and more hazardous than theirs, and the University Wits were all a lost generation. Having made their contribution within a decade, more or less, they were soon written out; and the upstart crow against whom Greene warned his fellows, the mother-wit William Shakespeare, was left in possession of the stage. To the extent — the prodigious extent — that he profited from the lessons they learned and taught, they had practiced the calling for which Cambridge and Oxford prepared them; they had been schoolmasters after all.

But the gulf between pedagogy and practice was widening again by the turn of the century, as we may infer from the Christmas trilogy produced at St. John's College, Cambridge. The first of those plays, *The Pilgrimage to Parnassus*, allegorizes the undergraduates' journey through the arts, hinting that their sojourn in the land of poetry might be a preparation for the ill-famed theatrical district of London — the district, incidentally, where Marlowe had sojourned:

> Here are entisinge Pandars, subtile baudes,
> Catullus, Ouid, wantome Martiall:
> Heare them whilest a lasciuious tale they tell,
> Theile make thee fitt in Shorditche for to dwell. (514–7)

For the graduates, the city holds more disappointment than temptation, corroborating a maxim paraphrased from Marlowe's *Hero and Leander*:

> Learninge and pouertie will euer kiss. (I, 76)

Consequently, the second and third parts of the trilogy, *The Return from Parnassus*, exhibit "the vnpleasing fortunes of discontented schollers" (II, 50). Having tried their hands at everything else unsuccessfully, they are reduced to "the basest trade," that of acting (II, 1846). The two leading actors of Shakespeare's company interview them in person and bear out, from the opposing side, the mutual distrust of town and gown. "Few of the vniuersity pen plaies well," says Will Kempe to Dick Burbage, "they smell too much of that writer *Ouid,* and that writer *Metamorphoses,* and talke too much of *Proserpina* & *Iuppiter*" (II, 1766–8). Forgetting that this passage satirizes the players rather than the would-be playwrights, we are likely to read it in the chilly light of our indifference to mythical allusion. We are so far removed from Latinity that we confound the classical with the scholastic. We tend to forget that conversely, in the ascetic lamplight of St. John's, it might not have been easy to distinguish the smells of Parnassus and Shoreditch; or that scanning a set of elegiacs could, to a susceptible Latinist, be an incantation for raising the spirit of Helen of Troy; or that if scholars were poets, as Nashe hoped they would be, the ancient metaphors would come alive.

When Caroline Spurgeon asserts that Marlowe's images are chiefly drawn from books, she includes the classics in that category. These comprise the largest single area of reference, to be sure; but the inference is misleading, since it assumes that Proserpina and Jupiter had no more sensuous immediacy for Marlowe than they have for Miss Spurgeon. She is concerned to emphasize the contrast between Marlowe's book-learning and Shakespeare's lore of nature. But nature, which is cosmic as well as domestic, embraces the starry regions of Marlowe's imagery as well as Shakespeare's gardens and hunting scenes. And Shakespeare's writing, during Marlowe's lifetime, was quite as heavily loaded with classical freight. It would seem that both writers started under the same poetic influence. Ovid, long exiled among the Goths, moralized by the Middle Ages, spoke again directly to the Renaissance; and his *Metamorphoses* supplied the Elizabethans with their favorite handbook of mythology. Where their Petrarchan sonnets dwelt upon the psychological tergiversations of courtship, Ovid's *Amores* brought a pair of lovers together in physical shamelessness, glorying like rediscovered sculpture in the naked contours of the body. Little of this erotic tension is lost in Marlowe's translation, posthumously published under the title of *Elegies* though probably undertaken as an academic diversion. Now and then he roves beyond the Ovidian situation — which is seldom other than a forthright proposal from the poet to his mistress — as when *ambitiosus amor* is translated "my ambitious ranging minde" (II, iv, 48). But when the poet feels guilty of having ignored more warlike themes, or bethinks himself of addressing some statelier muse than wanton Elegia, Ovid speaks rather for Marlowe than for himself:

Then with huge steps came violent *Tragedie*.   (III, i, 11)

Tragedy, it would seem, was preceded by a glance in the direction of the epic: by Marlowe's English version of the first book of Lucan's *Pharsalia*. That poem, according to the dean of rhetoricians, Quintilian (X, i, 90), was a better model for orators than for poets. Marlowe may well have felt a temperamental kinship with the brilliant Lucan, Seneca's short-lived nephew, who had repudiated myth for history; and who had celebrated, in lurid and sanguinary hexameters, the struggle for power between Cæsar and Pompey — those "Captaines emulous of each others glory" (120). His portrait of the cruel and self-seeking tyrant, Julius Cæsar, along with the omens and roll calls, the martial oratory and Near Eastern coloring, the strident alarums and spectacular excursions, would have heralded *Tamburlaine* even if Marlowe had not gone out of his way to insert the phrase, "conquering swords," into the invocation as a kind of signature, or replaced *signis* a few lines later with "trumpets, and drums." He could not have selected two Roman exemplars more unlike each other than Lucan, the clangorous laureate of civil war, and Ovid, the mellifluous singer of the loves of the gods. His own strain would modulate back and forth between those two registers, lyric seduction and epic conquest, between the respective modes of Venus and Mars. Ovid's elegiacs, rendered into heroic couplets, must have helped Marlowe afterward to set and sustain the elegant pace of *Hero and Leander*. A sensitive metrist, Ezra Pound, would argue that they also helped to establish the formalized cadence of eighteenth-century classicism. But, metrically speaking, Marlowe's rendering of Lucan carries vastly greater significance; for the fact that the Latin is rendered line-by-line sets the pace for his clear-cut articulation; and here presumably are his first attempts at mastering a line which, by virtue of his mastery, would become the standard meter of English drama.

The Earl of Surrey had utilized blank verse for a similar purpose when he had introduced it into English poetry some forty years before, in translating the second and fourth books of Vergil's *Æneid*.

His translation was published ten years after his death, along with Tottel's *Miscellany* of 1557, which also contained two poems in Surrey's "straunge meter," epic fragments translated from the neo-Latin by Nicholas Grimald. The crucial step was taken upon an emergent occasion, when the experimental tragedy of *Gorboduc* was acted before the Queen by members of the Inner Temple in 1562. One of its coauthors, Thomas Norton, had made previous use of blank verse in the course of a prose translation which quoted a few lines from Vergil. Thus it seems to have been accepted as a rough equivalent for the Latin hexameter and to have met halfway the demands of prosodists like Harvey, who were striving to classicize the vernacular. In other ways, it could be regarded as continuing the basic rhythm of English verse, since Chaucer wrote largely in rhymed iambic pentameters. Sometimes it seemed a reversion to the conditions of Anglo-Saxon prosody, with alliteration heavily compensating for lack of end-rhymes and a tendency for lines to break into doubly accented halves. So, in 1576, George Gascoigne could write his satire, *The Steel Glass*,

> In rymeless verse, which thundreth mighty threates.

For, explains "The Author to the Reader,"

> rimes can seldome reache,
> Unto the toppe, of such a stately Towre.

Gascoigne, at Gray's Inn in 1566, had collaborated on *Jocasta*, another tragedy in rhymeless verse. But mighty threats, on the popular stage, still resounded in fourteeners — in rhyming couplets which, when the thunder had died away, sounded exactly like the old ballad quatrains. This is *Cambyses'* vein, which Falstaff mentioned but did not illustrate:

> Doo not intreat my grace no more, for he shal dye the death!
> Where is the execution-man him to bereave of breath?   (433–4)

No effort to employ the new measure seems to have been made by the University Wits before the advent of Marlowe, with one significant exception. That was Peele's *Arraignment of Paris*, which is written primarily in decasyllabic couplets, but drops into blank verse two or three times when characters are required to make formal orations. Peele seems to have shared a general feeling that unrhymed iambic pentameter was the right poetic idiom for public speech, as he later exemplified in his scenario for a tournament at court, *Polyhymnia*. Such a view must also have affected the authors and producers of *Gorboduc*, lawyers whose forensic training disposed them to state an issue through a sequence of arguments *pro* and *contra*. Their successor to *Gorboduc* was *Gismund of Salerne*, which happened to be elaborately rhymed; but significantly it was transposed into blank verse "according to the decorum of these daies," when it was revised for publication in 1591.

Marlowe's intervention had, in the meanwhile, fixed the measure so decisively that other playwrights had perforce to adopt it. Greene, reluctantly following, admitted that he could not make his verses "iet vpon the stage in tragicall buskins . . . daring God out of heauen with that Atheist *Tamburlan*," and pointed the blame at mad and scoffing poets, "bred of Merlin's race . . . that set the end of scollarisme in an English blank verse." His resentful wordplay hit a mark, if it assigned to Marlowe the dual role of heretic and magician, upsetting an older order while casting spells of his own. This is no less evident in Marlowe's versification than in his ideas and activities. The decasyllabics of his predecessors, contrasted with his, sound tentative and irregular. Lopping and stretching words in Procrustean fashion, they fumble toward the norm of regularity. *Tamburlaine* achieves it with perfect ease and authoritative sonority, hitting each note upon the beat as it were, pausing for breath in the middle of the line and again more sharply at the masculine ending. Once the fundamental stress is established, shifts become possible and indeed desirable. Marlowe's subsequent writing begins that process of reiteration, syncopation, and variation which ramifies into Shakespeare's enjambments, Fletcher's feminine endings, and Milton's disciplined irregularities. Marlowe not only catches the melody of Spenser, as T. S. Eliot has remarked; he orchestrates it for the theater. There are no dissonances in either poet, but their harmonies can be too obvious. Both of them confronted the English language when it had just ripened to offer poets the optimum of possibilities, its unique combination of simplicity and variety, a highly flexible syntax and an incomparably rich vocabulary.

Marlowe's diction, profiting from this richness, attains its speed by means of polysyllables and its resonance by means of proper names. Whenever these two join forces at the end of a line, the emphasis is particularly strong, as *Tamburlaine* will repeatedly demonstrate. It is a far cry from the homely archaism of Surrey, where one verse often bogs down into ten harsh monosyllables, to what Nashe aptly termed "the spacious volubilitie of a drumming decasillabon," where the mouth-filling Latinate phraseology is continually amplified by mythological and geographical reverberations. All this is kept under firm control by the line itself, which — largely through Marlowe's avoidance of run-overs — becomes a syntactic as well as a metrical unit, coinciding with a single clause from a periodic sentence of as many as a dozen lines. By piling one such unit on top of another, he builds up those larger structures of discourse which, therefore, ought to be called verse-sentences rather than verse-paragraphs. When Nashe speaks of botching out verses with "ifs" and "ands," he indicates how the momentum of a speech can be suspended by conditional clauses and prolonged by a series of double predicates and appositional phrases. Their effect is to pad the sharp grammatical skeleton; whence the Elizabethan term for padding, "bombast," is applied not merely to actors' costumes but to their locutions. Again, when Nashe speaks of "the swelling bumbast of bragging blanke verse," he illustrates how Marlowe keeps an internal balance by modifying nouns with participles. The adjective is energized by the verb when he characteristically substitutes "shining" for "bright" or "mounting" for "high" or "fainting" for "low." The parts of speech, like the spheres that form his cosmos, are ever-moving.

The dynamism of Marlowe's language is slightly dulled for us, perhaps, by the fact that his imitators could soon reduce it to a bombastic formula. To recapture something of its impact, and of the difference between the printed word and the vocal projection, we are approaching him by way of his forerunners. At a jump he recapitulated their evolution by basing his early tragedy, *Dido, Queen of Carthage*, upon the opening books of the *Æneid*. These books, comprising the most dramatic part of Vergil's poem, were to reëcho in the theater. When Gorboduc's queen rebukes their guilty son, she echoes Dido's parting rebuke to Æneas:

> Ruthelesse, vnkinde, monster of natures worke,
> Thou neuer suckt the milke of womans brest,
> But from thy birth the cruell Tigers teates
> Haue nursed thee, nor yet of fleshe and bloud
> Formde is thy hart, but of hard iron wrought.   (IV, i, 71–5)

THE END OF SCHOLARISM   13

This is much smoother than Surrey's English, which falters awkwardly when it comes up against classical names. *Gorboduc*, in this domesticated passage, can leave them out; but it cannot avoid the rigidity of inversion; whereas *Dido* can assimilate them into its easy flow and decisive beat. Marlowe leads his queen rather self-consciously into the speech:

> And wilt thou not be mou'd with *Didos* words?
> Thy mother was no Goddesse periurd man,
> Nor *Dardanus* the author of thy stocke:
> But thou art sprung from *Scythian Caucasus*,
> And Tygers of *Hircania* gaue thee sucke. (1563-7)

Those Hyrcanian tigers, symbols of inhumanity, are common enough in the Elizabethan bestiary; but Marlowe's exoticism adds an extra touch with "Scythian"; and his appositions are paired off, almost too symmetrically, as if they were couplets. The illustration is even more graphic if, taking one step forward, we go back two steps to Surrey:

> Did I not him, thrown vp vpon my shore
> In neede receiue, & fonded eke inuest
> Of halfe my realme, his nauie lost, repair;
> From deathes daunger his fellowes eke defend? (485-8)

Here, where the alliterative pattern seems natural, the blank verse seems unaware of its commitments. It hesitates between the iamb and the spondee; it stops short for the cæsura and pushes on past the last foot; it "ekes" out disparities, in a painfully literal sense, by overworking that archaic monosyllable. Marlowe's Dido is clearly a different person:

> Wast thou not wrackt vpon this *Libian* shoare,
> And cam'st to *Dido* like a Fisher swaine?
> Repairde not I thy ships, made thee a King,
> And all thy needie followers Noblemen? (1569-72)

This time we hear the voice of the adapter, not simply in the accelerated rhythms or the interpolated names, but in a personal twist of exaggeration. The seagoing shepherd, climbing not to a share in a kingdom but to kingship, with rewards — not rescues — for his companions-at-arms, bears a closer resemblance to Scythian Tamburlaine than to pious Æneas. Marlowe goes on, where Vergil invokes the Olympians, to interpolate the moral emblem of the serpent warmed in one's bosom, and mitigates Dido's curses with farewells more passionate than anything in the original. The Marlovian line may not yet have gathered the full might that Ben Jonson would attribute to it, but in *Dido* its characteristics are manifest.

Such blessed words as "Mesopotamia," which so comforted Charles Lamb's old lady, should be a solace to Marlowe's readers and hearers. Sound effects are always difficult to separate from associative overtones, and not less so with poetry that depends upon a sesquipedalian nomenclature abounding in both. The introduction of strange vocables into a familiar rhythmical framework may be the sort of magic that functions best within circles of remote association. The spell may vary as subtly and as overwhelmingly as

> *La fille de Minos et de Pasiphäé*

varies from

> O *Priamus*, O *Troy*, oh *Hecuba*!   (400)

If Marlowe's pentameter is less suggestive than Racine's alexandrine, it is more assertive; for it accompanies the sigh of Æneas, calling up the underlying vision that haunted the European imagination. Each western capital considered itself, like Carthage, "a statelier *Troy*" (1410); every beauty could claim to be, like Dido, "a second *Helen*" (1552); and Æneas, the survivor of the legend, was its narrator. On the stage his narration became a declamation, not unlike those gloomy announcements delivered by Seneca's messengers, a set piece requested by Hamlet from the First Player. Marlowe's narrative, by taking up more than a tenth of his dramatization, turns his drama back toward its epic source. Though he adds a sprinkling of bloody details to the monologue, his dialogue reverts at the climax to direct quotations from Vergil's Latin. Such an evasion smells of the university, where he was probably still in residence when he wrote the play. Nashe, his junior at Cambridge, is credited with having been his collaborator; though Nashe's conscientious editor confirms the opinion that would ascribe it almost wholly to Marlowe. The title page of the quarto likewise states that it was performed by the Children of the Chapel, the group of boy actors whose courtly repertory included Lyly's plays and Peele's *Arraignment of Paris*. This would account for the number of women's and children's parts in the cast and for the mistaken identities, the pairing of rival lovers, the pert repartee, and other tricks more appropriate to comedy than to the Vergilian theme.

But Marlowe was concentrating upon an amorous episode which, in Vergil's scheme of things, had been a digression. Æneas, a hero at Troy and again in Latium, cuts an unheroic figure at Carthage, where he is not so much the romantic lover as the capricious object of Dido's passion. Dido, Marlowe's only feminine protagonist, is an answer to those critics who contend that he was unable to portray a convincing heroine. It is she who makes the advances, does the wooing, and — surrounded by royal suitors of her own — plays the thankless role of the lavish provider. Her attachment to Æneas is not much less maternal than that of his actual mother, Venus herself. Venus, who is motherly rather than voluptuous, not to say grandmotherly in the presence of young Ascanius, lives up to the matriarchal conception of Lucretius. The eroticism that motivates the characters is engendered by the charms of her younger son Cupid, confused through disguise with the grandson Ascanius, and even allowed to excite a comic warmth in the withered breast of the latter's elderly nurse. A key to these ambiguous complications is imparted by the prologue, a luxurious piece of mythical machinery, elaborated *con amore* by Marlowe out of half a line from the *Æneid.* The curtain is pulled aside to discover Jupiter himself, dallying with "that female wanton boy," Ganymede, and thus to furnish an Olympian precedent for the dalliance of Æneas, as well as an unambiguous comment upon the sexual climate of the play — its tenderness toward youths, its passivity with women, its childish delight in the presents and promises of courtship.

The prevailing mood is set by a curious word. Dido refers to Helen of Troy as a "ticing strumpet" (595), and in her turn is described by Achates as a "ticing dame" (1181). Like the persuasive Sinon, the fatal bearer of gifts from the Greeks, she possesses a "ticing tongue" (440). So does Jupiter, with his "earth threatning haire" (10), when he entices the petulant Ganymede, with his "fire darting beames" (25). Ganymede's stipulation is "a iewell for mine eare" (46). Jupiter's condition is "if thou wilt be my loue" (49). So Venus lures Ascanius:

> Ile giue thee Sugar-almonds, sweete Conserues,
> A siluer girdle, and a golden purse. (600–1)

And so the nurse beckons Cupid into a garden overflowing with fruits and flowers. Similarly, but with a difference, temptations are dangled before the faithful Achates on condition that the Trojans embark without Æneas.

> Ile giue thee tackling made of riueld gold, (750)

Dido promises, and into the bargain she tosses crystal anchors, silver masts, and linen sails. Having promised Æneas more wealth than "twentie thousand Indiaes can affoord" (727), it is quite in character for her to envisage the sirens trying to founder the ship with their counterattractions. Which of her enchantments is more seductive, her munificence or her eloquence or her person, is not altogether clear. Æneas is reluctant to take his leave because

> Each word she sayes will then containe a Crowne,
> And euery speech be ended with a kisse. (1203–4)

His choice, however, is between her kisses and another crown. Wavering — like Shakespeare's Antony — between Africa and Italy, between the enticements of love and the duties of war, he allows the gods to solve his dilemma for him. Venus is in the ascendant but Mars must have his day. For the nonce the poet is content to dwell in the pastures of Ovidian lyricism, but the epic clangor of Lucan, the call of Roman destiny, and the rumbling of Cæsarism are heard in the distance. Just as Æneas is conscious of his imperial mission, so Marlowe seems ready to invade a more heroic field. And as his hero — speaking "like a Conqueror" (1299) — moves out of her lyrical realm, his twice-widowed heroine enters the realm of tragedy, realizing herself in her desolation: "*Dido* I am . . ." (1672).

The youthfully lyrical phase of Marlowe's talent is crystallized in his sole surviving lyric, "The Passionate Shepherd to His Love." Here in a song, at its purest, is the pastoral tune on which the *Elegies* are variations, the mood of enticement that predominates in the tragedy of *Dido* and will reappear as a secondary motive in Marlowe's other plays:

> Come liue with me, and be my loue . . .

Every lover has addressed this plea to his beloved in so many words, but Marlowe seems to have chosen the shortest and simplest and smoothest. Their appeal, which is as obvious as his rhymes —

"rocks" and "flocks," "roses" and "posies" — has been constantly renewed by anthologies and tested by imitations and parodies. Unlike other educated lyrics, singing *vivamus atque amemus* to their coy mistresses, this one eschews both flattery and philosophy. His arguments are bribes, naïve, concrete, and pictorial; he proposes a way of life which is essentially a bed of roses, plus a series of inducements which are useful as well as ornamental. The highly generalized landscape seems to be an earthly paradise, where rivers are shallow and birds sing madrigals. The prospective sharer in these pleasures remains a listener and spectator, of whom we know no more than is suggested by the proffered items of shepherdess's attire. These are properly rustic for the most part, though the woolen gown and straw belt are decorated in proper Elizabethan fashion

> With Corall clasps and Amber studs.

The one hint of rigor, the slippers lined "for the cold," is quickly alleviated by "buckles of the purest gold." If such extravagance seems inconsistent with the simple taste set forth in the remainder of the poem, it is worthy of mention that the stanza containing this courtly refinement does not appear in the earliest printed version. As the refrain was repeated, it was bound to invite accretions, expressing less primitivistic notions of earthly felicity. Later versions interpose further embellishments, more in keeping with Olympus than with Arcadia perhaps, yet not devoid of a certain Marlovian ring:

> Thy dyshes shal be filde with meate
> such as the gods doe use to eate.

Marlowe's Epicureanism, which is simplified to the point of sheer delightful wish-fulfillment by "The Passionate Shepherd," develops into its fullest realization with the unfinished torso of *Hero and Leander*. The latter differs so much from his other writings, both as experiment and as parable, that it requires a place for itself in our study; but, in passing, we are bound to note that it elaborates and rationalizes an attitude struck in the apprentice work of his university days: the invitation to love. Like *Dido*, and unlike his other dramas, *Hero and Leander* has its origin in classical myth. Though it is rather a paraphrase from the Greek than a translation from the Latin, it is suffused with an Ovidian fragrance.

That men should need the authority of books to celebrate, if not to recover, the enjoyment of their senses is a paradox of the Renaissance which has nowhere been more vividly set forth. The asceticism professed by the Middle Ages, the Christian ideal of chastity, was enshrined in the cult of the Virgin Queen and glorified in such figures as Spenser's Britomart. In attacking Hero's virginity as an "idoll" (I, 269), Leander was therefore committing *lèse-majesté* as well as undermining the constraints of monasticism. Hero embodies this conflict between innocence and experience, cloistered virtue and sensual pleasure, through her paradoxical office as "*Venus* nun" (I, 45). Leander, the scholar turned lover, is himself a sexual novice; but the logic of the schools is irresistible when it is reinforced by love at first sight. Better versed in dialectic than blandishment, he is supremely apt at "Rhethoricke to deceiue a maid" (I, 338). He has mastered, as have all of Marlowe's spokesmen, the art of persuasion. As for their listeners:

> Maids are not woon by brutish force and might,
> But speeches full of pleasure and delight.   (I, 419–20)

After Hero is wooed and won in the first and second Sestiads, the poem breaks off; and Leander's tragedy is forever averted, but not until it has been foreshadowed by signs portending the envy and rivalry of the gods. Despite Marlowe's protestation that his pen is unfit to "blazon foorth" such matters (I, 70), he digresses to spy upon Neptune courting Leander and hints that Hero rejected the suit of Apollo. Furthermore, Leander dares to tell Hero that in beauty she exceeds the goddess she serves. This boldness was licensed by the *Elegies*, where Ovid pronounced his Corinna greater than Venus (III, ii, 60). Ovid's *Metamorphoses* likewise abounded in rhetorical stratagems for the enterprising suitor. Even the unpersuasive Cyclops, inviting the nymph Galatea to live with him and be his love, lavished poetic cajoleries which would scarcely be improved by the exuberant fancy of Góngora, and which Arthur Golding could Elizabethanize:

> More whyght thou art then Primrose leaf my Lady *Galatee*,
> More fresh than meade, more tall and streyght than lofty Aldertree,
> More bright than glasse, more wanton than the tender kid forsooth,
> Than Cockleshelles continually with water worne, more smooth . . .
>   (XIII, 929–32)

The distinctive feature of these comparisons is that they are actually stated in the comparative degree. Not "swift as lightning" but "swifter than lightning," not "bright as crystal" but *splendidior vitro*, neither "lovely as Venus" nor "mighty as Mars" but "lovelier than Venus" and "mightier than Mars" — this, if once more we may borrow a descriptive phrase from Nashe, is "to embowell the cloudes in a speech of comparison," to "get *Boreas* by the beard and the heauenly Bull by the deaw-lap." Thus the hero of *The Taming of a Shrew*, an anonymous play which approximates Shakespeare and parodies Marlowe, addresses the heroine:

> Sweete *Kate*, thou louelier then Dianas purple robe,
> Whiter then are the snowie Apennins,
> Or icie haire that grows on Boreas chin. (II, i, 148–50)

Marlowe habitually prefers the invidious comparison to the more usual kind of simile. Similes and metaphors are links, explicit or implicit, which connect the plane of literal reality with a plane of figurative cross-reference. Marlowe's habit is to abolish the boundaries between these two planes, elevating the human to the divine or vice versa, and freely and frankly pitting the moderns against the ancients. He restores the classical pantheon only to despoil it; he seeks out the great archetypes of humanity in order to challenge them, one by one, on the very grounds of their mythological fame. He storms the heavens by piling Pelion on Ossa.

The Greeks had occasionally permitted themselves such audacities, though Homer's Calypso admonishes Odysseus that they are improper (V, 211–13). Sappho, in her famous lyric describing the lover's emotions, had imagined the favored rival as a peer of the gods. Catullus, paraphrasing with Roman caution, had nevertheless gone farther:

> *Ille mi par esse deo videtur,*
> *Ille, si fas est, superare divos.* (LI, 1–2)

To surpass the divinities of Greece and Rome could be no sacrilege in the Christian era. Petrarch, giving his Laura the primacy over all other ladies, proclaimed her to be as pleasing as Diana; and, proceeding in triumph from myth to military history, likened her powers of resistance favorably with those of Julius Cæsar. Shakespeare, through the mockery of Mercutio, reversed the *tertium com-*

parationis; Laura, compared with Juliet, is a kitchenmaid, *"Dido a dowdie, Cleopatra a Gipsie, Hellen and Hero*, hildings and Harlots" (II, iv, 45–7). But the dramatized compliment had to be taken seriously when Juno, Pallas, and Venus stepped aside before the superior charms of Queen Elizabeth in Peele's *Arraignment of Paris*. And when Marlowe faced his own situations and characters, he continued to ransack the classics for precedents to break and parallels to outdo. There were always, and would be, the unquiet shades of Troy. Seeing them again when he beholds Carthage, Æneas unburdens a grief more poignant than Niobe's. Tamburlaine cannot plan to beautify his native Samarkand without hoping to "cast the fame of *Ilions* Tower to hell" (4092). He himself is metaphorically identified with Æneas by his bride, Zenocrate, who identifies herself with Æneas' destined wife, Lavinia, and her rejected suitor with the ill-starred Turnus. Battle, as Tamburlaine conducts it, is hotter than Cæsar's at Pharsalia, as Lucan had related it. Zenocrate, at her death, is worthier to be immortalized than Ovid's Corinna, Catullus' Lesbia, or Homer's Helen. Albeit this smacks of youthful bookishness, the scholar-poet is casting aside his books; and, even while trading scholarship for blank verse, he is asserting that literature cannot vie with life itself. But even Gabriel Harvey, in the unguarded intimacy of his *Letter-Book*, could babble:

> I challenge the, Aretino,
> Or any other Unico;
> Nether thy Angelica,
> Nor Petrarches Lauretta,
> Nor Catullus Lesbia, alias Clodia;
> Nor Tibullus Delia, alias Plautia;
> Nor Propertius Cinthia, alias Hostia,
> Nor Oviddes Corinna, alias Martials Julia;
> Nor any other famous Donna
> Comparable with my Ellena.
> No, not Paris Helena
> Comparable with my Ellena.

Marlowe can also emulate the Greeks in viewing nature under the aspect of mythology. When he calls, as he frequently does, upon Cynthia, we are never quite certain whether he is invoking the moon itself or its tutelary deity — or whether, indeed, the personification carries an overtone of homage to Elizabeth. When Tamburlaine's foes uneasily scan the Bosporus, visualizing the opposite shore as "faire *Europe* mounted on her bull" (2367), the loves of the gods are metamorphosed into parts of the map. The sweeping yet measurable horizons extended to Marlowe by geography, along with a wealth of precious substances and exotic objects, will be unfolding before us as we proceed. His predilection for the brightest vistas and widest ranges, "the dazzling heights and vast spaces of the universe," has been marked by Miss Spurgeon as "the dominating note of his mind." Another student of Shakespeare's imagery, Wolfgang Clemen, has located Marlowe's "upward thrust" more concretely in his inclination toward such verbs as "mount," "climb," "soar," and "rise." Ovid, speaking for the poet in his *Amores*, boasts that he will survive; Marlowe caps this, in his *Elegies*, by promising to "mount higher" (I, xv, 42). He rejoices in the epic rumble of large, round numbers, promising the heirs of Æneas more than a thousand years, where Vergil did no more than refer to their future. Quantities are quickly multiplied beyond the reckoning of mere arithmetic.

> *Æneas* may commaund as many Moores,
> As in the Sea are little water drops . . .   (1268–9)

— which is exactly the estimated number of Turks and renegades opposing Tamburlaine. Beyond this there can be nothing except infinity, which is not infrequently Marlowe's goal. He attains it, too, whenever he attaches the privative suffix to root-words denoting limits; when Æneas alludes to "quenchles fire" (481) and "toples hilles" (1162), the effect is to open up unlimited possibilities. At the other extreme — for Marlowe is nothing if not an extremist — the effect of rarity and of uniqueness is conveyed by the generous employment of superlatives. It is not enough for his heroes and heroines to be better than their literary prototypes; they must be the best of their kind; and, more than paragons, they must be nonpareils, beyond compare, resembling only the phoenix. Typically, the lines that characterize them commence with "The only . . ." and conclude with ". . . the world." Creatures of this sort, since they are matchless, are of necessity unrivaled. For them, accustomed to win, unwilling to lose, it is Cæsar or nobody. When they deign to play the games of their fellow men, the stakes are all or nothing.

Their typical gesture is to pose an absolute alternative, to impose an intransigent choice between uncompromising extremes. Sink or swim, live or die, with the Duke of Guise in *The Massacre at Paris*, they stand pledged to hazard everything for an inestimable prize:

> And with this wait Ile counterpoise a Crowne,
> Or with seditions weary all the worlde.   (115–6)

Now all these modes of expression are forms of a single trope, which in itself is the exaggerated form of many different tropes, hyperbole. Rather a figure of thought than a figure of speech, it relates Marlowe's speech to his thought, his manner to his matter. It presupposes a state of mind to which all things are possible, for which limitations exist to be overcome. Because of its vehemence it is better adapted to youth than to age, according to Aristotle's *Rhetoric* (III, xi, 15–6). And Aristotle cites a Homeric example involving both innumerable quantity and invidious comparison: Achilles in his wrath, rejecting gifts as numerous as the sands and refusing to wed, though the maiden vie with Athene in skill and Aphrodite in loveliness. Such hyperboles magnify their subject matter, though others can just as cavalierly diminish it and may — as Quintilian cautioned — give rise to laughter. The Elizabethans, however, responsive to youthfulness and to every manifestation of verbal exuberance, seriously welcomed the device and gave it effective employment upon the stage. Rhetoricians like Abraham Fraunce recommended it for amplification and heightening, for making the language "very loftie and full of maiestie." George Puttenham, in his staunch endeavor to Anglicize the ancient rhetorical categories, renamed hyperbole "the Ouer reacher, otherwise called the loud lyer." He defined it as "by incredible comparison giuing credit," and justified his slur by conceding that all too often it strained belief. The other epithet may not have been his coinage, since the Oxford dictionary cites a parliamentary comment of a decade earlier, 1579, in which "hyperbole" is equated with "overreaching speech." It could not have been more happily inspired to throw its illumination upon Marlowe — upon his style, which is so emphatically himself, and on his protagonists, overreachers all. Their ethos of living dangerously, between the alternatives of aspiration and sedition, again is well represented by the Guise, the chief exponent of Marlowe's Machiavellianism:

That like I best that flyes beyond my reach.
Set me to scale the high Peramides,
And thereon set the Diadem of Fraunce,
Ile either rend it with my nayles to naught,
Or mount the top with my aspiring winges,
Although my downfall be the deepest hell. (99–104)

This is Marlovian tragedy in stark outline. The overreaching image, reinforced by the mighty line, sums up the whole dramatic predicament and affords the actor a maximum of opportunity. The stage becomes a vehicle for hyperbole, not merely by accrediting the incredible or supporting rhetoric with a platform and sounding board, but by taking metaphors literally and acting concepts out. Operating visually as well as vocally, it converts symbols into properties; triumph must ride across in a chariot, hell must flare up in fireworks; students, no longer satisfied to read about Helen of Troy, must behold her in her habit as she lived. Whereas poetry is said to transport us to an imaginative level, poetic drama transports that level to us; hyperbolically speaking, it brings the mountain to Mohammed. Marlowe seems to have admired the ceremonies, if not the dogmas, of the Catholic Church; and behind his plays, as behind all drama, loom the elemental configurations of ritual. Yet while glimpsing them, we should be misled if we did not also discern that, unlike some of our contemporaries who have turned back toward the liturgical tradition, Marlowe was engaged in breaking away from it. Whenever he returns to it, his tone is satirical. In so far as he worked within the universal framework of the moralities, he was filling in particulars, subordinating abstraction to individuality. His protagonist is never Everyman but always *l'uomo singolare*, the exceptional man who becomes king because he is a hero, not hero because he is a king; the private individual who remains captain of his fate, at least until his ambition overleaps itself; the overreacher whose tragedy is more of an action than a passion, rather an assertion of man's will than an acceptance of God's.

That such a figure could be a mouthpiece for his epoch is borne out independently — among other places, in a notation of Gabriel Harvey's, where heroic vigor is coupled with hyperbolic impetus. This comes close to the *hubris* of the Greek tragedians, that arrogance of heroes which fatally provokes the jealousy of gods. "Pride goeth before a fall," the proverbial formula for tragic irony, seems to hold good regardless of changing epochs. None the less the emphasis changes crucially; whereas the classics and the Renaissance emphasized "pride," the Middle Ages lingered over "fall." The precariousness of the balance is brought home to us by the earliest English morality still extant, the fourteenth-century fragment known as *The Pride of Life*. There the King of Life, in his vainglorious prime, is predestined to be cut down by his stalking enemy, Death; for, though the conclusion is missing, we are well enough aware of a denouement in which we shall all be participants, the *danse macabre*. But death, which is necessarily more tragic to skeptics than to believers, had far from the last word in medieval drama. Though it impends in the mysteries of Abraham and Isaac, the angel averts it melodramatically. Man's lot was viewed less as tragedy than as the first act of a divine comedy, wherein the mistakes of this life could be rectified by the next. Tragedies so-called were not written to be enacted; they were tales in verse lamenting the falls of princes. To read them was to intensify one's consciousness of mutability and mortal vicissitude: how are the mighty fallen! They were also supposed to propound an object lesson for rulers and divers others in high positions. Hence the principal Elizabethan collection of exemplary monologues in this vein was the *Mirror for Magistrates*, whose best-known contributor, Thomas Sackville, also collaborated in *Gorboduc* to teach Elizabeth herself the lessons of transitory pomp and "lust of kingdome" (III, Chorus, 1).

For their refusal to believe in the soul's immortality, Dante ironically entombed the Epicureans among the heretics in his Inferno (X, 13–6). It was their belief — paraphrased by an Elizabethan commentator, Philemon Holland, who deplored "these wretched daies, wherein Epicurisme beareth up the head as high as at any time euer before" — "That all things roll and run at a venture, and that there is no other cause of the good and euill accidents of this life, but either fortune or els the will of man." Dante was able to fit that chaotic picture into his cosmic order by believing that God had deputed worldly affairs to a "general minister and guide" (VII, 78). Fortuna, blindly fickle, notoriously jealous, yet all-powerful among men, alternately worshiped by them as a goddess and cursed as a bitch, regulated the fates of kings and beggars by the casual revolution of her wheel. Whether the Roman empire had owed its greatness to her favor or to some quality of its citizens — this was a mooted question which Machiavelli pondered in his discourses on Livy. He answered by stressing the very quality that he extolled and expounded throughout *The Prince*, that virtue of virtues, *virtù*. Although our cognate word seems comparatively pallid, we can catch the vibrations in such rough transatlantic equivalents as "initiative," "self-reliance," and "rugged individualism." For the good Christian — or, for that matter, the Stoic — virtue might reside in suffering, in accepting one's condition; but the less one trusted in providential design, the more one relied on free will, the more one acted for one's self. One could meet the occasion by actively rising to it rather than by passively falling with it. Rulers and magistrates might still have their ups and downs, but the angle of observation was rotating from the downward to the upward movement. The cycles of prosperity and adversity, as they now revolved, did more to incite ambition than to instill humility.

Which, then, was true virtue: to suffer the slings and arrows of an outrageous fortune or to take arms against them, defying the stars and entrusting one's own fortune to one's own hands? It was to this dilemma that Marlowe's tragedies delivered their challenging response. Tragedy is grounded upon mortality; and in obscuring the prospect of a hereafter, it enhances the perception of here and now. Moreover, in exalting the individual to heroic stature, it frees him to act, but measures his acts by a scale of values; and the stature of Marlowe's heroes is so exalted that we shall be wondering whether it does not jeopardize the scale. By conquering kingdoms or amassing fortunes or scrutinizing the cosmos, they challenge the more settled ways of living. And, just as they break down the barrier between realities and figures of speech, so they seem to override distinctions between this world and any other. Orthodox Christianity, with Saint John (First Epistle, ii, 16), had preached contempt for "all that is in the world, the lust of the flesh, the lust of the eyes, and the pride of life." But concupiscence, curiosity, and vainglory — temptations which men become saints by resisting — are leading motives of humanistic drama, which — in more affirmative terms — would be inconceivable without fullness of life, freedom of will, and the inevitability of death. The unholy trinity of Marlowe's heresies, violating the taboos of medieval orthodoxy, was an affirmation of the strongest drives that animated the Renaissance and have shaped our modern outlook. In the stricter categories of theology, his Epicureanism might have been *libido sentiendi*, the appetite for sensation; his Machiavellianism might have been *libido dominandi*, the will to power; and his Atheism *libido sciendi*, the zeal for knowledge. Singly and in combination he dramatized these ideas — these "highest reaches of a humaine wit" — pushing them to limits beyond which no writer had gone, and toward which we shall follow him with mixed feelings of exhilaration and temerity.

Chapter **II**

THE PROGRESS OF POMP

From iygging vaines of riming mother wits,
And such conceits as clownage keepes in pay,
Weele lead you to the stately tent of War,
Where you shall heare the Scythian *Tamburlaine*
Threatning the world with high astounding tearms
And scourging kingdoms with his conquering sword.

So runs the prologue, concluding:

View but his picture in this tragicke glasse,
And then applaud his fortunes as you please.   (1–8)

Clearly this is the confident manifesto of a man who knows what
he is doing. He can be no more than twenty-three years old; and
he has just come down from Cambridge to London; but he invades
the theater like the conqueror whose conquests he has chosen to
dramatize. Though he has set the end of scholarism in blank verse,
he remains the arrogant young scholar-poet, with all the disdain
of a University Wit for the mother-wit of the popular stage, as he
sweeps aside the doggerel rhymes and clownish jigs of his predecessors. Henceforth, he proudly announces, English actors will speak
a language and portray a hero worthy of tragedy. The ringing words
that convey the announcement are calculated to support it. The regular cadence of each line is strengthened by pauses after the second
foot and the final beat. The verse-sentence mounts climactically
through a sequence of virtual couplets. The lines break cleanly into
hemistichs, which are bombasted out by participial adjectives: "jig-
ging" and "rhyming," "astounding" and "conquering." Consciously
we are asked — or, rather, allowed — to participate in an adven-
turous undertaking of the theatrical imagination. We are invited
to listen, to hear the threats and scourges of war. The invitation
is addressed explicitly to our ears, and subsequently to our eyes.
Though the author does not solicit our applause, he whets our ex-
pectation with images which will serve to project his overreaching
ideas. Here and elsewhere he reiterates a traditional view of his
medium, visualizing his subject "as in a mirrour" (2258). But he
promises to hold, as it were, this looking-glass up to certain phases of
experience which the drama has never presented before.

Where the *Mirror for Magistrates* darkly reflected the falls of
princes, Marlowe exhibits the rise of commoners. His heroes make
their fortunes by exercising virtues which conventional morality

might well regard as vices. For the most part, they are self-made men; and, to the extent that they can disregard the canons of good and evil, they are supermen. They are continually active and, up to a point, incapable of suffering. All of Marlowe's plays are dominated by the animus of such individuals, and by the resultant conflicts between virtue and fortune: that is to say, between the energies of the protagonist and the circumstances into which he hurls himself. As it is repeated, the pattern is varied and elaborated; the characterization, starting with the crudest and broadest strokes, increasingly registers subtlety and depth. Of this extraordinary development *Tamburlaine the Great* is the barbaric prototype. If its garish colors and exaggerated proportions had not made an impact, certainly nothing else could have done so; and once he had demonstrated the sheer magnitude, Marlowe could go on to cultivate the inherent qualities of his medium. The play would not have been so successful if it had been less spectacular, and it would not have been so spectacular if it had been less external. Let us accept it, then, for what it is: a resonant fanfare and a pictorial spectacle, pure action uninhibited by passion, and — by no means least — an actor's showpiece. Aptly, Marlowe's emergence as a playwright seems to have coincided with the vogue of Edward Alleyn, an actor whose commanding voice and impressive stature must have amply qualified him to wear the crimson breeches and copper lace that went with the title role.

It is probably more than a coincidence that the most remembered role in the mysteries had been that of another famous tyrant. Herod foreshadows Tamburlaine strikingly when, in the Wakefield cycle, he boasts that his supremacy extends from India to Italy, from Norway to Normandy, from Padua to Paradise. And Tamburlaine, when he proscribes the Virgins of Damascus, emulates Herod's slaughter of the Innocents. Like the Turkish Knight of folk drama or the braggart soldier of classical tradition, Herod was essentially a Ruffler — an aggressive boaster whose vainglorious ranting is the prelude to his ironic discomfiture. This can be tragic in the religious sense, as when Death stalks into Herod's banquet hall in the *Ludus Coventriæ*. More often than not, the outcome is a reduction to comic absurdity. But nemesis, be it comic or tragic, was less immediately interesting than the *hubris* that brought it on, the gestures of man challenging his destiny. Such was the interest taken in "Ercles' vein," the impious rage of Seneca's Hercules, which most of us remember through Shakespeare's burlesque. Tamburlaine, outdoing the rants and rages of his forerunners, was therefore, in his very inhumanity, as proud a figure as human presumption could frame. That he was not born to high estate, but had risen through his innate capability, further augmented his pride. His ascent from "Scythian Shephearde" to "mightye Monarque," emphasized on the title page of the play, suggests one basis of its appeal to a middle-class audience. It also suggests the course that Marlowe was taking, leaving the pastoral fields of Ovidian lyricism and proceeding in the direction pointed by Lucan's epic imperialism.

It was actually a vulgar error, which Sir Thomas Browne would duly expose, to assume that Tamburlaine the Great had begun his career as a humble shepherd. His original, Timur the Lame, had begun as the leader of a nomadic Tartar tribe which reckoned property by flocks of sheep. A brilliantly cruel general and brutally efficient administrator, he constructed a far-flung and short-lived regime out of the ruins of the Mongol Empire. Against the Turks at Angora in 1402, he fought one of the decisive battles in the history of the world. Shortly thereafter he was visited by the Spanish emissary Clavijo, who beheld a man so old his eyelids had fallen, dozing amid the bright tiles and luxuriant gardens of Samarkand. That was far removed from the Michelangelesque vigor of Marlowe's portrait, which is more classical than Asiatic and in some traits is modeled on Homer's Achilles. Meanwhile, the European impression of Timur had been shaped at Byzantium, where it was his intervention that kept the Turks from capturing the city for another fifty years. Christian historians naturally interpreted the Turkish defeat as a manifestation of Providence and looked upon the victorious infidel as a supernatural instrument: *flagellum dei*, the scourge of God verily prophesied by Isaiah and prefigured by Attila. But their emphasis centered upon his principal victim, the Sultan Bajazet, whose downfall afforded a luminous example of tragedy in its medieval outline. To be the Great Turk in the morning and, before the day was over, to become the footstool of Timur — had anyone since antiquity been so suddenly and completely foiled by the instability of Fortune's wheel? Even Marlowe's friend Ralegh would ascribe it to God, "the Author of all our tragedies," and would draw the moral

"That the change of fortune on the great Theater, is but as the change of garments on the lesse."

Now the demi-revolution that plunged Bajazet from the heights to the depths had obviously carried Timur from the bottom to the top. Thence he might have expected a similar reversal. But unlike Fortune's erstwhile favorites, he seems to have felt no remission of her favors, and his uniqueness in this respect was recognized by the versions of his life that appear in such standard works of the sixteenth century as La Primaudaye's *French Academie*. Hence, more appropriately than any other hero that Marlowe could have picked, Tamburlaine could be viewed as "Fortunes maister" (490) and could proclaim:

> I hold the Fates bound fast in yron chaines,
> And with my hand turne Fortunes wheel about. (369–70)

Bajazet's misfortunes, which were generic, could still exemplify the old, sad story of "fickle Empery" and "earthly pompe" (2134–5). The novelty, the unique individuality of Tamburlaine, lay in the fact that his was a success story. If he was really a historical character and not a legendary agent of divine wrath, what was the motive that propelled his upward journey through the tottering monarchies? Perondinus, his humanistic biographer, speaks of *insatiabilis sitis*. That quenchless thirst, of which Marlowe had spoken in *Dido*, is for Tamburlaine *libido dominandi*, boundless ambition in its grossly material aspect. Frankly he avows his "thirst of raigne" (863), while enemies deplore him as a "fiery thirster after Soueraingtie" (842). Therein he was not so much an exception as an exponent of the new age, and had been named as its very type and model by Louis Le Roy some twenty years before Marlowe's interpretation. Le Roy's philosophy of history, tracing "the concvrrence of Armes and Learning," stressed the chronological linkage between the ascendancy of Timur in the East and "the restitution of the tongues; and of all sciences," the Renaissance in the West. "Yet fortune hauing allwaies fauoured him, without euer hauing bin contrary unto him," Le Roy concludes his eulogy of Tamburlan, "seemeth among so many admirable euents, which exceed the ordinary course of Conquerours, to haue denyed him an Historyographer of excellent learning, and eloquence; agreeable to his vertues: to celebrate them worthily."

Fortune granted that crowning favor in 1587; and, though his dramatic historiographer proved less fortunate, the dramatic history survived as a leading attraction in the repertory of the troop that would perform at the Fortune Theater. If, as seems likely, the First Part was originally performed on improvised stages at innyards, that would explain its ambulatory construction. The pageants of the guilds had formed street processions, and Elizabethan pageantry delighted in exhibiting the sovereign and her court on royal progresses or tours of duty. Elements of both intermingle with military pomp in "the warlike progresse" of Tamburlaine (3525), the triumphal procession of a conquering hero, whose coach is preceded and followed by kings he has made and unmade. To watch this parade is to see the *Mirror for Magistrates* come to life, to hear the sad stories of their deaths acted out — with the difference that all of these plaintive monarchs have been deposed by the same usurper, for whom each usurpation has been a milestone on the highroad to world dominion. Cæsar, who rose with Pompey's fall, fell in his turn; but Tamburlaine's rise, step by step, is predicated upon a succession of falls from higher and higher places. Nothing succeeds like success, and nothing can stop him until "death cuts off the progres of his pomp" (2320). The drama is built up on rivalries like a tournament, where each new contender is more formidable than the last. The unseasoned challenger, by defeating the champion, acquires his standing and must defend it against all comers, just as in the first part of Shakespeare's *Henry IV*. Thus Tamburlaine assumes the titles and dignities of Bajazeth, which he promises to "maintaine . . . against a world of Kings" (1525).

The earliest victory is the easiest. It takes place in the decadent empire of Persia, which Spenser describes in *The Faerie Queene* (I, iv, 7) as "the nourse of pompous pride," against a background of dynastic intrigue. The king, Mycetes, is the weakest of rivals; and he is soon replaced by his stronger brother, Cosroe; yet, even as the latter is crowned, there is ominous allusion to the rout of Darius; and, out of the fratricidal struggle, Tamburlaine gains his initial crown at Persepolis. This is a little drama in itself, the substance of the first and second acts. The third act not only introduces the central antagonism but virtually completes it by routing the Turks, leaving the agony of Bajazeth to be prolonged as a minor theme into the fourth and fifth acts. These develop a major theme introduced near the outset, Tamburlaine's courtship of Zenocrate. Her father,

THE OVERREACHER

the Sultan of Egypt, and her betrothed, the King of Arabia, join their clamorous efforts to the opposition, which collapses after the siege of Damascus. Despite the many incidental tragedies, the kingly casualties along the way, the First Part is not a tragedy; it is a heroic play or romantic drama, in the manner of Corneille, where the hero stands between the conflicting claims of love and honor. Unlike Æneas, Tamburlaine chooses both; and unlike Dido — indeed, like Lavinia — Zenocrate has a share in the happy ending. Sweeping all before him triumphantly, thoroughly exhausting his antagonists, Tamburlaine also exhausted Marlowe's source material; and when the play's unprecedented success demanded a sequel, he was thrown back upon his own imaginative devices. He was forced, by the very impact of his creation, to face the genuinely tragic conflict that was bound to destroy the monster he created.

Since the Second Part starts with a hero who is all but invincible, it cannot rely upon its mounting roster of enemies to keep up the suspense. They do their best and worst to combine against Tamburlaine; but the coalition is made up of Mohammedans and Christians, who before too long are at each other's throats. The hero is in abeyance, above the battle, while in the foreground their plot and counterplot eke out the first two acts. Again, as in the preceding play, the structure is tripartite, and the central act pits Tamburlaine against a Turkish foe; this time it is Callapine, the son of Bajazeth, crowned and accompanied by an avenging host. Again, the last two acts march toward the culminating siege; and where the locale was Damascus in the First Part, it is now Babylon. Marching from strength to strength, from Persepolis to Damascus and from Samarkand to Babylon, Tamburlaine finally seeks to storm the gates of heaven itself. It is then that "murdrous Fates throwes al his triumphs down" (2321). The death of Zenocrate, in the second act, should have been an intimation of his vulnerability. Their three sons, who have managed to be born and grow up during the interval between the two parts, should be further warnings of some Achilles' heel. The cowardly petulance of one of them, Calyphas, is ironically contrasted with the filial enterprise of Callapine. Tamburlaine, vicariously wounded through the misfortunes of those nearest to him, is enraged and aroused to strike his final attitudes of pride and doubt: the chariot drawn by kings and the burning of the Koran. "Proud

Fortune," in the manner of his death, seems to resume "her olde inconstancie" (3140).

The headlong imperative that unites and dominates both parts is, for better or worse, *libido dominandi*. Yet each is counterbalanced, to some degree, by an impulse of its own. In the First Part it is *libido sentiendi*, the romance and beauty incarnate in Zenocrate. In the Second Part, with her passing and Tamburlaine's defiance of heavenly powers, Marlowe's *libido sciendi* reveals itself. To sum it up in a paradigm: the first treats of love and war, the second of war and death. Throughout, the bravado of the hero persists unaltered; but as his relationship with the cosmos alters, his tone acquires deeper undertones. Defying his fellow men, he seems a "God or Feend" (826); defying the gods, he is nothing more or less than a man. The Second Part, transcending the first, follows logically from it — though historically it rests on a slighter foundation, and the critical scene with the Koran is one of Marlowe's most characteristic inventions. Though the episode of the broken alliance is true enough, it actually happened among the foes of Scanderbeg, a generation after Timur. In a rather ineffectual effort to fill the vacuum caused by the loss of his heroine, Marlowe adapted from Ariosto the underplot treating the suicide of Olympia. As he went along he amplified his thundering ultimatums and expanding itineraries, but not in the vein of bombast. On the contrary, it has been noted that his geographical excursions were grounded upon the latest maps of that elegant cartographer, Abraham Ortelius. His long-drawn-out digression on military tactics, in the third act of the continuation, was so well informed and up-to-date that much of it seems to have been derived from the manuscript of a book which had not yet been published, Paul Ive's *Practise of Fortification*.

This work provided the technical terminology for a lecture which, slowing down the action at its midpoint, seems to us a tedious affair. But to the Elizabethans, living in daily apprehension of the Spanish Armada, the problem of defense was not less vital than it has latterly become. England, through the successful prosecution of its war with Spain in both hemispheres, was decisively emerging as an imperial power and imposing its hegemony over the seas. Marlowe, with England, is ready to take the offensive:

> . . . to vndermine a towne,
> And make whole cyties caper in the aire.   (3250–1)

In celebrating the idea of conquest, in dramatizing geopolitics, Marlowe was striking the note of timeliness as loudly as it ever has been struck. What is more, while catching the momentum of Elizabeth's most triumphant decade, he was enlarging his medium beyond the scope of all other forms. His success was immediately echoed by a chorus of playwrights, hitherto in search of a clear directive, who turned simultaneously to blank verse and to the imperial theme. Greene's *Alphonsus, King of Aragon*, Lodge's *Wounds of Civil War*, Peele's *Battle of Alcazar*, the pseudo-Shakespearean *Locrine*, and the anonymous *Selimus* reaped — from the dragons' teeth *Tamburlaine* had sown — a whirlwind of emulous dynasts and termagant potentates. How strategically these theatrical heroes were allied to the naval heroes of the day is evident from Peele's *Farewell to Norris and Drake*:

> Bid theatres and proud tragedians,
> Bid Mahomet's Pow and mighty Tamburlaine,
> King Charlemagne, Tom Stukely, and the rest
> Adieu. To arms, to arms, to glorious arms!

Thus in the late 1580's and early 1590's, an epoch of rising empires and falling dynasties, Marlovian tragedy voiced aspirations which were collective as well as individual. It looked to the east, through the Near East and toward the Indies, as western Europe traditionally did for its sources of richness and strangeness. Yet the vantage point had shifted since the days of crusades and romances, when the oriental had been the opaque. It was still exotic, but it was no longer far-fetched, with voyagers returning to render accounts of it which would be gathered together by Hakluyt and Purchas. As for the other hemisphere, it was claiming a larger and larger place within the expansive orbit of English nationalism. Though Tamburlaine's native sphere is Asia, his vision travels westward,

> Euen from *Persepolis* to *Mexico*.   (1353)

Whether it be upon the personal or the national or the international plane, there are two paths to power. Machiavelli indicated them, with his maxim that the complete prince should possess both the courage of the lion and the cunning of the fox. Marlowe embraces the same alternative when Cosroe, in his opening speech, attributes the Persian dominion to "prowesse" and "pollicies" (16).

When Tamburlaine is first mentioned, as a thieving interloper, he is compared to a fox; shortly thereafter, when he first wears armor, he is described as a lion. Thenceforth it is the lion's part that he consistently acts, and the play is primarily a study in prowess; whereas *The Jew of Malta* and *The Massacre at Paris* will be studies in the more distinctively Machiavellian realm of policy. From the beginning, Tamburlaine is obsessed with his destiny as "Monark of the East" (380). So is Cosroe, who makes use of his help in dethroning Mycetes, and thereby teaches Tamburlaine how to unseat him in his turn. No sooner has Cosroe left to "ride in triumph through *Persepolis*" (754) than Tamburlaine picks up the reëchoing phrase and, after a battle as brief as the intervening scene, crowns himself with that "Emperiall Diadem" which he has all too lately obtained for Cosroe (147). Thereupon he pronounces his apologia, citing the precedent of Jove himself, and the dethronement of Saturn and the Titans by the gods who founded the reigning Olympian order. In envisaging the mind as a microcosm of nature, where the elements meet each other in martial strife, Marlowe could have brought the authority of Lucretius — and behind him Empedocles — to the support of his hero's restlessness. But the upward reach of the verse, along with the dynamic force of the diction, is more likely to remind us that Galileo was Marlowe's exact contemporary or that Giordano Bruno was in England during his lifetime:

> Our soules, whose faculties can comprehend
> The wondrous Architecture of the world:
> And measure euery wandring plannets course,
> Still climing after knowledge infinite,
> And alwaies moouing as the restles Spheares,
> Wils vs to weare our selues and neuer rest,
> Vntill we reach the ripest fruit of all,
> That perfect blisse and sole felicitie,
> The sweet fruition of an earthly crowne.   (872–80)

Except for the cæsura at the beginning, and for the enjambment that carries the first line so breathlessly into the second, these nine lines are the suspended periods of a sentence which climbs with its subject to a climax. The last line, however, has had the opposite effect on some of Marlowe's warmest enthusiasts; A. H. Bullen labeled it an anticlimax, and Havelock Ellis denounced it as "Scythian bathos." Such denunciations have resulted from an evident failure to read the passage in its historical context. Reading Ellis and Bullen in their historical context, we can well understand how Marlowe's values fail to accord with the esthetic idealism of the late Victorians. The humanism of the Renaissance led directly from contemplation to action; intellectual curiosity was a means toward a higher end; and the highest end of all the sciences was what Sir Philip Sidney terms *Arkitecktonike* — an illuminating term in this connection, as it is in connection with *The Advancement of Learning*, where Bacon discusses the "Architecture of Fortune" (II, xxiii, 37). Sidney's *Apology for Poetry* places the goal of thought "in the knowledge of a mans selfe, in the Ethicke and politick consideration, with the end of well dooing and not of well knowing onely." Marlowe's ethics may diverge from Sidney's as drastically as Machiavelli diverges from Plato; but Marlowe would agree that knowledge was virtue, even while interpreting knowledge as *libido sciendi* and virtue as *libido dominandi*. Tamburlaine's conception of bliss is not less climactic because it is heresy. Spenser rebukes an overambitious shepherd, whose July motto is *In summo fœlicitas*, and Hamlet equates felicity with heaven. But, whereas a heavenly crown was the pious hope of every Christian, an earthly crown is the notorious emblem of worldliness, heterodoxy, and pride of life. In short, it is not bathos but blasphemy.

A God is not so glorious as a King,

for Tamburlaine, as for his followers, one of whom adds,

I thinke the pleasure they enioy in heauen
Can not compare with kingly ioyes in earth.   (762–4)

Coronation, even more than deposition, sets the key for the play; and "crown" is the all-powerful monosyllable that is bandied back and forth from scene to scene, no less than fifty times. Marlowe was feeding the audience what it wanted when, for a banquet, he dished up a "*course of Crownes*" — he was exploiting the most favored property in the Elizabethan tiring house. The slapstick of the foolish king Mycetes, hiding his crown, is no less symbolic than that earnest scene where the Prince tries on the crown in the second part of *Henry IV* — or, for that matter, the coronet of *King Lear* or the vision of future dynasties in *Macbeth*. The crowning of Zenocrate, whose brows shadow "Triumphes and Trophees" (2295), brings to its close a dramatic progression which might otherwise be endless. Earlier in the fifth act, Tamburlaine has likened those starry eyes of hers to planets; and their tears have evoked his longest monologue, which, we might say, expatiates upon *libido sentiendi*. Having just decreed a massacre of innocent maidens, he feels no pity for his enemies. But, since they are headed by Zenocrate's father, she suffers for them; and, since Tamburlaine is esthetically — if not morally — sensitive, he is touched through her vicarious feeling. His soliloquy rises to the occasion, not unlike the bravura performance of Corneille's *Cid* at a comparable moment. But, where Don Rodrigue's dilemma is love and honor, Tamburlaine's is rather beauty and virtue. "What is beauty?" the hardened warrior pauses to inquire, and he answers by making imagination itself the subject of an overwhelming hyperbole:

> If all the pens that euer poets held,
> Had fed the feeling of their maisters thoughts . . .   (1942-3)

And the conditional clauses, the "ifs" and "ands," ascending in couplets, spiral toward the "highest reaches" until they almost meet the situation. Almost, but not quite, and therein lies the point: that poetry can express more and more of experience, but never all that clamors for expression. Poets still unborn, racking "their restlesse heads" with Heinrich Heine, will long to pluck more pens from a forest of fir trees and use a burning volcano for an inkstand. Yet Marlowe succeeds, by straining the limits of rhetoric, in conveying a sense of the inexpressible,

> Which into words no vertue can digest.   (1954)

Tamburlaine, after this contemplative flight, apologizes for having wandered afield from his soldierly character. Within his soul he now discovers an aptitude for "conceiuing" as well as "subduing." According to the psychology of Marlowe's time, the will could be stirred in two directions by appetite, irascible or concupiscible. Though anger is Tamburlaine's predominant humor, desire is his relation with Zenocrate; for fame and valor need "Beauties iust applause" (1959), and Jupiter has "masked in a Shepheards weed" (394). He ends his meditation by reminding himself and us that his mission is to show the world, in spite of his birth,

That Vertue solely is the sum of glorie,
And fashions men with true nobility.   (1970–1)

The antithesis between virtue and nobility, native capacities as
against inherited advantages, is common enough in the sixteenth
century; even earlier it had been debated in the first English secular
play, *Fulgens and Lucres*; and, of course, the question is only raised
when sentiment favors the hopes of the rising talents. But Marlowe
expressed the sentiment so strongly that he approximated Machiavelli, and encouraged such critics as W. J. Courthope to single
out Tamburlaine as the "incarnation of *virtù*."

Zenocrate, the incarnation of beauty, is visually conceived. While
we look upon her, she is looking at Tamburlaine, who consistently
apostrophizes her eyes; these are "brighter than the Lamps of
heauen" (1218), and his apostrophes to them bedazzle us with
astronomical images. His wooing speech is a *locus classicus* of invidious comparison, redounding lavishly to their mutual credit.
Swayed by the double assault of force and flattery, she does not
acknowledge until he later neglects her that his talk is "sweeter than
the Muses song" (1035) and that she desires nothing more felicitous
than to "liue and die" with him (1009). She dies with him to the
fullest implication when, after her soul has departed, her embalmed
body continues to grace his entourage. It might be said that the
Second Part, like the second sequence of Petrarch's sonnets, is dedicated to a dead heroine. But it could also be said that, like the
beautiful corpse in the Appian Way, discovered so many centuries
after interment, Zenocrate embodies a sensuous ideal. She is the
perfect embodiment of the senses in their very imperfection; her
presence is a continual reminder of the closeness between the carnal
and the charnel. Her melodious weeping accompanies Bajazeth's
downfall, and her own deathbed presents the crucial instance of
"this fraile and transitory flesh" (3011). Tamburlaine's way of
lamenting her is to challenge the classic portrayals of feminine
loveliness:

And had she liu'd before the siege of *Troy*,
Hellen, whose beauty sommond Greece to armes,
And drew a thousand ships to *Tenedos*,
Had not bene nam'd in *Homers* Iliads.   (3054–7)

This might be called the hyperbole pedantic. It figures in the next
act when Tamburlaine, to "ouerdare" the Turks, identifies himself

THE PROGRESS OF POMP   41

with Hector visiting the Grecian camp. Tardily he seems to realize —
for previous portrayal has identified him with Achilles — that he is
not heralding himself with a favorable omen:

I doe you honor in the *simile*.   (3571)

Such evocations do not conjure up myths; they exorcise a youthful
poet's literary self-consciousness. The shades of Troy, which hovered
on the edge of actuality for Dido and Æneas, grow more remote
in juxtaposition with Zenocrate and Tamburlaine. The latter is much
more closely related to Spenser's Prince Arthur, from whose eques-
trian portrait Marlowe borrows a plume or two. Yet, in the midst of
those five borrowed lines, a sixth appears which is unmistakably
Marlowe's:

With bloomes more white than *Hericinas* browes.   (4101)

The wonder is that Marlowe's originality has already manifested
itself, that the style of *Tamburlaine* is so fully fledged. As a matter
of fact, we have no explicit evidence for connecting the play with
him; yet no one has seriously doubted his authorship, because each
verse is so strongly marked by the impress of his personality; and
such Marlovian words as "clang" and "ceaseless" seem to be neol-
ogisms here. Habits of speech and thought which pervade his work
are enunciated here most densely and most emphatically. Thus
Professor F. I. Carpenter, studying Marlowe's similes and metaphors, found no less than 400 in both parts of *Tamburlaine*, as
against a total of some 250 from all the later plays, where his idiosyncrasies are controlled and modified. Where they spontaneously
assert themselves, sounding out the medium and testing possibilities,
and where repetitions and totals are of the essence, statistics can be
revealing. Thus in *Tamburlaine*, the amplest vehicle for Marlowe's
fascination with proper names, we can count 1,410 of them. More
than a third of these, 545, gain peculiar stress by coming at the end
of a line. This means that 12 per cent of the lines of the two plays
terminate with such a colorful polysyllable. The impression that
Tamburlaine makes — speaking a third of the time, and spoken
about during much of the remainder — is underlined by repeating
his name more often than any other. It is noteworthy too that, under
the influence of Marlowe's symmetrical rhythms, 15 per cent of the
lines commence with "and." The strongest lines are those in which

this conjunction is the first syllable and the two last feet are rounded out with a proper name. Characteristically:

> And ride in triumph through *Persepolis?* (755)

Clanging at the gates of Memphis, marching on to Babylon, Marlowe conducts a grand tour of falling capitals, each one an object lesson like Ninevah or Troy. Like the wanderings of Io, recounted to Prometheus, they give the setting immense geographic extension. Proclamations and treaties interpolate further place names until so much distance has been covered that Tamburlaine, resolving to "confute those blind Geographers" (1715), seeks to map regions hitherto unexplored. Provinces merge into continents:

> All *Asia* is in Armes with *Tamburlaine.* (2397)
>
> All *Affrike* is in Armes with *Tamburlaine.* (2401)

Local color, at this stage, is less important than hemispheric size. "All" and "every" are indispensable words, and many a list trails off in an ampersand, the breathless phrase, "and the rest." As suspense gathers with the mustering armies, drama and poetry hinge upon arithmetic, and numbers are multiplied by roll calls and epic catalogues. "Let thousands die" (1236), cries Bajazeth, whose cunning is reckoned as "millions infinite" (1131) and whose successors reckon with "numbers more than infinit" (2875). There, where enumeration breaks down, we may turn back to nature, which is frequently called upon to assist Tamburlaine with pathetic fallacies. Just as Zenocrate's beauty is mirrored in the skies, so his prowess is registered by the earth; and more than once his assembled host

> Makes Earthquakes in the hearts of men and heauen. (2865)

It is not for nothing that the original octavo refers to the two plays as "Tragicall Discourses." Theatrical makeshifts, alarums and excursions, a ringing bell and an occasional party of supernumeraries could scarcely have set such world-shaking battles in motion, had it not been for what Ben Jonson — in his prologue to *Every Man in His Humour* — called the "helpe of some few foot-and-halfe-foote words." Driven by an impetus toward infinity and faced with the limitations of the stage, the basic convention of Marlovian drama is to take the word for the deed. Words are weapons; conflict perforce is invective, verbal rather than physical aggression; through musters and parleys, wars of nerves are fought out by exchanging boasts or parrying insults. They resemble those flytings of the Middle Ages, where warriors undertook to outdare each other, or the *agon* of Aristophanic comedy, where the Sausage-Seller overreaches the Demagogue. The braggadocio of the antagonists matches the tall talk of our American frontiersmen, when they yawped about whipping their weight in wildcats. Dialogue does not flow in *Tamburlaine*; characters converse in formal monologues, accumulating to rhetorical lengths; the text consists mainly of set pieces or purple passages, rather loosely strung together by short bits of awkward verse and functional prose. We are reminded of how, in grand opera, the arias deliquesce into recitative. We are not surprised that Hector Berlioz composed two operas on themes which Marlowe had rendered; what may be surprising is that no composer has attempted a musical rendering of *Tamburlaine*. But that would be a work of supererogation; for Marlowe contrives his own sound effects, manipulating a language which is not simply a means of communication but a substitute for representation. Magniloquence does duty for magnificence.

Hence the hero is a consummate rhetorician and, conversely, weakness is represented as speechlessness. The weakling Mycetes, since he is king, has the prerogative of opening the play; but, since this requires "a great and thundring speech," he confesses that he is "insufficient to expresse the same" (10). Thereupon, preparing us for his subsequent displacement, he yields the floor to his more articulate brother. Afterwards, habitually depending upon the eloquence of others, he dispatches an envoy to Tamburlaine:

> Go, stout *Theridimas*, thy words are swords
> And with thy lookes thou conquerest all thy foes. (82–3)

And in the next scene, after seeing and hearing Tamburlaine, Theridamas responds:

> Won with thy words, & conquered with thy looks,
> I yeeld my selfe, my men & horse to thee. (423–4)

Tamburlaine, after capturing and courting Zenocrate, has decided — against the advice of his lieutenants — to "play the Orator" with Theridamas (325) and to "tice" the Persians by displaying his treasure at a parley (419). The argument becomes visual as well as vocal, and is reinforced by looks which "menace heauen and dare the Gods" (352) and notably by "his piercing instruments of sight" (468). He is shown to be "the king of men," more particularly, by his ability to "perswade at such a sodaine pinch" (491). If he did not move Theridamas by "perswasions" (406), he would try to intimidate him by "vaunts" (408) — which could, if worst came to worst, be made good on the battlefield. The testimony of his fallen opponents substantiates his own menacing employment of the future tense:

> For Wil and Shall best fitteth *Tamburlain*. (1139)

On the other hand, we have just seen and heard him playing the passionate shepherd:

> Disdaines *Zenocrate* to liue with me? (278)

he has pleaded, and spread out before her a vista of enticement which, *ex hypothesi*, surpasses anything that any other lover could possibly offer. Theridamas, trying the same approach in the Second Part, only succeeds in driving Olympia to mortal desperation. Marlowe's Ovidian strain, the invitation to love, is richly latent in the First Part, though it is gradually drowned out by a harsher sound, the challenge to battle. Tamburlaine commands both modes of rhetoric, the plea and the threat, the poetry of Venus and the oratory of Mars. Vaunt and persuasion combine when enemies are converted to allies by his "woorking woordes" (623). The convention is so securely established by the opening of the Second Part that it can be comically handled. The imprisoned Callapine begins to elaborate a set speech:

> By *Cario* runs. (2506)

Whereupon his jailer, Almeda, interrupts the blank verse:

> No talke of running, I tell you sir. (2501–7)

Beyond the trivial quip, Almeda's serious assumption is that, if he listens, he will inevitably be persuaded. And so he is. Callapine begins again, and goes on with promises of a crown and a coach and endless erotic delights. Forthwith Almeda decamps with him to enjoy those pleasures, and to burlesque the exploits of Tamburlaine.

The prize of an earthly crown, by the time Almeda attains it, has been considerably cheapened. As soon as Tamburlaine has attained his kingship, it is not enough for him to be a king; he must be kingmaker, and reward his faithful friends with contributory kingdoms. The petty kings of Fez, Morocco, and Algiers, who pay tribute to the Sultan of Turkey, must surrender their crowns to Techelles, Usumcasane, and Theridamas, whose euphonious names accomplish as much as their swords to swell the chorus of Tamburlaine's following. Viceroys, like all the other configurations of his universe, go by threes. Since words are the moral equivalent of deeds, and since he must have rivals worthy of his mettle, each of them must rant in the fashion of Herod and then be out-Heroded by Tamburlaine. Bajazeth has his own grandiloquence, and complacently savors the oriental hyperboles of his pashas. Tamburlaine is never persuaded by others, and never intimidated by their speeches. "Tush," he says, and the scornful interjection becomes a habit with Marlowe's protagonists,

> Tush. Turkes are ful of brags
> And menace more than they can wel performe. (1101–2)

Shortly thereafter, when he has become an emperor, the incense of adulation ascends to his nostrils; while Bajazeth's empress, Zabina, has forfeited the attributes of majesty:

> The pillers that haue bolstered vp those tearmes,
> Are falne in clusters at my conquering feet. (1327–8)

Historically, it was the Battle of Angora that undermined those terms and spelled the difference between Turkish menace and military performance. Dramatically, this great event occurs offstage; and though a few sorties are indicated, the stage direction makes *"the battell short."* On stage we witness a battle of Billingsgate between Zabina and Zenocrate, entrusted meanwhile with the crowns of their respective countries, and instructed to "manage words" as their husbands are managing arms (1229). Marlowe's stratagem of out-Heroding Herod, which builds up Tamburlaine into a king of kings by breaking down the others, is absurdly reversed when these tragedy-queens tirade like fishwives, each threatening to make the other the servant of her servants. With the victors enthroned and the victims encaged, their intercourse is reduced to taunts and curses. Bajazeth, finding the humiliation "expreslesse",

(2063), brains himself against his cage; Zabina does likewise, but not before her emotion has come to the surface in madness. Here Marlowe has ventured on one of his most effective innovations; he has broken away from verse altogether and utilized the more supple cadencing of prose to catch the distracted stream of her consciousness. This device would be adopted for the conventional treatment of mad scenes in Elizabethan drama. We can trace its adoption through *The Spanish Tragedy*, which was written in elaborately regular blank verse and afterwards seasoned with interpolations in the newer style. And Ophelia's last words will reëcho Zabina's:

> Streamers white, Red, Blacke, here, here, here. Fling the meat in his face. *Tamburlaine, Tamburlaine*, Let the souldiers be buried. Hel, death, *Tamburlain*, Hell, make ready my Coch, my chaire, my iewels, I come, I come, I come. (2096–100)

There is a poignance in these few broken lines which is lacking in the grandiose scenes they recapitulate, and which again contrasts with the stately formality of Zenocrate's ensuing scene. Her threnody over the bodies, with its moralistic refrain and its incremental repetition, is rhythmically and thematically linked with her husband's lamentation over her in the Second Part and with the choric lament of his lieutenants upon his death. The plea and the threat, the strains of love and war, are resolved in the lament, the mode of death.

In tracing the declamatory technique of the two plays, we ought not to neglect their scenic structure. "Marlowe's keen eye for spectacular effect" — in the phrase of the keen-eyed theatrical historian, W. J. Lawrence — was second only to his mighty lines in shaping a form and attracting an audience. Here his contribution was to devise stage business as sensational as his astounding terms. Looks and words, those two components of drama, the blood and the thunder, had been rigidly kept apart at the Inns of Court, where tragedy was still a kind of legal or parliamentary debate. Good and bad counselors argued in *Gorboduc*, choruses moralized, and orations brought home how ill advised it was

> To hazarde life for conquest of a crowne. (V, i, 157)

Between the acts, which were so pervasively oratorical, came dumb shows — pageant-like interludes or allegorical pantomimes with music, wherein the ethical purport of the dialogue was mutely but

THE PROGRESS OF POMP 47

spectacularly symbolized. Thus the goddess Fortune, crowning slaves and uncrowning kings, appeared at a pertinent interval in *Jocasta*. What was even more to Marlowe's purpose, the prologue to that tragedy was a dumb show,

> Representing vnto vs Ambition, by the hystorie of *Sesostres* king of *Egypt*, who beeing in his time and reigne a mightie Conquerour, yet not content to haue subdued many princes, and taken from them their kingdomes and dominions, did in like maner cause those Kinges whome he had so ouercome, to draw in his Chariote like Beastes and Oxen, thereby to content his vnbrideled ambitious desire.

The parable was not an unfamiliar one. Marlowe would have seen it signalized as a warning to Cæsar, had he looked ahead from his translation to the tenth book of Lucan. And if he had read Le Roy on *The Variety of Things*, he had seen the footstool of Timur coupled with the chariot of Sesostris. Nothing in Timur's adventures had gone quite so far; and in the First Part it is Bajazeth's notion that he should be "horsed on fower mightie kings" (1522) and that Tamburlaine should "draw the chariot" of Zabina (1178). No preparation could have eased the shock of Tamburlaine's triumphal entrance in the Second Part, literally scourging his enemies, out-Heroding his regal steeds with a vengeance, and shouting hyperbolically:

> Holla, ye pampered Iades of *Asia*:
> What, can ye draw but twenty miles a day,
> And haue so proud a chariot at your heeles . . . ? (3980-2)

The absence of actual horses from the stage, and the problem of Shakespeare and others in getting around them, throw a special light on Marlowe's ingenuity. But his audacity lay in taking a metaphor and acting it out, in turning a manner of speaking into a mode of action, in concretely realizing what had theretofore subsisted on the plane of precept and fantasy. It meant breaking through the artificial compartments that divided speech from spectacle in the tragedies of the Inns of Court, and making drama a much more flexible instrument for mirroring as well as echoing life.

Gigantic marionettes with iron mouths, but with no more than two or three simple and violent gestures — so a French critic, Jules Lemaître, has characterized the dramatis personæ of *Tamburlaine*. And it is perfectly true that Tamburlaine's character shows no change or growth or development; his metamorphosis from low birth to lofty position is completed by his very earliest gesture, when he sweeps aside his shepherd's weeds and steps forth in full armor. Always the actor bidding for our attention, he can also be the spectator and amuse himself by making pageants of his enemies. Though his wrathful glance does not literally kill, when for once he "*sayes nothing*" it terrifies the stoical Agydas into stabbing himself. Tamburlaine's moods are expressionistically symbolized in the "*streaming collors*" of his tents and his costumes, white and peaceable upon the first day, red and bloody on the second, black "*and verie melancholy*" on the third. The whole work is painted in this lurid color scheme, in the shades of love, war, and death, successively — with two exceptions borrowed from Homer and Spenser, the amber of the hero's locks and the verdure of his plumes. Otherwise there are no greens or yellows, and no browns or blues, none of the hues of the landscape, of ordinary nature. The contrast with Shakespeare could not be more vividly illustrated; for black and white are hardly colors at all, but an alternation between darkness and brightness, often associated with the glitter of metals; while red, the color of blood, for Marlowe is tinged with the dazzlement of fire and highlighted with flashes of lapidary and astronomical imagery. It is less a question of coloring than of lighting in Tamburlaine's threnody over Zenocrate:

> Blacke is the beauty of the brightest day,
> The golden balle of heauens eternal fire,
> That danc'd with glorie on the siluer waues . . .
> Ready to darken earth with endlesse night.   (2969–75)

Every scene offers the hero a new pedestal and stimulates him to strike another posture, as when he wounds himself and compels his sons to dip their hands in his blood. Symbols of domination and subjection are used as stage properties: his cage, his scourge, his chariot, his plethora of crowns. His emotions are so thoroughly extroverted that he expresses his final grief for his queen by burning the town where she died. This is an opportunity for fireworks; and there are other signs of elaboration in the staging of the Second Part, as distinguished from the processional movement of the First. Yet the restless caravan keeps moving, joined by her hearse, and despite another defection along the way. Tamburlaine has observed that his sons take after their mother: "their looks are amorous, / Not martiall . . ." (2590–1). Two of the three, in response to paternal discipline, vie with each other to become little scourges and terrors of the world. But Calyphas, the third, is a cynical Epicurean who shuns the battle, professing remorse of conscience. The exposure of his cowardice is a turning point — not because his father instantly slays him, which almost goes without saying, but because it scourges the scourger; and it inspires Tamburlaine, as did the death of Zenocrate, to flout the gods of Olympus. Jove, whom he had been naming as his exemplar and patron, now seems to be his rival and enemy. Whereas he has justified his subversions by recalling how the Olympians overthrew Saturn, now he would seem to be on the side of the Titans. At the start, motivated by "Giantly presumption" (813), he anticipated "more than Cyclopian warres" (619). By the end of the First Part he is a candidate for apotheosis. But the Second reveals the self-proclaimed god as a mortal, a human being whose strength is his inhumanity and whose weakness is his mortality,

Rauing, impatient, desperate and mad. (3080)

In the First Part, when Tamburlaine conquers the Turks and frees the galley slaves, he acts as an avenger — if not a defender — of Christendom. In the Second Part he is opposed by the Christians, who league against him with the Turkish armies. With some misgiving, the King of Hungary is convinced by his generals that "necessary pollycy" (2832) dispenses those who profess the true religion from honoring the oaths they have sworn to infidels. Marlowe is dealing here with the casuistical argument that led to the Battle of Varna in 1444, when the papal legate absolved the crusaders of the Holy Roman Empire from a truce they had just signed with the Ottoman forces. Their equivocation was sometimes considered a test case for the morality of that famous or infamous chapter where Machiavelli had pondered the ways of princes in keeping and breaking faith. The outcome, though it discredited the Christians, could be said to have vindicated Christianity, or might, as Marlowe again implies, be blamed upon "the fortune of the wars" (2952). At all events, the faithless allies are punished, zealously slaughtered and syncretistically consigned to a hell of "quencelesse flame" (2945) and "quenchlesse fire" (3529), in which Christian and Mohammedan features are blended with a classical paganism. Similarly, heaven seems to coexist with Elysium and with the

THE OVERREACHER

Mohammedan paradise; and if Mohammed is styled "the friend of God" (2462), Christ is envisioned as "son to euerliuing *Ioue*" (2898), who seems in this regard — as in the Miltonic usage — to be consubstantial with Jehovah. Under his pantheistic immanence, which approaches Spinoza's doctrine that the existence is the essence of God, Christ and Mohammed look down together dispassionately from the Empyrean. And Marlowe puts his loftiest religious sentiments into the mouth of an infidel, when the King of Natolia prays to both, defining God as

> he that sits on high and neuer sleeps,
> Nor in one place is circumscriptible,
> But euery where fils euery Continent,
> With strange infusion of his sacred vigor . . .   (2906–09)

At the other extreme, abjuring Mohammed, Tamburlaine orders the Koran to be burned, and even doubts the revenging God — "if any God" (4312) — whose scourge he has heretofore considered himself. The epithet has always been ambiguous, and now it is divinity which is flagellated. The bonfire of "supersticious bookes" (4285) was, to some of Marlowe's contemporaries, a self-dramatized confession of his Atheism; it meant, to Robert Greene, daring God out of heaven. Yet the scene, though ambivalent in its dramatic shock, is by no means heretical. In so far as its target is Mohammedanism, it conforms to the doctrines of orthodox Christianity. In so far as it aims at nearer targets, it anticipates Voltaire's discovery that, under pretense of attacking Islam, the rationalistic playwright could attack all organized religions. Yet Marlowe resolves this dangerous question with such oracular ambiguity that even Mohammed has a chance to vindicate his prestige. A moment after the sacrilege, after the drowning of the Babylonians has been reported to Tamburlaine, he feels himself "distempered sudainly" (4329). Next, his only foe who is still at large, Callapine, supplicates Mohammed to revenge the overthrow of Bajazeth. Then the three comrades-in-arms open the final scene with a sort of apocalyptic chant; for them the whole cosmos is turned upside down, the head of heaven significantly crowned with the "foot-stoole" of hell (4421). To Tamburlaine, stricken at the height of his megalomania, divine intervention is the real audacity.

> What daring God torments my body thus . . . ?   (4434)

he asks, and rallies to make his ultimate gesture. Alexander the Great, seeking more worlds to conquer, had thought of besieging the heavens — a supreme instance of desire for rule, *late dominandi cupiditas*, according to Lorenzo Valla. In Boiardo's *Orlando Inamorato* (II, i, 64), the Saracens boast that, when they have beaten Charlemagne and subjugated the earth, they will carry the battle into paradise. Such a Titanic dare is Tamburlaine's climax of climaxes:

> Come let vs march against the powers of heauen,
> And set blacke streamers in the firmament,
> To signifie the slaughter of the Gods.   (4440–2)

In the last act of the earlier play, Tamburlaine has peremptorily commanded his soldiers to hand the Damascene Virgins over to his servant, "imperious Death" (1892). Now, though he still regards "the vglie monster death" as his slave (4459), he is aware that he himself can no longer be master. The overreacher has out-Heroded himself: "the Scourge of God must die" (4641). The wheel of Fortune, which seemed to spin at his pleasure, has come full circle. Whereas he boasted of binding the Fates in his chains, now it is they who overthrow his triumphs. The iron logic that justified his many victories now justifies his one defeat,

> Since Fate commands, and proud necessity.   (4598)

His deathbed is surrounded with trophies of conquest. The conquest of beauty, his esthetic impulse, which seems to have waned with Zenocrate, is preserved unwithered in her hearse. Knowledge is summed up by the map of his conquests, whereon he traces the boundaries of territories unconquered and uncharted, looking west to the mines of Eldorado and even looking ahead to the Suez Canal. The conquered crown and the conquering scourge are perquisites of an unsated will to power, and his elder son is duly invested with them. But the dominating symbol is his proud chariot, and the dominant image is "the pride of *Phaeton*" (4637). Will his successor be able to harness royalty or will he go plunging down in a blaze of vainglory? And is it not himself that he discerns in the fatal rashness of "*Clymenes* brainsicke sonne" (4624)? After humbling Bajazeth, he portentously vaunted his own repute to be

> As was the fame of *Clymenes* brain-sicke sonne,
> That almost brent the Axeltree of heauen.   (1493–4)

Phaëthon's sudden descent, as the archetypal fate of the tragic hero, had been evoked by the chorus of *Gorboduc* and would be recalled at a poignant moment in *Richard II*. It was linked with the defeated Armada in *Elizabetha Triumphans* by James Aske, a blank-verse pamphlet contemporaneous with *Tamburlaine*. The Elizabethan court knew how to celebrate such occasions, and of its masques and tournaments Bacon wrote: "The Glories of them, are chiefly in the Chariots." But the vehicles of Marlowe's imagination — the Roman processions that ride out of Lucan and Ovid into *Dido* and *Edward II*, the daydreams of triumph that culminate in *Tamburlaine* — went beyond the panoply of state. Life was conceived, in the pageants of the Renaissance, as a sequence of triumphs; all too quickly, however, they pass by; and the car of the triumphant is inevitably flanked by those he has triumphed over. Petrarch's *Trionfi* are devoted not only to Love and Chastity and Fame, but also to Time and Death and Divinity. *Sic transit gloria mundi*. We are temporarily bedazzled by the "Sun-bright armour" of Tamburlaine's troops (620) and by the resplendent array of solar images which traditionally radiate from kingship. Planning to ride in triumph up the Milky Way, he saw his coach as Jupiter's "shining chariot, gilt with fire" (4105). And now his triumphal chariot is seen as a fiery chariot — not bearing him like Elijah off to heaven, but classically prefiguring the delusion of grandeur, the *hubris* that goes before a meteoric fall.

Perhaps we have gone far enough, yet modern interpretation has ventured farther. Poe has made *Tamerlane* a Byronic hero, "A diadem'd outlaw" who has isolated himself by abandoning love for ambition. The artist who paints the subject, in George Eliot's *Middlemarch*, has a post-Darwinian explanation: "I take Tamburlaine in his chariot for the tremendous course of the world's physical history lashing on the harnessed dynasties (II, xxii). From that distance, Timur may have seemed more credible as a force of nature than as a historical figure. Yet Arnold Toynbee has more lately vouched for the credibility of Marlowe's portraiture and has instanced Timur's accomplishment as "a supreme example of the suicidalness of Militarism." To the most civilized mind of Marlowe's century, Montaigne, much the same lesson could already be drawn from the same example, proving that arms and arts did not flourish side by side, that the art of war was fundamentally barbarous, and that

"the most warlike nations . . . are the rudest and most ignorant."
It is a sobering comment on our age, if not on Marlowe's tragedy,
that, after having all but dropped out of the repertory for more than
three hundred years, its recent revival has been greeted as peculiarly
meaningful and appropriate. The massing of armies, the breaking
of treaties, the cult of despots, the regimentation of satellites, the
clashing extremes of East and West — hyperbole seems powerless
to exaggerate the commonplaces of our daily news. Marlowe seems
comparatively innocent, a boyish scholar indulging his spellbound
fancy in heroics, making destruction a basis for creation. Not that
his panorama, wide as it is, has room for moral compunctions: only
the esthete Calyphas feels "what it is to kil a man" (3700), and
merely the weakling Mycetes curses the man "that first inuented
war" (664). Since they and their fellow tragedians are so patently
engaged in wars of words, we are not deeply touched; and, after
the reëchoing captains and rhetorical kings have made their exeunt,
their verbalism rings hollow. But, in retrospect, the very hollowness
adds a reverberation of irony. To Shelley we may turn for a doubtful
epitaph:

> And on the pedestal these words appear:
> "My name is Ozymandias, king of kings:
> Look on my works, ye Mighty, and despair!"
> Nothing beside remains. Round the decay
> Of that colossal wreck, boundless and bare
> The lone and level sands stretch far away.

Chapter **III**

MORE OF THE SERPENT

What next? That has always been the crucial question for the creative mind. How can it continue to surprise the audience captured by its early boldness? The Renaissance could offer more in the way of unrealized potentialities, could open wider and smoother channels to innovation, than the age of Joyce, Picasso, and Stravinsky. But Marlowe, like the most original artists of our century, strives to surpass himself with every effort. After his triumphant arrival with *Tamburlaine*, all his viceroys — Peele, Lodge, Greene, and the rest — duly gained their contributory crowns. But Marlowe's own hyperbolic impetus had carried him as far as he could possibly go on the naïvely imperialistic plane. The next step he took, in whatever direction, would involve some kind of strategic retreat *pour mieux sauter*. Because his works were produced within so brief a span, we are not quite certain which of them came next. Each of them, however, introduces novelties of conception and execution which range them in a fairly logical order, proceeding from simplicity toward complexity and coinciding with the chronological sequence, as nearly as it can be inferred from the external evidence. *Tamburlaine*, the simplest, laid down the outline of a new dramatic genre, the tragedy of ambition — an ascending line propelled by the momentum of a single character, whose human relationships are incidental to his ulterior goal, and whose conflicts are literal, overt, and invariably successful. If Tamburlaine had been more evenly matched against other characters, if his victims had been presented more sympathetically, if his path had been crossed by more effectual foes, if Callapine rather than heaven had avenged the death of Bajazeth, *Tamburlaine* would have fitted into a more elaborate and conventional genre, the tragedy of revenge.

That form arrived, not long after *Tamburlaine*, with Marlowe's gloomy colleague, Thomas Kyd, and his *Spanish Tragedy*. It gave to the enlarging repertory a role of comparable stature and much greater emotional range; for, while Tamburlaine threatened and acted, it remained for Hieronimo to lament and suffer, to "shew a passion" (III, xiia, 145). While Tamburlaine was a superhuman antagonist, driven by some sort of inner urge, Hieronimo is more of a human protagonist, responding to the outer situation; but since he is rather the challenged than the challenger, it is the situation that predominates — the vendetta thrust upon him when his son is murdered while seeking to avenge a previous murder. While Marlowe had been concerned with the individual who is a law unto himself, Kyd's concern was with the more general laws of God and man. *Tamburlaine* is an esthetic spectacle, framed by an equivocal morality, which is flouted more emphatically than it is asserted. *The Spanish Tragedy*, though it is intermittently heroic, is consistently ethical; in subordinating love and war to revenge, it measures private motives against public sanctions. To take the law into one's own hands may be "a kinde of Wilde Iustice," as Bacon defined it; but it implies an ethos, however primitive, which the hero imposes on others instead of rejecting. It was ambition that animated character, on the vast scale of Elizabethan drama; but it is revenge that motivates plot; and plot is the main thing, for technicians like Aristotle. For the Elizabethans, a plot was originally a piece of ground or the design of a house; and Shakespeare is fully conscious of the metaphor, when his plotters conspire in the second part of *Henry IV* (I, iii, 42). Thence the term was used more abstractly for any scheme, especially for a conspiracy against the established order, as when "the plot is laide" in *The Massacre at Paris* (165). By a later extension, after many such intrigues had been hatched upon the stage, it was neutrally applied to the plan of a literary work.

Thus plot is a moral as well as a technical concept, which presupposes some responsible agent. As George Meredith, in *Modern Love*, discerned:

> In tragic life, God wot,
> No villain need be! Passions spin the plot:
> We are betray'd by what is false within.

But when the heroine of *The Spanish Tragedy* cries out, "We are betraide" (II, iv, 50), the hero is eminently justified in suspecting malice aforethought. So is Navarre, when the same cry goes up in *The Massacre at Paris* (202). In short, we are in the presence of the villain — that ingenious theatrical figure who, by pulling the wires of the story, determines the structure of the play. Properly, his name has a low origin in the feudal term *villein*, a peasant or base fellow, which was easily transferred from a social to a moral context, and thence to the theater. The role that it stigmatizes is closely related to that of the Vice, the mischievous tempter in the moralities, or to the clever slaves and parasites who manipulated

Roman comedy. Where Tamburlaine enacted the *Alazon* or proud man, your villain must enact the *Eiron* or sly man. The irony lies in the difference between his conduct upstage and his machinations behind the scenes, as it were. But what he conceals from the other characters must be revealed directly to the audience, and this convention tends to be less and less convincing. Thus Richard III, the Shakespearean heir of Marlovian invention, soliloquizes at his first appearance:

> I am determined to proue a Villaine. (I, i, 30)

Life would be considerably less tragic, God wot, if villainy announced itself in such resounding tones. The villains of actuality are readier to invest themselves, like Tamburlaine, with the sense of a lofty mission. Few, if any, of them are cold-blooded hypocrites; what is false in our world is largely perpetrated by men who sincerely believe that it is true, and launch indignant countercharges at all who doubt the nobility of their intentions. The problem of evil would be no problem at all, if good and bad were clearly labeled in black and white. The difficulties of choice are the source of tragedy. "In the twilight," Jean-Paul Sartre has reminded us, "it takes sharp eyesight to distinguish God from the Devil." To Macbeth, confounding the colors of good and evil, fair seems foul and foul seems fair. When Othello puts his trust in honest Iago, it is the blackamoor who is truly noble, the white man who is black-hearted. Yet when Shakespeare attempted his first tragedy, *Titus Andronicus*, he explicitly painted his Moorish villain as black as the traditional devil. By the time he came to *Julius Cæsar*, he had acquired his comprehensive awareness of the endless jar between right and wrong. A contemporary witness, John Weever, tells us:

> The many-headed multitude were drawne
> By *Brutus* speach, that *Cæsar* was ambitious,
> When eloquent *Mark Antonie* had showne
> His vertues, who but *Brutus* then was vicious?

Antony's vices would be shown up by Octavius, with the next revolution of Fortune's wheel; and Brutus, retrospectively, could claim to have been revenging Pompey's death. The question of war guilt can be pushed back indefinitely, and the blood feud is handed on from one generation to another. So it goes, with ambition and revenge acting as stimulus and reacting as response. The rising and falling lines are crisscrossed and paralleled in a symmetrical pattern of motivation. Sympathies shift when the erstwhile villain is hailed as a fallen hero, or when the revenger turns out to be a villain. With the give-and-take of injuries, gore is bound to flow in ever-increasing amounts. The ethic of revenge is the *lex talionis*, the Mosaic code of an eye for any eye, a thumb for a thumb. On the grim but equable assumption that "blood asketh blood," *Gorboduc* sacrifices a life for a life, a Ferrex for a Porrex (IV, Chorus, 17). But to right a grievous wrong by retaliating is to provoke the loss of further lives. Furthermore, revengers usually try to better the instruction, as Shylock would, if not for the intervention of a more merciful kind of justice.

> Thou never dost enough revenge the wronge,
> Exept thou passe,

says Atreus in Jasper Heywood's translation of Seneca's *Thyestes*; and his cruelty to his brother's children is so surpassing that it brings down a curse upon the heads of his own. Warmed over by Shakespeare, it provides the cannibalistic catastrophe for *Titus Andronicus*. Though Kyd's Hieronimo is more punctilious, he cannot rest until he is "reuenged thorowly" (IV, iv, 172). And Kyd's Soliman, at a similar consummation, rejoices in having revenged a friend's death "with many deaths" (V, iv, 148) — a total of thirteen in the play, *Soliman and Perseda*, as compared with eleven in *The Spanish Tragedy*. The fact that nine of the dramatis personæ do not survive the last act of *Hamlet* evinces Shakespeare's relative moderation. There are sixteen corpses in the two parts of *Tamburlaine*, not counting the casualty lists from the battlefields. Apart from the offstage carnage in *The Massacre at Paris*, such as the hundred Huguenots drowned in the Seine, twenty characters are killed *coram populo* during an unusually abbreviated play — an average of one killing for every sixty-three lines.

Numbers, at that rate, mean all too little; it is taken for granted that an Elizabethan tragedy will terminate in many deaths; there is more significance in the manner of them. Here the fine Italian hand of Machiavellianism is discernible; and *The Jew of Malta* is notable, not for its twelve fatalities — exclusive of the poisoned convent and the exploded monastery — but for the perverse ingenuity with which they are conceived and executed. Marlowe might well be expected to outdo Kyd's theatricalism, to sharpen the formula for the tragedy of revenge, to discipline its wallowing emotions by his ruthless intellectuality. But, in the process, he seems to have learned a good deal from *The Spanish Tragedy*: from its complicated plotting, its interplay of motive, and above all its moralistic tone. He was still too much of an intellectualist to let himself be constricted by this framework, and too much of a hero-worshiper to let his hero suffer very acutely. Barabas the Jew is a man with a grievance, but his retaliation outruns the provocation. His revenges, augmented by his ambitions, are so thoroughgoing that the revenger becomes a villain. He is not merely less sinned against than sinning; he is the very incarnation of sin, the scape-goat sent out into the wilderness burdened with all the sins that flesh inherits. *Tamburlaine* dealt with the world and the flesh, but not with the devil; that was to be the sphere of *Doctor Faustus*. Somewhere between the microcosm of *Doctor Faustus* and the macrocosm of *Tamburlaine* stands *The Jew of Malta*. Contrasted with the amoral Tamburlaine, Barabas is an immoralist, who acknowledges values by overturning them. Contrasted with the devil-worshiping Faustus, he is more consistently and more superficially diabolical. His is a test case for the worldly logic, if not for the spiritual consequences, of the Satanic decision: "Evil be thou my Good" (*Paradise Lost*, IV, 110).

In Shakespeare, as critics have noted, it is the villains who expound free will and take a skeptical view of planetary influences. In Marlowe the villains are heroes, by virtue — or perhaps we should say *virtù* — of their unwillingness to accept misfortune. As soon as he is left "to sinke or swim" (503), Barabas defies his "lucklesse Starres" (495). Like Tamburlaine and the rest, he considers himself to be "fram'd of finer mold then common men" (453). His attitude toward others is that of Lorenzo, the villain of *The Spanish Tragedy*:

Ile trust my selfe, my selfe shall be my freend. (III, ii, 118)

This fundamental premise of egoism is stated even more incisively by Richard III:

Richard loues *Richard*, that is, I am I. (V, iii, 184)

Barabas makes the same affirmation, somewhat more deviously, by misquoting slightly from the *Andria* of Terence:

Ego mihimet sum semper proximus. (228)

The articles of his credo have been more bluntly set forth in the prologue, where Machiavel makes a personal appearance to bespeak the favor of the spectators for his protégé. It was a bold stroke, which undoubtedly thrilled them, with a different thrill from the one they felt at beholding Marlowe's resurrection of Helen of Troy. Marlowe based his speech on a Latin monologue by Gabriel Harvey, and both scholar-poets were in a position to know how grossly they distorted Machiavelli's doctrine and personality. Yet, in misrepresenting him, they voiced a state of mind which he anticipated and which Nietzsche would personify: the impatience with words and ideas, the special fascination with brutal facts, that marks the disaffected intellectual. Might could be right, snarls Machiavel, and fortification more important than learning. Marlowe must also have enjoyed the occasion for shocking the middle class, which wanted improving precepts from the drama. Instead, with Cæsarian flourishes and Draconian precedents, he propounds a series of maxims which Blake might have included in his "Proverbs of Hell." These reflect the English suspicions of popery and of other Italianate observances, recently intensified by the persecution of the French Protestants and by the indictment that Gentillet had itemized in his *Anti-Machiavel.*

I count Religion but a childish Toy,
And hold there is no sinne but Ignorance. (14–5)

This last is a Machiavellian corollary to the Socratic equation of knowledge and virtue. As for religion, it is dismissed by Atheism with a peculiarly Marlovian monosyllable. Just as polysyllables are a means of aggrandizement, "toy" — which in Marlowe's day meant trifle or frivolity — is the ultimate in belittlement.

The Jew of Malta, continuing Marlowe's studies in *libido dominandi*, emphasizes conspiracy rather than conquest — or, in the terms laid down by *Tamburlaine*, policy rather than prowess. From the roaring of the lion we turn to the wiles of the fox. "Policy," the shibboleth of political realism, is mentioned thirteen times, and serves to associate Barabas with Machiavelli. Barabas is well qualified to speak for himself, speaking more lines than any of Marlowe's other characters, indeed, about half of the play. Whereas Machiavel has his "climing followers," they have theirs, from Támburlaine's viceroys to Edward's favorites; and even Barabas, in his egoistic isolation, takes up with an alter ego. The knight of Lope de Vega has his *gracioso*; the rogue of the picaresque novel commonly squires a fellow-traveler; and Barabas the Jew finds a roguish accomplice in Ithamore, the Turkish slave. They are well aware, from their first encounter, of what they have in common: "we are villaines both . . . we hate Christians both" (979–80). Barabas announces another key-word when he asks Ithamore's profession, and the answer is "what you please" (931). For "profession," like "vocation" or "calling," signified a way of life in a double sense: religious conviction and practical employment. The ambiguity is the key to much controversy, which dwelt with particular bitterness on what was known as "the profession of usury." Barabas confides to Ithamore what professions he has practiced, starting in Italy as a Machiavellian doctor who poisoned his patients, carrying on the self-appointed task of destruction as a military engineer in the wars of the Empire, and reaching the climax of this protean and predatory career as "an Usurer." After mastering all the shady tricks of all the dubious trades, his culminating crime has been the taking of interest. Later we learn the percentage: "A hundred for a hundred" (1563).

The paradox of his notorious harangue is that it so crudely expresses a vaunted subtlety:

> As for my selfe, I walke abroad a nights
> And kill sicke people groaning under walls.   (939–40)

And, in the same vein of horrific gusto, further revelations are divulged. Reality is so callowly assailed that the modern reader thinks of the so-called comic books. These, we think, are the nightmares of spoiled children rather than the misdeeds of wicked men. Yet we know how audiences were impressed, and that Marlowe again was paid the compliment of imitation by Shakespeare. The parallel monologue of Aaron the Moor in *Titus Andronicus* throws light back upon *The Jew of Malta*, since it is wholly preoccupied with pointless mischief:

> Tut, I haue done a thousand dreadfull things
> As willingly, as one would kill a Fly.   (V, i, 141–2)

If this conveys any point, it is an echo from an earlier scene, where Titus objects to the killing of a fly. Though the cross-reference seems to bring out the worst in both Shakespeare and Marlowe, it manages to be characteristic of both. The real basis of distinction is that, while Aaron is merely gloating over his macabre practical jokes — including one which has been borrowed from an episode in *The Jew of Malta* — Barabas is trenchantly satirizing the professions and institutions of his day. In sketching such a violent self-portrait, he belatedly lives up to the introduction of his Florentine patron and departs from the tragic dignity that he has maintained throughout the opening scenes. There we hear the note of lamentation that we heard in the threnodies of *Tamburlaine*; but it has been transposed to the minor harmonics of the Old Testament, notably the Book of Job. When the three Jews fail to comfort Barabas, he invidiously compares himself with Job, who, after all, lost a less considerable fortune; and Marlowe even diminishes Job's five hundred yoke of oxen to two hundred.

> For onely I haue toyl'd to inherit here
> The months of vanity and losse of time,
> And painefull nights haue bin appointed me.   (429–31)

By catching the lilt — and, in this case, the very language — of the Bible, Marlowe has modulated and deepened his style. Barabas is lighted with scriptural grandeur at the beginning of the second act. There he is still in part what Edmund Kean was apparently able to make him: a sympathetic figure, the injured party about to seek redress, no Atheist but an anti-Christian praying to the wrathful deity of his tribe, a prophet imprecating the avenging Jehovah. The darkness of the night is accentuated by the flicker of his candle, and the heavy images are sustained by the tolling rhythms:

> Thus like the sad presaging Rauen that tolls
> The sicke mans passeport in her hollow beake,
> And in the shadow of the silent night
> Doth shake contagion from her sable wings;
> Vex'd and tormented runnes poore *Barabas*
> With fatall curses towards these Christians.
> The incertaine pleasures of swift-footed time
> Haue tane their flight, and left me in despaire.   (640–7)

This is an extraordinary departure from the swiftness and brightness of Tamburlaine's forensics. It has more in common with the speeches of Dr. Faustus — and with the lamenting Kyd, the infernal Seneca, the nocturnal *Macbeth*. Shakespeare's puzzling reference to "the School of Night" in *Love's Labour's Lost* (IV, iii, 255) may indeed be a side glance at such rhetorical tendencies. But Marlowe looks upward, with the imprecations of Barabas:

> Oh thou that with a fiery piller led'st
> The sonnes of *Israel* through the dismall shades,
> Light *Abrahams* off-spring. (651-3)

Marlowe was never more the devil's advocate than when he chose a wandering Jew for his hero. His working model was less a human being than a bugbear of folklore, inasmuch as the Jews were officially banished from England between the reign of Edward I and the protectorate of Oliver Cromwell. In certain regions of the Mediterranean, Jewish financiers and politicians had risen to power in the sixteenth century; and Marlowe, whose play has no literary source, must have come across anecdotes about them. In his selection of a name there is a deeper significance, for Barabbas was the criminal whom the Jews preferred to Jesus, when Pilate offered to release a prisoner. One of the witnesses against Marlowe's Atheism, Richard Baines, quotes his assertion: "That Crist deserved better to dy then Barrabas and that the Jewes made a good Choise, though Barrabas were both a thief and a murtherer." It could also be said that, if Christ died for all men, he died most immediately for Barabbas; and that Barabbas was the man whose mundane existence profited most immediately from Christ's sacrifice. From the perspective of historical criticism, Barabbas actually seems to have been an insurrectionist. Marlowe, in instinctively taking his side, identifies his Jew with the Antichrist. Hence the crude cartoon becomes an apocalyptic monstrosity, whose temporal kingdom is the earth itself. It is no idle jest when Ithamore remarks of Barabas: "The Hat he weares, *Iudas* left vnder the Elder when he hang'd himselfe" (1988). When Alleyn wore it with the accustomed gabardine, the red beard, and the hyperbolic nose, he must have seemed the exemplification of guile, acquisitiveness, and treachery.

Nature seemed to be imitating art when, a year after Marlowe's death, the Jewish physician, Roderigo Lopez, was executed for plotting against the Queen. This had some bearing on the success of the play; and, what is more, the play may have had some bearing on the outcome of the trial — where doubtful evidence was strengthened by prejudice. The animus that flared up on such occasions was kindled by the twofold circumstance that many Jews, forbidden to hold property, lived by trading in money; and that the profession of usury stood condemned by the orthodox tenets of Christianity. The gradual adaptation of Christian tenets to the rise of modern capitalism, through the diverging creeds of the Protestant Reformation, has been much scrutinized and debated by social historians. There seems to be little doubt that Jewish moneylenders, whose international connections enabled them to organize some of the earliest stock exchanges, performed an indispensable function in the developing European economy. The myth of the elders of Zion, controlling Europe from their treasuries, finds some degree of confirmation in Barabas.

> Thus trowles our fortune in by land and Sea, (141)

he exults, cognizant that this blessing of Abraham entails the curse of anti-Semitism.

> Or who is honour'd now but for his wealth? (151)

he retorts, to the assumption that there have been other standards. Yet, as a self-made merchant prince, he speaks not so much for his race as for his epoch — an epoch when consumption was more conspicuous than it had ever been before. This timeliness keeps him from being quite alien in mercantile England. Though Malta was not to be a British colony for more than two centuries, it occupied a strategic position on the old trade routes and in the new struggle for markets. The polyglot Maltese, descended from the Phoenicians, mixed in their Levantine melting pot with Italians and Spaniards, were mainly Semitic in blood and Latin in culture. On their island, if anywhere, East met West. The Knights Hospitallers of Saint John — formerly of Jerusalem — had settled at Malta when Rhodes fell to the Turks in 1522, and successfully held out when besieged in 1565, presumably the period of the drama. Their baroque capital, with its bastioned port, was both an outpost of Christendom and a citadel against Islam; but the spirit of the crusaders who founded it had yielded to the emergent interests of the merchant adventurers.

The starting point of the play is the exit of Machiavel, who pulls back the arras that curtains the inner stage and thereby discovers

Barabas in his counting-house. We are not asked to believe that this shallow recess is anything more than concretely strikes the eye. This is a back-room, not the façade of a palace. True, the stage direction indicates heaps of coins; but we are less impressed by them than by Barabas' gesture of dismissal.

> Fye; what a trouble tis to count this trash. (42)

We are dazzled, not because riches are dangled before us, but because they are tossed aside; because precious stones are handled "like pibble-stones" (58). Not that Barabas is indifferent to them; soon enough he makes it evident that gold is to him what the crown is to Tamburlaine, "felicity" (689); and he completes that blasphemy by marking his buried treasure with the sign of the cross. But it vastly increases the scale of his affluence to reckon it up so dryly and casually. Barabas out-Herods Tamburlaine by making hyperboles sound like understatements; he values the least of his jewels at a king's ransom. His will to power is gratified less by possession than by control. In this he does not resemble the conqueror so much as he adumbrates the capitalist; and Marlowe has grasped what is truly imaginative, what in his time was almost heroic, about business enterprise. To audit bills of lading for Indian argosies, to project empires by double-entry bookkeeping, to enthrone and dethrone royalties by loans — that is indeed "a kingly kinde of trade" (2330). In the succinct formulation of Barabas,

> Infinite riches in a little roome, (72)

Marlowe sublimates his expansive ideal from the plane of economics to that of esthetics. The line itself is perfect in its symmetry; each half begins with the syllable "in" and proceeds through antithetical adjectives to alliterative nouns; six of the ten vowels are short *i*'s; and nothing could be more Marlovian than the underlying notion of containing the uncontainable. It is hard to imagine how a larger amount of implication could be more compactly ordered within a single pentameter. Ruskin once categorically declared that a miser could not sing about his gold; James Russell Lowell, on the contrary, has described this line as "the very poetry of avarice"; and if that be a contradiction in terms, it matches the contradictions of Marlowe's theme.

To pursue this theme, *libido dominandi*, we now take the fox's path through the realms of high finance. Barabas warns us that it is more complex, if less spectacular, than the lion's path across the battlefield:

> Giue vs a peacefull rule, make Christians Kings,
> That thirst so much for Principality. (172–3)

His policy spins a plot for *The Jew of Malta* which can be pursued on three interconnecting levels. The conventions of English drama prescribed an underplot, which is ordinarily a burlesque of the main plot; clowns are cast as servants and play the zany to their respective masters; and the stolen sheep is a symbolic counterpart of the infant Jesus in the *Second Shepherds' Play* of Wakefield. With the full development of tragedy, there is a similar ramification upwards, which might conveniently be called the overplot. That is the stuff of history as it impinges upon the more personal concerns of the characters; thus the events of *The Spanish Tragedy* are precipitated by wars between Spain and Portugal. Thus, with *Hamlet*, the overplot is conditioned by the dynastic relations of Denmark with Norway and Poland; while the main plot concentrates upon Hamlet's revenge against Claudius; and the underplot — which, in this instance, is more romantic than comic — has to do with the household of Polonius, and most particularly with Ophelia. *The Jew of Malta* is similarly constructed, and probably helped to fix this triple method of construction. The overplot, framed by the siege, is the interrelationship between the Christians and Jews, the Spaniards and Turks. It is connected with the main plot through the peculations of Barabas, who is caught up in the underplot through his misplaced confidence in Ithamore. The bonds of self-interest connect the central intrigue, which involves usury, with power politics upon the upper level and with blackmail upon the lower. Blackmail is the tax that Barabas pays on his ill-gotten hoards; but his rear-guard actions against the blackmailers are more successful than his efforts to beat the politicians at their own game.

Morally, all of them operate on the same level, and that is precisely what Marlowe is pointing out. In order to sell a cargo of Turkish slaves, the Spanish Vice-Admiral talks the Governor into breaking the treaty between Malta and the Turks. It is not merely in the slave market, but in the counting-house and the senate chamber, that men are bought and sold. As for the traffic in women,

Ithamore becomes ensnared in it; soon after Barabas buys him, he falls into the hands of the courtesan Bellamira and her bullying companion, Pilia-Borza — whose name, meaning "pickpurse," denotes the least sinister of his activities. The confidence game that this nefarious couple practices on Barabas, through their hold over Ithamore, was known in the Elizabethan underworld as "crossbiting." By whatever name it goes, it reduces eroticism to chicanery; it debases Marlowe's *libido sentiendi* to its most ignoble manifestation. Ithamore addresses Bellamira as if she were Zenocrate or Helen of Troy, instead of a woman whose professional habit is to do the persuading on her own behalf. The invitation to love, as he extends it, is sweetened for vulgar tastes; the classical meadows of Epicureanism now "beare Sugar Canes"; and rhetorical enticements sink into bathos with a couplet which burlesques "The Passionate Shepherd":

> Thou in those Groues, by *Dis* aboue,
> Shalt liue with me and be my loue.   (1815–6)

The subversion of values is finally enunciated in *Tamburlaine* when, with the chorus of lesser Kings, "hell in heauen is plac'd" (4408). Here the confusion that exalts to the skies the god of Hades, and of riches likewise, is a final commentary upon an ethos turned upside down. When everything is ticketed with its price — an eye, a thumb, man's honor, woman's chastity — values turn inevitably into prices. The beauty of Helen herself is devalued, a decade after Marlowe's apostrophe, with the epic degradation of *Troilus and Cressida*:

> Why she is a Pearle,
> Whose price hath launch'd aboue a thousand Ships,
> And turn'd Crown'd Kings to Merchants.   (II, ii, 81–83)

The principle of double-dealing, which prevails on all sides in Malta, is established in the scene where the Governor summons the Jews to raise funds for the Turkish tribute. Distinguishing somewhat pharisaically between his profession and theirs, he offers the alternative of conversion, which none of them accepts. When he mulcts them of half their estates, the other Jews comply at once; and since Barabas refuses, his wealth is entirely confiscated. To him, therefore, his co-religionists are Job's comforters; yet, from the outset, his devotion has centered less on his race than on his selfish interests. He finds a justification in observing that Christians preach religion and practice opportunism.

> What? bring you Scripture to confirm your wrongs?
> Preach me not out of my possessions. (343–4)

From one of the Knights, he picks up the catchword that seems to explain the disparity between what they profess and what they really do:

> I, policie? that's their profession. (393)

In endeavoring to recover his lost fortune, he resolves to "make barre of no policie" (508). He justifies his next stratagem on the grounds that "a counterfet profession" (531), his daughter's pretended conversion, is better than "vnseene hypocrisie," than the unexposed perfidies of professed believers. He admonishes his daughter that religion

> Hides many mischiefes from suspition. (520)

His cynicism seems altogether justified when the Knights break a double faith, refusing to pay the Turks the money they have seized for that purpose from Barabas. Their argument, the one that the Christians used in *Tamburlaine* when they violated their oath to their Mohammedan allies, proves a useful rationalization for Barabas:

> It's no sinne to deceiue a Christian;
> For they themselues hold it a principle,
> Faith is not to be held with Heretickes;
> But all are Hereticks that are not Iewes. (1074–7)

Ithamore, going over to the other side, can quote this dangerous scripture against his master:

> To vndoe a Iew is a charity, and not sinne. (2001)

After the Christians have broken their league with the Turks, Barabas leagues with the Turks against the Knights. His fatal mistake is to betray his new allies to his old enemies, the Christians, by whom he thereupon is promptly betrayed. He is repaid in kind; but his Turkish victims have been comparatively honorable; and he ends as an inadvertent defender of Christendom. Meanwhile, by craftily pitting infidels against believers, one belief against another, fanaticism against Atheism, Marlowe has dramatized the dialectics of comparative religion.

Is there, then, no such thing as sincere devotion? Perhaps some unfortunate person, Barabas is willing to allow,

> Happily some haplesse man hath conscience. (157)

If so, he does not appear on the Maltese horizon. But by chance, by that ironic destiny which Thomas Hardy calls "hap," there is one woman,

> one sole Daughter, whom I hold as deare
> As *Agamemnon* did his *Iphigen*. (175–6)

Though Agamemnon is less relevant than Jephtha might have been, the simile is an omen for Abigall, the single disinterested character in the play, who is characterized by the first four words she speaks: "Not for my selfe . . ." (462). Her father lovingly repeats her name as David repeated the name of Absalom. His policy dictates her profession, when in filial duty she reënters his former house, which has been converted into a nunnery. When she recognizes that she has been the unwitting instrument of his revenge, "experience, purchased with griefe," opens her eyes to "the difference of things" (1285). She now experiences a genuine vocation, perceiving that

> there is no loue on earth,
> Pitty in Iewes, nor piety in Turkes. (1270–1)

By taking the veil, she extinguishes the latent spark of tenderness in Barabas, who retaliates by poisoning all the nuns. Stricken, she has the moral satisfaction of confessing that she dies a Christian. But the pathos of these last words is undercut by the cynical dictum of her confessor:

> I, and a Virgin too, that grieues me most. (1497)

Abigall's honesty, in the Elizabethan sense of chastity as well as sincerity, is confirmed by her death; but she finds no sanctuary among the religious. Her innocent lover, Don Mathias, has been slain while slaying the Governor's son, Don Lodowick, in a duel contrived by the vengeful Barabas. This contrivance gives a Marlovian twist to one of the strangest obsessions of the European consciousness, the legend of the Jew's daughter, who serves as a decoy in luring a Christian youth to his doom by her father's knife in their dark habitation. The story is deeply rooted in those accusations of ritual murder, which seem to result from misunderstandings of the Jewish Passover rite, and have left a trail of bloodier revenges — across whole countries and over many centuries — than could ever be comprehended within the theatrical medium. Created out of hatred to warrant pogroms, thousands of lurid effigies swing behind Barabas; and Abigall's sacrifice is one of millions, which have not yet atoned for the Crucifixion. In medieval versions the martyrdom commonly flowers into a miracle, as in the ballad of Hugh of Lincoln or the tale of Chaucer's Prioress. The latter points an old moral, "Mordre wol out," which is expressly rejected by Marlowe's Machiavel:

> Birds of the Aire will tell of murders past;
> I am asham'd to heare such fooleries. (16–7)

But Barabas invokes the birds of the air, the raven before and the lark after Abigall has aided him to regain his moneybags. The night scene, in its imagery and staging, curiously foreshadows the balcony scene in *Romeo and Juliet*. When Abigall — who, like Juliet, is "scarce 14 yeares ˄f age" (621) — appears on the upper stage, Barabas exclaims:

> But stay, what starre shines yonder in the *East*?
> The Loadstarre of my life, if *Abigall*. (680–1)

When Shakespeare copies this picture, he brightens it, in accordance with the more youthful and ardent mood of Romeo:

> But soft, what light through yonder window breaks?
> It is the East, and *Iuliet* is the Sunne. (II, ii, 2–3)

There is another moment which looks ahead to Shakespeare's romantic tragedy; and that comes after the duel, when the Governor eulogizes the rival lovers and promises to bury them in the same monument. If this midpoint had been the ending, the drama might have retained its equilibrium; there would have been enough grievances and sufferings on both sides. With the disappearance of the fragile heroine and of the lyrical touches that cluster about her, tragedy is overshadowed by revenge. But we might have realized, when Abigall introduced herself to the Abbess as

> The hopelesse daughter of a haplesse Iew, (557)

that Marlowe was shaping his play by the sterner conventions of *The Spanish Tragedy* and Kyd's Hieronimo,

> The hopeles father of a hapless Sonne. (IV, iv, 84)

Between revenge and romance, between tragedy and comedy, *The Merchant of Venice* provides a Shakespearean compromise. It gives the benediction of a happy ending to the legend of the Jew's daughter; and it allows the Jewish protagonist, for better or for worse, his day in court. Legalism both narrows and humanizes Shylock, in contradistinction to Barabas, who for the most part lives outside the law and does not clamor for it until it has overtaken him. In rounding off the angles and mitigating the harshness of Marlowe's caricature, Shakespeare loses something of its intensity. The mixed emotions of Shylock, wailing, "O my ducats, O my daughter" (II, viii, 15), are muted by being reported at second hand. We see and hear, we recall and recoil from the unholy joy of Barabas:

> Oh girle, oh gold, oh beauty, oh my blisse! (695)

If the comparison is not with Shakespeare but with Marlowe's earlier writing, *The Jew of Malta* registers enormous gains in flexibility. Except when Barabas mutters to himself in a *lingua franca* of Spanish and Italian, the diction is plainer and much saltier. The average length of an individual speech is no more than 2.8 lines, as differentiated from the second part of *Tamburlaine*, where it runs to 6.3. This implies, theatrically speaking, more than twice as many cues in the later play, with a consequent thickening of the dialogue and a general quickening of the action. It follows that there are fewer monologues, although Barabas delivers a number of them — in that Biblical vein which transforms the basic modes of Tamburlaine's rhetoric, the threat and the plea, into the curse, the jeremiad, the prophecy. The Prophets had spoken English blank verse in Greene and Lodge's *Looking-Glass for London*, as had the Psalmist in Peele's *David and Bethsabe*. But *The Jew of Malta* requires some means of private comment, as well as public speech, to express the cross-purposes between policy and profession, deeds and

THE OVERREACHER

words. It leans much more upon the soliloquy, which the extroverted Tamburlaine hardly needed, and its characteristic mode is the aside. Marlowe did not invent this simplistic device; actors had voiced their thoughts to audiences before they had exchanged them with each other; and characterization of the villain was, for obvious reasons, peculiarly dependent upon that convention. It could not be disregarded by a playwright who had to guide introverted characters through the Machiavellian province of false declarations and unvoiced intentions. "*I must dissemble,*" says Barabas (1556), and the italics alert the reader to what the spectator feels when the spoken words are aimed at him in a stage whisper. The actor is professionally a dissembler, etymologically a hypocrite. The histrionics of Barabas are not confined to his role in the disguise of a French musician. Except for his unwarranted confidences to his daughter and to his slave, he is always acting, always disguised. We, who overhear his asides and soliloquies, are his only trustworthy confidants. We are therefore in collusion with Barabas. We revel in his malice, we share his guilt. We are the "worldlings" to whom he addresses himself (2332).

This understanding is the framework of Marlowe's irony. When Barabas is first interrogated by the Knights, his replies are deliberately naïve; we know that he knows what they want from him; but he dissembles his shrewdness, plays the *Eiron*, and fences with the Governor. Often he utters no more than a line at a time, and engages in stichomythy — in capping line for line — with his interlocutors. Repartee is facilitated by Marlowe's increasing willingness to break off a speech and start upon another at the cæsura, without interrupting the rhythm of the blank verse. Speeches of less than a line are still rather tentative, and prose is a more favorable climate than verse for the cultivation of pithy dialogue. Possibly the most striking advance beyond *Tamburlaine* is the transition from a voluble to a laconic style, from Ciceronian periods to Senecan aphorisms. Effects depend, not upon saying everything, but upon keeping certain things unsaid. The climax of ironic dissimulation comes with the scene where the two Friars "exclaime against" Barabas (1502). In their association with the nuns, Marlowe has lost no opportunity for anticlerical innuendo; now the "two religious Caterpillers" hold the upper hand over Barabas, since they have learned of his crimes from the dying Abigall; but since they are bound by the seal of confession, they cannot lodge a downright accusation. He has both these considerations in mind, as do we, when he parries their hesitating denunciations.

Thou art a —, (1539)

says one Friar; and Barabas admits what is common knowledge, that he is a Jew and a usurer.

Thou hast committed —, (1549)

says the other, and again the admission is an evasion:

Fornication? but that was in another Country:
And besides, the Wench is dead. (1550-1)

For anyone else there might be, for others there have been, romance and even tragedy in the reminiscence. For Barabas it is simply an alibi, a statute of limitations. He is content to remind the Friars, with a legalistic shrug, that the Seventh Commandment is not to be taken as seriously as the Sixth. Deploring his callousness, we are tempted to admire his cheerful candor, and are almost touched by the emotional poverty of his life.

At this impasse he takes the initiative, with the dissembling announcement that he stands ready to be converted. His renunciation is actually a temptation, to which the Friars easily succumb, enticed by his Marlovian catalogue of the worldly goods he professes to renounce.

Ware-houses stuft with spices and with drugs,
Whole Chests of Gold, in *Bulloine*, and in Coyne . . .
All this I'le giue to some religious house. (1573-84)

Pretending to be persuaded, it is he who persuades and they who do the courting. Their courtship is the most grotesque of Marlowe's variations on the tune of "Come live with me and be my love." The vistas of opulence that Barabas has just exhibited contrast with the cheerless asceticism of their monkish vows. While Barabas ironically aspires toward grace, they fall into the trap of worldliness that he has so lavishly baited for them.

You shall conuert me, you shall haue all my wealth, (1590)

he tells one. Whereupon the other tells him,

Oh *Barabas*, their Lawes are strict . . .
They weare no shirts, and they goe bare-foot too, (1591-3)

and is told in turn,

You shall confesse me, and haue all my goods. (1595)

By playing off one monastic order against the other, he divides and conquers. He murders one Friar and pins the blame on the other, with a threadbare trick which Marlowe may have encountered in a jestbook. The fact that the same trick occurs in a play of Thomas Heywood's, *The Captives*, plus the fact that Heywood sponsored the publication of *The Jew of Malta*, have led some commentators to infer that he may have added these scenes to Marlowe's play. It would seem more probable that *The Jew of Malta* influenced *The Captives*. Clearly it influenced *Titus Andronicus*, where the jest of a leaning corpse is mentioned by Aaron in his imitative monologue. Since we owe the text of *The Jew of Malta* to Heywood's quarto of 1633, published more than forty years after the drama was written, it may well have been retouched here and there. But the Friars are integral to Marlowe's design; Abigall's death would go unrevenged without them, and Machiavel's contempt for the clergy would go undemonstrated. Furthermore, in the canon of Heywood's extant works, there is no passage which is comparably sharp in tone or audacious in matter. Closer affinities might be sought in the sardonic tragicomedy of Marston or in the baroque tragedy of Webster.

It seems wiser — and is certainly more rewarding — to accept *The Jew of Malta* as an artistic whole, noting its incongruities and tensions, than to take the easy course of ruling them out as interpolations by a later hand. Criticism is warranted in stressing the disproportion between the two halves of the play; but the very essence of Marlowe's art, to sum it up with a Baconian phrase, is "strangenesse in the proportions." The "extreme reuenge" (1265) of Barabas runs away with the play, egregiously transcending the norms of vindictiveness; but it is the nature of the Marlovian protagonist to press whatever he undertakes to its uttermost extreme. As Barabas progresses, the Old Testament recedes into the background, and the foreground is dominated by *The Prince*. Effortlessly, his losses of the first act are made good by the second; and the third repays, with compound interest, his grudge against the Governor. Here, with the disaffection of Abigall, he abandons any claim upon our sympathy and vies with his new accomplice, Ithamore, in the *quid pro quo* of sheer malignity. In the fourth act he is blackmailed, not only by Bellamira and her bravo, but by the pair of Friars. His counter-measures lead him, in the fifth act, upward and onward into the realms of the higher blackmail, where Turks demand tribute from Christians and Christians from Jews.

> Why, was there euer seene such villany.
> So neatly plotted, and so well perform'd? (1220–1)

Ithamore asks the audience. Yet who should know, better than he, that the performance of each plot somehow leaves a loose end? Murder is not postponed from act to act, as it is in the bungling *Arden of Feversham*; rather, as in a well-conducted detective story, every crime is its own potential nemesis. Barabas does not count on Abigall's love for Mathias when he calculates the killing of Lodo-wick. He does away with her and her sister religionists without expecting the Friars to inherit his guilty secret. When he silences them, he comes to grips with the complicity of Ithamore and with the extortations of Pilia-Borza. In settling their business, he incriminates himself; and, though he survives to betray the entire island, his next and final treason is self-betrayal.

To show the betrayer betrayed, the engineer hoist in his petard, the "reaching thought" (455) of Barabas overreached, is the irony of ironies. Marlowe's stage management moves toward a *coup de théâtre*, a machine which is worthy of all the machination that has gone before. Barabas can kill with a poisoned nosegay, can simulate death with "Poppy and cold mandrake juyce" (2083), and — thrown to the vultures from the walls of the town — can let the enemy in through the underground vaults, the subterranean corridors of intrigue. His hellish broth for the nuns is brewed from the recipes of the Borgias, seasoned with "all the poysons of the Stygian poole" (1405), and stirred with imprecations from the classics. "Was euer pot of Rice porredge so sauc't?" comments Ithamore (1409). The sauce of the jest is that poetic justice takes, for Barabas, the shape of a boiling pot. He is shown *"aboue"* — from which coign of vantage he likes to look down on the havoc he engineers — *"very busie"* in his "dainty Gallery" (2316), explaining his cable and trap-door to the Governor. When the signal is given, and the monastery blown up with the Turks inside, it is Barabas who falls through the trap. The curtain below is flung open, *"A Caldron discouered,"* and in it Barabas fuming and hissing his last. He implores the Christians to help him, but they are "pittilesse" (2354). Once he merely professed "a burning zeale" (850), but now he feels "the extremity of heat" (2371). He dies cursing. The steaming caldron in which he expires, like the "hell-mouth" of *Doctor Faustus*, was a property in the lists of Alleyn's company. But, like the human pie in *Titus Andronicus*, today it excites more ridicule than terror. In the age of *Macbeth*, however, a caldron was no mere object of domestic utility. It was the standard punishment for the poisoner. It had betokened a city of abomination in the flaming vision of Ezekiel. And in the *Emblems* of Geoffrey Whitney, printed in 1586, it illustrates the humbling of aspiration and amplifies the gospel of Luke (xviii, 14), *Qui se exaltat, humiliabitur*:

> The boyling brothe, aboue the brinke doth swell,
>   And comes to naughte, with falling in the fire:
> So reaching ,heads that thinke them neuer well,
> Doe headlong fall, for pride hathe ofte that hire:
>   And where before their frendes they did dispise,
>   Nowe beinge falne, none helpe them for to rise.

Barabas stews in the juice of his tragic pride, foiled and foiled again, like the melodramatic villain he has become. Malta is preserved; murder will out; crime does not pay; the reward of sin is death; vengeance belongs to the Lord. This is exemplary but commonplace doctrine, and we have clambered through a labyrinth to reach it. Can Machiavel's introductory proverbs of hell be conclusively refuted by such copybook didacticism? Barabas is a consistent Machiavellian when, at the very pinnacle of his career, he soliloquizes on Turks and Christians:

> Thus louing neither, will I liue with both,
> Making a profit of my policie. (2213–4)

The words "live" and "love" jingle strangely amid this concentration of cold antipathy. Yet they are in character — or rather, Barabas steps out of it at the crisis, when he willfully departs from the teaching of his master. Machiavelli, in his chapter on cruelty and pity, had counseled: "Both dowbtlesse are necessarie, but seinge it is harde to make them drawe both in one yoake, I thinke it more safetie (seinge one must needes be wantinge) to be feared then loved, for this maybe boldlie sayde of men, that they are vngratefull, inconstante, discemblers, fearefull of dayngers, covetous of gayne." This may unquestionably be said of Barabas, and he is all too painfully conscious of it; he is conscious of being hated, and wants to be loved. To be loved — yes, that desire is his secret shame, the tragic weakness of a character whose wickedness is otherwise unflawed. His hatred is the bravado of the outsider whom nobody loves, and his revenges are compensatory efforts to supply people with good reasons for hating him. Poor Barabas, poor old rich man! That he should end by trusting anybody, least of all the one man who wronged him in the beginning! He has authority now, but Malta hates him. Instead of playing upon the fear of the islanders, he proposes to earn their gratitude by ridding them of the Turks. As Governor, he is anxious to make his peace with the former Governor, to whom he says: "Liue with me" (2192). It is worse than a crime, as Talleyrand would say; it is a blunder.

The original miscalculation of Barabas was his failure to reckon with love. Then Abigall, sincerely professing the vows she had taken before out of policy, declared that she had found no love on earth. Having lost her, holding himself apart from the "multitude" of Jews, Barabas must be his own sole friend: "I'le looke vnto my selfe" (212). Yet he would like to win friends; he needs a confidant; and for a while he views Ithamore, much too trustingly, as his "second self" (1317). It is the dilemma of *unus contra mundum*, of the egoist who cannot live with others or without them. Since he conspires against them, they are right to combine against him; but their combinations frequently break down, for each of them is equally self-centered.

> For so I liue, perish may all the world. (2292)

When every man looks out for himself alone and looks with suspicion on every other man, the ego is isolated within a vicious circle of mutual distrust. The moral of the drama could be the motto of Melville's *Confidence-Man*, "No Trust." Without trust, sanctions are only invoked to be violated; men live together, not in a commonwealth, but in an acquisitive society, where they behave like wolves to their fellow men. Barabas, who is fond of comparing himself to various beasts of prey, announces in his most typical aside:

> Now will I shew my selfe to haue more of the Serpent
> Then the Doue; that is, more knaue than foole. (797–8)

This is taking in vain the injunction of Jesus, when he sent forth the Apostles "as sheepe in the middest of wolues" (Matthew, x, 16). They were enjoined to remain as innocent as doves, but also to become as wise as serpents, so that they might distinguish between vice and virtue. Bacon amplified this precept in his *Meditationes Sacræ*, but in his career he did not exemplify it very happily. The innocence of the dove can scarcely preserve itself unless it is armed with the wisdom of the serpent; but it is difficult to acquire such worldly wisdom without being somewhat corrupted in the process. *Columbinus serpens: serpentina columba*, by whichever name Gabriel Harvey designates that hybrid creature, it is engendered in the humanist's mind by the crossbreeding of innocence and experience. Experience, as the dovelike Abigall discovers, is purchased with grief. The serpentine Barabas, too, comes to grief; and the difference between his caldron and Tamburlaine's chariot, between feeling pain and inflicting it, may well betoken Marlowe's advancing experience in the ways of the world. He is awakening to a vision of evil, though he innocently beholds it from the outside. The devil obligingly identifies himself by wearing horns and a tail.

But the devil is no diabolist; he sees through himself; he knows that men have invented him to relieve themselves of responsibility for those woes of the world which the Governor attributes to "inherent sinne" (342). The devil's disciple, Machiavel, holds that there is no sin but ignorance; and Machiavel's disciple, Barabas, prefers the role of the knave to that of the fool. Thus, in letting other knaves get the better of him, he commits the only sin in his calendar, the humanistic peccadillo of folly. He acts out the Erasmian object lesson of a scoundrel who is too clever for his own good, the cheater cheated, wily beguiled. In getting out of hand, his counterplots exceeded the proportions of tragedy, and his discomfiture is more like the happy endings of melodrama. T. S. Eliot endows the play with a kind of retrospective unity by interpreting it as a comedy, a "farce of the old English humour." Though the interpretation is unhistorical, it has the merit of placing *The Jew of Malta* beside the grotesquerie of Dickens and Hogarth and — most pertinently — Ben Jonson's *Volpone, or the Fox*. Jonson's comedy of humours begins where Marlowe's tragedy of humours leaves off; Volpone and Mosca continue the misadventures of Barabas and Ithamore; and the Fox of Venice has learned not a few of his tricks from the Jew of Malta.

The atmosphere of both plays is conveyed, and both playwrights are linked together, by a couplet upon an earlier comic dramatist which Jonson revised from Marlowe's translation of Ovid:

> Whil'st Slaues be false, Fathers hard, & Bauds be whorish,
> Whilst Harlots flatter, shall *Menander* flourish. (I, xv, 17–8)

The hard-bitten types of New Comedy are perennially recognizable: miser, impostor, parasite, prostitute. Whether in Malta or Venice, Athens or London, their outlook is always a street and never a landscape. Social intercourse is, for them, a commercial transaction; self-interest is the universal motive; everything, every man's honesty and every woman's, has its price; all try to sell themselves as dearly, and to buy others as cheaply, as possible. The moral issue is the simple choice between folly and knavery – in Elizabethan terms, the innocence of the gull and the wisdom of the coney-catcher. The distance between these extremes, as *The Jew of Malta* demonstrates, can be precariously narrow. Barabas, for all his monstrous activism, inhabits a small and static world. Though Marlowe would not be Marlowe without a cosmic prospect, he seems to be moving centripetally through a descending gyre toward a core of self-imposed limitation. But, even as potentialities seem to be closing in, actualities are opening up. The room is little, the riches are infinite.

Chapter **IV**

STATE OVERTURNED

The tragic view is never a simple one. It is not a spontaneous reaction to a given situation, but a gradual recognition of the sternest facts that govern the whole of life. It came as the hard-won guerdon of maturity to Sophocles and Shakespeare; and even Marlowe, for all his precocity, had to ripen into it. *The Jew of Malta* provokes less pity than terror; most of its terrors, indeed, are merely horrors; and in so far as it subordinates everything else to contrivance, it deserves to be classed as a farce — or, at any rate, a melodrama. That little room, that self-contained island are quite incommensurable with the geopolitical expanses of *Tamburlaine*; but their angularity and narrowness frame a more realistic picture of society, as scaled down by the law of diminishing returns. The tragedy that overtakes Tamburlaine is almost an afterthought, although his centrifugal route is strewn with lesser tragedies. Similarly, *The Tragedy of Dido* is incidental to the epic adventures of Æneas. In those plays which we have thus far considered, Marlowe seems to stand like his Leander, poised upon the very brink of tragedy. He has provided a *sine qua non* by creating extraordinarily powerful protagonists; had he stopped there, his genre would have been monodrama; and though effective drama has been built around single figures — Eugene O'Neill's *Emperor Jones*, Büchner's *Dantons Tod*, to some extent *Macbeth* — the overbalance is too precarious to be long sustained. Marlowe has taken another step, and introduced a framework of ethical reference, by stigmatizing his hero as a villain. If he does nothing else in *The Massacre at Paris*, he exorcises this devil that he has raised. And in *Edward II* he sets forth his discovery that tragic life needs no villains; that plots are spun by passions; that men betray themselves.

Meanwhile, his imagination has been traveling closer to home, sweeping from Asia and Africa through the Levant, and thence to western Europe. In the prologue of *The Jew of Malta*, Machiavel announces that he has crossed the Alps from Italy toward England, and that he has crossed over from France after the assassination of his most enterprising disciple, the Duke of Guise. That event, which happened late in 1588, furnishes the climactic episode in *The Massacre at Paris*, which was produced as a new play four years later. Marlowe gathered his material out of the flux of current history, much as he had done in *The Jew of Malta*; and on his brief excursion into the troubled realm of French politics, he discovered a vein which would afterward be exploited by the tragedies of George Chapman. The massacre of Marlowe's title was the notorious holocaust of Saint Bartholomew's day, 1572, sometimes called Machiavelli's holiday by Protestants — who, hating Catherine de Medici as the chief disseminator of Italian influence beyond the Alps, called *The Prince* the Queen-Mother's Bible. For the subjects of Queen Elizabeth, who is thrice saluted as the leading defender of the Protestant faith, the play is by implication a tale of two cities, Paris and London. Huguenots are referred to as Puritans, and suspicion is directed toward the English Catholic exiles at Douai and Reims. It is not surprising that the French government objected to its performance on one occasion. If Marlowe had lived a few months longer, he would doubtless have been surprised to learn that Henry of Navarre, the spokesman for his anticlericalism, had joined the Catholic church. Marlowe's own attitude toward the Pope is intensified in two lines assigned to the previous king, Henry III:

Ile fire his crased buildings and inforse
The papall towers to kisse the holy earth.   (1214–15)

The same lines occur in *Edward II*, with "lowlie ground" instead of "holy earth" (397) — a difference which suggests that an actor's fallible memory is responsible for our text of *The Massacre at Paris*. Notwithstanding, the speech is more appropriate to the latter play than it is from the mouth of the ineffectual Edward. His expulsion of the Templars is not mentioned in Marlowe's account, which concentrates its antireligious sniping on Edward's humiliation of the Bishop of Coventry. At a time when hatred of the papacy ran so high in England that King John could be something of a hero upon the popular stage, Marlowe could enjoy immunity in expressing Barabas' impulse to burn churches. The recurrence is peculiarly Marlovian in its juxtaposition of prideful towers and purging fires.

Heretofore the protagonist has been an infidel: an Atheist or a pagan, a Mohammedan or a Jew. To this rule the Guise is no exception, since his religious fanaticism is a thin disguise for political opportunism. His "aspiring thoughts" (930) reflect the anti-Machiavellian presumption that Catholics were really Atheists who professed to believe in Christ for reasons of policy — what John Donne would call "perfidiousenesse or dissembling of Religion." Where Barabas believed in Jehovah and emulated the Christians in failing to practice what he preached, the Guise is a complete unbeliever at heart. "Religion: *O Diabole*," he snarls in the candor of soliloquy (123), even as his master, Machiavel, counts religion but a childish toy. Nevertheless, through lip-service he commands the infiltrating ranks of the priesthood, and draws upon the sinister gold that his Catholic majesty, Philip of Spain, is currently extracting from the Americas. The Guise is a born gambler, ever ready to stake his all for the prize of the hour, to pose the absolute alternative: *Aut Cæsar aut nullus*. With all his cards in his hand "to shuffle or cut" (147), he coolly reckons on dealing himself a king. Yet the crown itself seems less desirable to him than the ceaseless conspiracy wherewith he strives for it. It is not so much *libido dominandi* as sheer appetency, *libido* unsated and insatiable, that drives him on. "For this," he reiterates, he has contrived his stratagems: not for the end but for the means, not for the fruit but for the experience. For this he builds upon his "quenchles thirst" (107), utilizing a curious metaphor which intermixes the acts of construction and consumption, as with the pyramid that he soon is promising either to climb or destroy. Truly, as he has stated at the outset, his thoughts are bursting into flames which can only be quenched with blood. Not only Marlowe's *Doctor Faustus* but even Goethe's *Faust* is foreshadowed by the Guise's doctrine

That perill is the cheefest way to happines. (95)

Except for this soliloquy, Marlowe's longest, and a few other speeches by or about the Guise, *The Massacre at Paris* is a singularly crude and unpoetic potboiler — at least in the abridged and garbled redaction that has survived. The upshot is a stronger emphasis than ever upon the force of a single personality, a heroic torso prone on a crumbling pedestal. In the original version, which must have been twice as long, this may have been counterweighted with the other parts; but the play, like all of Marlowe's, was known by its title role and listed as *The Guise* on the books of his theatrical manager, Philip Henslowe. In *Tamburlaine* character is destiny; in *The Jew of Malta* destiny is character; perhaps there is not enough plot in the one and too much in the other. In *The Massacre at Paris* there seems to be a schism between character and plot. The restless egoism of the Guise cuts through the tangled motives of the others; three successive kings are dwarfed by his failure to attain the throne; the one who sits upon it through most of the play, Henry III, closely resembles Edward with his minions and his "pleasure vncontrolde" (127). But the Guise too has his soft spot; his isolation from everyone else is confirmed when his wife betrays him; he gains a pair of horns, if not a crown; and that brutal irony is the theme of the one comic scene — a scene which, as chance or forgery will have it, survives in extended detail from an early transcript. The Guise regains his dignity at his death, after the classical moment of exultation:

> As ancient Romanes ouer their Captiue Lords,
> So will I triumph ouer this wanton King,
> And he shall follow my proud Chariots wheeles. (989–91)

But there is to be no triumphal procession for him. It is not in a little room, but in an apartment of the palace, that he is finally trapped. He responds to the royal challenge and strides through the claustral seclusion: "Yet *Cæsar* shall goe forth" (1005). Cæsar has been his epithet for himself, and it is no less apt for his fate than for his ambition. Whether *Julius Cæsar* echoed this line, or whether the Shakespearean line was interpolated into Marlowe's script, is one of the many uncertainties that hedge *The Massacre at Paris*. The Guise, drawing back in aristocratic aloofness from his assassins, dies with a Senecan declaration of identity in the midst of adversity:

> But they are pesants, *I* am Duke of *Guise*. (1007)

What he likes best, he has boasted, is what flies beyond his reach. Now we behold, the King points out, "traiterous guile outreacht" (969). And, since no one is more abject than the opportunist who has missed his opportunity, the overreaching Guise now devolves to the very nadir of fortune. It is left for Shakespeare to formulate an epitaph in *Antony and Cleopatra*:

> Tis paltry to be *Cæsar*:
> Not being Fortune, hee's but Fortunes knaue. (V, ii, 2–3)

With this final spin of Fortune's wheel, Cæsarism exhausts its possibilities. Marlowe already had gone on to investigate the problem of kingship from the other side, the side of the legitimate monarch who forfeits his crown, the unheroic hero at whose expense the interloper achieves his self-made greatness, the weak and unambitious inheritor of high place caught in the conflict of strong and ambitious men. Marlowe's cult of strength, from the beginning, carried along its explicit corollary, the scorn of weakness. *Tamburlaine* begins with a sketch of the weakling Mycetes, lacking in wit but interested in poetry, esthetically preoccupied with the sight of blood on the battlefield, wistfully clinging to the smooth-spoken courtier whom he terms his "Damon" (58). Though Tamburlaine is all that Mycetes is not, the strain of effeteness turns up again in Calyphas, the Phaëthon-like son who proves incapable of taking over his father's reins. Tamburlaine's virtue is capable of both conceiving and subduing, as he asserts in one of his rare moments of introspection; but his behavior is so externalized that we scarcely see him when he is not subduing. The conceiving is actually done by Marlowe, who accompanies his conqueror — as poets do — "in conceit" (260). As his dramaturgy matured, he would concentrate more upon passion and less upon action, less upon externals and more upon feeling. *The Jew of Malta* glanced behind obvious surfaces and purchased with grief its glimpse of experience. But with Barabas, as with Tamburlaine and the Guise, the impact is registered on us — as on their victims — from the outside; whereas with Edward, because he is the victim, we feel the effect of people and circumstances on him. Because he is passive rather than active, he cuts much less of a figure; but he is more deeply grounded within the psychological range of his creator; and his sensations are relayed to us more fully and faithfully.

Above all, he is a man who lives by his senses, an exponent of *libido sentiendi*. Being a king, he has no need to seek power; it is thrust upon him; and, being a hedonist, he wants to enjoy it. He is kept from doing so by the agitations of those careerists who surround and harass him. In his vacillations with them, his yearning for affection, and his continual yielding, he utterly reverses the pattern of *Tamburlaine*. Tucker Brooke stresses the fact that *Edward II*, unlike Marlowe's more characteristic plays, was not performed by Henslowe's companies; and draws the interesting inference that Marlowe, unable for once to count upon Edward Alleyn for a dominating role, was attempting to distribute the equilibrium more evenly among the dramatis personæ. This is the kind of functional

THE OVERREACHER

sidelight that is seldom irrelevant to our understanding of Elizabethan drama; it illuminates both the technique of the one-man
play and the emergence of an ampler and more varied characterization. But it should not deflect our attention from Marlowe's
increasing flexibility, his maturing sympathies, and his unexpected
insight into human frailties. Nor should it, within the precincts of
the theater, persuade us that Edward's part is somehow negligible.
Rather, what is envisaged may be a new style of acting, more
rounded and subtle than Alleyn's elocution, ultimately to be associated with Richard Burbage and the major Shakespearean roles. We
are reminded, as we enter the 1590's, that Shakespeare will soon be
catching up with Marlowe. He will be imitating his contemporary,
out-Marlowing the Marlovian idiom, in *Richard III*. But Shakespeare may have meanwhile established, with *Henry VI*, a dramatic
balance and a lyrical modulation which Marlowe may well be
emulating in *Edward II*.

During the patriotic decade between the rout of the Spanish
Armada and the downfall of the Earl of Essex, between *Tamburlaine* and Shakespeare's *Henry V*, the dramatic repertory was dominated by the vogue of the chronicle history. In trying his hand at
it, Marlowe addressed his iconoclastic talent to a highly traditional
form, which was fast becoming a quasi-official vehicle for keeping
tradition alive. Tragedy, which was also founded on some historical
matter, differed from the history play by being set in some other
country than England. Hence, while the tragic playwright could take
many liberties in the interest of his artistic conception, the historical
playwright was obliged to respect the common preconception of his
material as crystallized by legend, if not by history more rigorously
construed. Much of this material, in fact, was taken from the Elizabethan historians, notably from the second edition of Raphael Holinshed's *Chronicles*, published in 1587. These chronicles are essentially annals, recording events as they happened, year by year and
reign by reign. The result, transferred to the stage, was bound to
be clumsily episodic in structure, and to derive such unity as it
possessed from the personality of the reigning monarch. Much could
be done if he was a popular hero, like Henry V. When he was
a villainous usurper, like Richard III, Shakespeare could blend in
him the qualities of Tamburlaine and Barabas, and motivate the
plot by the interplay of ambition and revenge. But those were the

great exceptions, and they remain among the few English kings who have continued to live in the theater. The long-drawn-out and unhappy reign of Henry VI was more difficult to resolve dramatically. Marlowe might have been attracted by that ill-fated ruler, who would so much rather have been a shepherd; but Shakespeare relegates him to the background, where he does all too little to unify the three plays treating York and Lancaster, Joan of Arc and Jack Cade, and a miscellany of problems, foreign and domestic.

The grand design of Shakespeare's histories is delineated through a series of lessons in ethics and politics. In general, the king can do no wrong; sometimes, alas, he is led astray by evil counselors and false favorites; yet nothing ever justifies the dethronement of God's anointed. On the other hand, the commons are usually right, except when they are misled by demagogues. The sovereign and the people working happily together, in a popular monarchy where the feudal barons are kept well under control, fulfill the Tudor ideal of commonwealth. The primary function of the dramatic chronicler is to reinforce such precepts as these by examples — as crudely and naïvely, more often than not, as Peele in his jingoistic *Edward I*. No one would or could have questioned this ethos, but Marlowe shows no special concern to apply it; he is not concerned with the state but, as always, with the individual; and, in this case, it is a poignant irony that the individual happens to be the head of a state. Where Shakespeare's rulers prefigure Queen Elizabeth in various ways, the court of Edward almost seems to anticipate the absolutism and favoritism of the Stuarts. Thomas Heywood claims, in his *Apology for Actors*, that the whole of English history has been dramatized, from the landing of the legendary Brut up to the day of writing in 1612. Out of that continuous procession, Marlowe's single choice is significant. Other University Wits, if they preceded him in taking up the chronicle history, brought to it techniques he had used in his tragedies: the blank verse, the pageantry, the handling of conquests and conspiracies. His unique contribution was to bring the chronicle within the perspective of tragedy, to adapt the most public of forms to the most private of emotions.

The prologue to *Doctor Faustus*, apologizing for the private nature of the story, casts a backward glance at certain other plays. One is about Carthaginians, though it can hardly be *Dido*; another might well be *Tamburlaine*, aptly summed up in "the pompe of

THE OVERREACHER

prowd audacious deedes" (5). Still another may be *Edward II*, whose issue is sharply presented when the Chorus speaks of

> sporting in the dalliance of loue,
> In courts of Kings where state is ouerturnd.   (3–4)

Love is an unseasonable motive, in the face of political responsibility, as Æneas demonstrated when he abandoned Dido. "*Quam male conueniunt*" — the fragment cited from Ovid in *Edward II* (308) is completed and translated when the effeminate Henry III in *The Massacre at Paris* speaks of "loue and Maiestie" (609). *Amor et maiestas* — how badly they suit each other! The complaint has been softened from Machiavelli's hard-boiled remarks on whether princes ought to be loved or feared. The pride of the Guise is conveyed, in an image of overeating, as a "surfet of ambitious thoughts" (960). The tragic flaw of *Edward II*, as Gaveston conveys it in his opening soliloquy, is to "surfet with delight" (3). Where the Guise exultantly contemplated the prospect of a Roman triumph over Henry III, Gaveston evokes it metaphorically as the measure of his relationship with Edward:

> It shall suffice me to enioy your loue,
> Which whiles I haue, I thinke my selfe as great,
> As *Cæsar* riding in the Romaine streete,
> With captiue kings at his triumphant Carre.   (171–4)

This was an actuality for Tamburlaine, and these last two lines appear to be echoes from both *Edward I* and *Henry VI*. There the procession is taken quite literally, whereas in *Edward II* amorous fulfillment is preferred to military victory. When the future Richard III panegyrizes the sweetness of a crown, in the third part of *Henry VI*, he outdoes Tamburlaine by exclaiming:

> How sweet a thing it is to weare a Crowne,
> Within whose Circuit is *Elizium*,
> And all that Poets faine of Blisse and Ioy.   (I, ii, 29–31)

Tamburlaine made the identical value-judgment, in equating the diadem with bliss and felicity, that Barabas did in evaluating his gold. Somewhat differently, the returning Gaveston salutes London as his Elysium and finds no greater bliss than to bask in the sunshine of royalty, to "liue and be the fauorit of a king" (5). Nemesis manages, when he is executed, to repeat the key-word in his final speech:

> O must this day be period of my life!
> Center of all my blisse! (1290-1)

His affinity with the King is reaffirmed, across an eventful interval, when Edward meets his fate:

> O day! the last of all my blisse on earth,
> Center of all misfortune. (1928-9)

Edward's admisison of defeat is a reversal for all that Marlowe's heroes have represented:

> To wretched men death is felicitie. (2114)

While other playwrights were following Marlowe's lead and dramatizing kingly success, he chose to occupy himself with conspicuous failure. There are no unhappier pages in English history than those which record "the pitifull tragedie of this kings time" — for even Holinshed so described the regime of Edward II. Holinshed sympathized with the baronial party in its internal struggle against the King, and deplored the loss of national prestige that England suffered in its wars with Ireland, Scotland, and France. Marlowe touches upon these very lightly, treats the King much more sympathetically, and centers his dramatization on Edward's relations with his antagonist, Mortimer, and his favorite, Gaveston. Since the latter has to be executed midway through the drama, Marlowe fills in the gap and preserves the dramatic continuity by introducing the two Spencers, as Gaveston's protégés, ten years before their historical models emerged as Edward's favorites. The chronological sequence, which extends from Edward's accession in 1307 to Mortimer's execution in 1330, is concentrated into a time scheme which seems fairly short and consecutive, albeit Edward progresses from youth to old age. Early editions, which yield a more satisfactory text than we have for any of Marlowe's other plays, indicate his emphasis on the title page: *The troublesome raigne and lamentable death of Edward the second, King of England: with the tragicall fall of proud Mortimer.* Edward's reign was a time of troubles, yet his death is to be lamented. His brother, Edmund of Kent, blames "the ruine of the realme" first on Gaveston and later on Edward (1011, 1832). But when Edward is deposed, "the murmuring commons," as Mortimer recognizes, "begin to pitie him" (962, 2334). Mortimer is emphasized, as a more distinctively Marlovian figure, in the octavo of 1594; but the quartos of 1598 and thereafter add another flourish to the subtitle: *And also the life and death of Peirs Gaueston, the great Earle of Cornewall and mighty fauorite of King Edward the second.*

With Gaveston, Marlowe goes beyond Tamburlaine and Barabas in charting a new and dangerous way to rise in the world, to out-Herod monarchs. To charm their affections is to be exposed to the hatred of all their other courtiers, as was the actual Piers Gaveston, the leader of the French party at the court of the Plantagenets. Mortimer voices the attitude of the barons when he scorns "that slie inueigling Frenchman" (264), and what is said about Gaveston's aspirations and extravagances seems to be historically warranted. But Marlowe goes out of his way to make Gaveston a baseborn social climber, a "night growne mushrump" (581), just as he makes parvenus out of the respectable Spencers, in order to humble the pride of their courtly rivals. Gaveston inaugurates the drama by reading aloud the "amorous lines," the welcoming letter of Edward,

> The king, vpon whose bosome let me die,
> And with the world be still at enmitie. (14–5)

Gaveston's insouciant hostility toward the peers is matched by his cynical contempt for the multitude, which he exhibits next in his encounter with the three poor men. This is not the right chorus for his mounting fortunes, he soliloquizes, as soon as he has dismissed them:

> I must haue wanton Poets, pleasant wits,
> Musitians, that with touching of a string
> May draw the pliant king which way I please:
> Musicke and poetrie is his delight,
> Therefore ile haue Italian maskes by night,
> Sweete speeches, comedies, and pleasing showes,
> And in the day when he shall walke abroad,
> Like *Syluan* Nimphes my pages shall be clad. (51–8)

Marlowe is here refining on Holinshed's description of Edward "passing his time in voluptuous pleasure, and riotous excesse," corrupted by Gaveston, who "furnished his court with companies of iesters, ruffians, flattering parasites, musicians, and other vile and naughtie ribalds, that the king might spend both daies and nights in iesting, plaieng, blanketing [sic], and in such other filthie and dishonorable exercises." Between that medieval brawl and Marlowe's Renaissance pageant, the contrast is brilliantly illuminating. Marlowe's anachronistic Gaveston, in anticipation of such entertainments as the Earl of Leicester gave for Queen Elizabeth at Kenilworth, becomes a lord of misrule, a master of the revels, as well as a stage manager of palace intrigue. The Machiavellian becomes an Epicurean, maintaining his sway through the elusive and disturbing power of the arts. The Marlovian flattery, the speech of esthetic persuasion, is embellished with scenery and choreography; sound and spectacle are bracketed together by the casual couplet that rhymes "night" with "delight." And Gaveston proceeds to imagine a masque which can be taken as a portent, since its hero, Actæon, was hunted down for having gazed on a sight forbidden to men.

Its heroine is sexually ambiguous, a "louelie boye in *Dians* shape" (61), like the epicene pages or — for that matter — the boys who took feminine parts in the Elizabethan theater. The heroine of the play, the Queen neglected by Edward, wishes that her own shape had been changed by Circe (469), while Gaveston himself is compared to "*Proteus* god of shapes" (708). Examples of metamorphosis are frequently adduced, along with such standard mythological prototypes as Phaëthon; and the elder Mortimer evokes a long series of classical precedents to show that heroes and wise men "haue had their minions" (688) — Achilles and Patroclus, Socrates and Alcibiades, and other names still cited by apologists. Comparisons of Gaveston to Ganymede, and to Leander as well, link *Edward II* with *Dido* on the one hand and with *Hero and Leander* on the other. But the most suggestive comparison looks back to Tamburlaine's lament for Zenocrate and ahead to Faustus' vision of Helen of Troy, when Lancaster addresses Gaveston as

> Monster of men,
> That like the Greekish strumpet traind to armes
> And bloudie warres, so many valiant knights.   (1182-4)

The epithet most commonly applied to Gaveston, "minion," is etymologically the French term of endearment, *mignon*, which now begins to acquire pejorative overtones. Though it is sounded only nine times, it charges the atmosphere, just as "policy" does in *The Jew of Malta*. The King, says Mortimer, "is loue-sick for his minion" (382). As the Queen says, "his minde runs on his minion" (806). And again, and always:

Harke how he harpes vpon his minion. (608)

His obsession is carefully underlined by the repetition of the proper name. "Gaveston." The very word is like a charm, like "Tamburlaine" and "Barabas" in their different ways; and all three are alike in being amphimacers, which fit so effectively into Marlovian verse: "Bajazeth," "Abigall," "Mortimer." Beginning with the first line, and largely confined to the first half of the play, "Gaveston" is sounded 110 times, fifty-six times at the end of a line. Thus Edward, posing the absolute alternative, will "eyther die, or liue with *Gaueston*" (138). He is perfectly willing to divide his kingdom among his nobles,

So I may haue some nooke or corner left,
To frolike with my deerest Gaueston. (367–8)

It is the old story, so often renewed by life and repeated by drama, of neglecting one's duty to realize one's individuality: *All for Love, or the World Well Lost*. By dwelling upon the emotional conflict between majesty and love, Marlowe resolves the technical conflict between the claims of history and of tragedy. Edward's infatuation, though it impels him in the opposite direction, is just as extreme as Tamburlaine's domination or Barabas' cunning. His irresponsibility is rendered peculiarly flagrant by the unsanctioned nature of his indulgences. It cannot pass without comment that this, the most wholehearted treatment of love in any of Marlowe's plays, involves the erotic attachment of man to man. Friendship, as classically illustrated by Richard Edwardes' tragicomedy of *Damon and Pythias*, was a major Elizabethan theme; but to glance no farther than Shakespeare's sonnets, the ardor with which both sexes are celebrated is such as to elude academic distinctions between the sensual and the Platonic. Gaveston is more and less than a friend to Edward, who devotes to him an overt warmth which Marlowe never displays toward the female sex. The invitation to love, "Come live with me," the mode of enticement so richly elaborated in Gaveston's monologue on music and poetry, soon found its echo in Richard Barnfield's amorous appeal of a swain to a youth, *The Affectionate Shepherd*, thereby joining a literary tradition of homoeroticism which can be traced through Vergil's second Eclogue to the Greek bucolic poets. To ignore the presence or to minimize the impact of such motivation in *Edward II*, as most of its critics discreetly tend to do, is to distort the meaning of the play. According to the testimony of Kyd, Marlowe dared to suspect "an extraordinary loue" between Saint John and Jesus — even comparing them, according to Baines, with "the sinners of Sodoma." It seems unlikely, when the chronicles hinted at such a scandal as he had read into the Gospels, that Marlowe should have looked the other way.

In Michael Drayton's *Legend of Piers Gaveston*, the monologuist adapts a familiar Marlovian symbol to characterize his relationship with the King:

> I waxt his winges, and taught him art to flye,
> Who on his back might beare me through the skye.   (281-2)

When the "mounting thoughts" (879) of Marlowe's Gaveston are blocked by the opposition, there is a residue of genuine pathos in his response to Edward's commiseration:

> Tis something to be pitied of a king.   (426)

Their dalliance, which could be profitable to Gaveston, can only be harmful to Edward, who is the lone disinterested character; or rather, as a lover, he projects his innate egoism into a second self which transcends the rest of the world. Pliant to the caprices of his flattering favorite, "the brainsick king" (125) is petulant with his "head-strong Barons" (1065), vainly commanding and pleading by turns, a spoiled child now cajoling and now capitulating. "Ile haue my will" (78), he declares on his first entrance, and a moment later: "I will haue *Gaueston*" (96). But Mortimer and the other nobles, taking their stand upon an absolute alternative, decide to be resolute,

> And either haue our wils, or lose our liues.   (341)

In the ensuing battle of wills, Edward is predestined to be "ouerrulde" by his "ouerdaring peeres" (333, 342):

> The Barons ouerbeare me with their pride.   (1315)

Every other speech of the King's is an order, which is generally flouted and countermanded, while the Mortimers issue orders of their own. When Edward decrees of the younger,

Lay hands on that traitor *Mortimer*, (315)

the elder Mortimer treasonably retorts,

Lay hands on that traitor *Gaueston*. (316)

Edward has the regal habit of likening himself, or being likened, to the king of beasts; he is a lion, not to be intimidated by the crowing of "these cockerels" (1005). Yet, after he has fallen, he is a wren, striving against "the Lions strength" of Mortimer (2299) — or, more appropriately, "a lambe, encompassed by Woolues" (2027). It is perversely characteristic of him that he reads his destiny in the emblems of eagles and flying fish, the heraldic devices of temporary reconciliation that Mortimer and Lancaster bear to his "generall tilt and turnament" (673).

Edward is good at such charades, his enemies concede, at "idle triumphes, maskes, lasciuious showes" (959). Mortimer understands him as well as Gaveston does, and Mortimer's reproach is as pertinent as Gaveston's artistic plan of campaign:

When wert thou in the field with banner spred?
But once, and then thy souldiers marcht like players,
With garish robes, not armor. (984–6)

For Edward is not a soldier or a commander, he is an esthete and a voluptuary. Glorified by masques or defamed by ballads, he is a king with the soul of an actor, where Tamburlaine was more like an actor in the role of a king. Rhetoric and pageantry existed on the surface in *Tamburlaine*, objective and unreal; but in *Edward II* they are of the essence, subjective and real. Here the theatricality is not conventional but psychological, conceived as a trait of Edward's character. No longer is it taken for granted that words and deeds must coincide; on the contrary, his chronic fault is his inability to substantiate his vaunts. He is steeled by the news of Gaveston's death to make the one vow that he is able to execute. Then, when the parasite is avenged at Boroughbridge, Edward must stage a triumphal ceremony in his memory and in honor of newer favorites:

> Thus after many threats of wrathfull warre,
> Triumpheth Englands *Edward* with his friends,
> And triumph *Edward* with his friends vncontrould. (1695–7)

But his triumph, like the Guise's, is short-lived, and shortly he has reason to complain that he is "contrould" by the Queen and Mortimer (2015). When his infelicitous crown is demanded, he prays that it be transmuted into "a blaze of quenchelesse fier" (2030). Then, in accordance with the stage direction, *The king rageth.* In his eagerness before the battle, he invoked the sun, with an invocation that Juliet would use at a happier juncture: "Gallop a pace" (1738). His vain command, on the point of abdication, is for the elements to stand still. Now he feels, as Gaveston did when banished, "a hell of greefe" (412, 2538). But, just as Gaveston nonchalantly surrendered with the maxim that "death is all" (1199), so Edward asserts in yielding that "death ends all" (2140). That is a pagan sentiment which sorts, at all events, with his prayer to "immortal *Ioue*." In the dark and muddy dungeon where he encounters his end, he pays the most ironic penalties for the frolicking prodigality of his kingship. Tortured physically and mentally, humiliated by the loss of his beard, shaved and washed in puddle water, he rises to a sense of his tragic role with his remembrance of a forgotten victory:

> Tell *Isabell* the Queene, I lookt not thus,
> When for her sake I ran at tilt in Fraunce,
> And there vnhorste the duke of *Cleremont*. (2516–8)

It is a far cry of triumph, more theatrical than chivalric; but Shakespeare must have borne it in mind when Othello, on the verge of suicide, remembered his victory over the Turk at Aleppo. The striking feature of Edward's catastrophe is the total absence of anything spectacular. After all the talk about pageants, the tourneys and processions, they seem to have completely melted away. We are left with a bare stage which pretends to be nothing more, and with a hero stripped of any claim to distinction except his suffering.

> Hence fained weeds, vnfained are my woes. (1964)

Edward, on his imaginative flights, is the heir of Marlowe's earlier and more exotic heroes.

> Ere my sweete *Gaueston* shall part from me,
> This Ile shall fleete vpon the Ocean,
> And wander to the vnfrequented Inde. (343–5)

Such is his vaunt, at least, but harsh reality tests and deflates the gorgeous hyperbole. The state rests secure, the island remains terra firma, while Gaveston is whirled away by the currents of lawless dalliance. And Edward's recognition of his own powerlessness, hyperbolic though it sounds, is quite literal:

> Ah *Spencer*, not the riches of my realme
> Can ransome him, ah he is markt to die. (1309-10)

The style of the play, toned down to accord with its subject matter, has its pedestrian stretches as well as its minor harmonies. Numerous commas indicate varying pauses, as well as improvement upon the other texts in punctuation, and lines run over more limpidly than before. The dialogue makes flexible use of short speeches, sharp interchanges, and subdivided lines; yet, in the later scenes particularly, it crystallizes again into monologues, soliloquies, and set pieces. Marlovian allusion sounds out of place when — to cite an anticlimactic example — the Queen, setting out for Hainault in near-by Belgium, avows her willingness to travel as far as the Don,

> euen to the vtmost verge
> Of *Europe*, or the shore of *Tanaise*. (1640-1)

The blare of Marlowe's nomenclature is subdued when his characters' names are domesticated, and the verse halts when the Earl of Lancaster boasts of his four other earldoms,

> Darbie, Salsburie, Lincolne, Leicester. (103)

Gaveston mocks at those titles in a subsequent scene which comprises a single speech, five lines of ironic exposition while he is crossing the stage with the Earl of Kent. Such is Marlowe's technical self-consciousness that, when the Queen breaks down in the midst of a formal utterance, she is interrupted by Mortimer:

> Nay madam, if you be a warriar
> Ye must not grow so passionate in speeches. (1762-3)

The Queen's rhetorical abilities are put to an even severer test when Edward forces her to plead for the repeal of her rival's banishment. The usual plea is reversed, and persuasion gives way to dissuasion, when she dissuades Mortimer and he dissuades the barons from standing by their resolve. He complies out of love for her, while she has complied out of love for her husband; and Gaveston, the object of her husband's love, completes the unnatural quadrangle of compliance by virtually driving her into Mortimer's arms. Meanwhile Edward, reconciled with her, ironically accepts the situation as "a second mariage" (632).

Isabell, his queen, is a split personality. Though she does not live up to the accusation of being "subtill" (1581), it would be unfair to assume that characterization of women had as yet been developed to any degree of subtlety. She is more alive, at any rate, than the corpse of Zenocrate or the wraith of Helen. The theater was still a man's world; its heroines, as played by boys, were not unnaturally somewhat androgynous; they could behave without effort like shrews or viragoes or the proverbial Hyrcanian tigresses. Somewhat more feminine, though awkwardly depicted, was the saintly, long-suffering type of the patient Griselda, like the women so consistently neglected by the men in the plays of Robert Greene. Isabell enacts both types with manic-depressive inconsistency. She is pathetically devoted to Edward when, prompted by Gaveston, he repels her as a "French strumpet" (441). Subsequently, it is he who talks of "outragious passions" and denounces her as "vnnaturall" (2003). But the interim, and the downfall of her rival, have changed the forlorn wife into the scheming adulteress; and the transition is abruptly made in two brief soliloquies, which stand no more than a page or a scene apart. Despite the modifications that have been effected in order to give the drama a semblance of unity, the elaborate construction that differentiates it from all the others, there is still a break in the middle of *Edward II*, a watershed which divides our sympathies. Up to that point, Edward's follies alienate us, and afterward his trials win us back; while Isabell, who starts by being ungallantly abused, ends by justifying his antipathy. Amid these bewildering shifts of the moral winds, Kent is a sort of weathervane whose turnings veer with the rectitude of the situation, not unlike his namesake in *King Lear* — or possibly a Shakespearean *raisonneur* like John of Gaunt or Humphrey, the good Duke of Gloucester.

Our impression of Mortimer, too, is jeopardized by the same discontinuity that splits the characters of Edward and Isabell. Originally, when the King is so unreasonable, Mortimer seems not merely reasonable but exceptionally downright and hearty, the very antithesis of the intriguing courtier. One of the play's most observant commentators, W. D. Briggs, has even observed in him a model for Hotspur. In that respect he is the natural spokesman for Gaveston's enemies, ultimately becoming a foil for Edward himself, and maintaining a hold upon Isabell that parallels Gaveston's ascendancy over the King. But, as the play moves from open hostilities to more devious conspirations, Mortimer becomes increasingly Machiavellian and thus more characteristically Marlovian. Whereas Edward and Gaveston cling to each other, he stands — and falls — by himself. When Edward, "Englands scourge" (1567), defeats the barons, and Mortimer is taken prisoner, the latter asks himself:

> What *Mortimer*? can ragged stonie walles
> Immure thy vertue that aspires to heauen? (1565–6)

Soon enough he "surmounts his fortune" and makes his escape from the Tower of London; before long he has dethroned the King and become the Lord Protector. In his quickly accumulating *hubris*, quoting a verse from Ovid, he declares that greatness has placed him beyond the reach of fortune; in Senecan terms, he is the Olympian oak, to whom all others are but humble shrubs: yet the shrub is safer than the lofty tree from the whirlwind. He exults, as Tamburlaine did, that he can make "Fortunes wheele turne as he please" (2197). But his own death, compressing three years of history into a crowded final scene, is the immediate consequence of Edward's. Young Edward, having succeeded his late father as King, at once denounces Mortimer as "Villaine" (2593). Mortimer's acceptance of the fatal decree is a belated recognition that his strivings do not exempt him from the common lot:

> Base fortune, now I see, that in thy wheele
> There is a point, to which when men aspire,
> They tumble hedlong downe: that point I touchte,
> And seeing there was no place to mount vp higher,
> Why should I greeue at my declining fall? (2627–31)

Mortimer has viewed himself, in his heyday, rather as Fortune's successful foe than as her erstwhile favorite. With her triumph and his decline, he still may depend on his virtue; but virtue, at this point, devolves from Machiavelli's conception back to Seneca's. The individual, in a narrowing world, has less room to act and more occasion to suffer. The ethical criterion is the stoical resignation with which he meets inevitable and overwhelming odds. Where

Barabas died cursing, Mortimer's last lines are profoundly meditative. In the seriocomic realm of *The Jew of Malta*, sin could be temporarily dismissed as something that happened in another country. Tragedy, however, must face consequences. Mortimer faces them with curiosity as well as fortitude, readily dismissing the limited sphere of his worldly activities and welcoming death as a further adventure, an Elizabethan voyage of exploration:

> Farewell faire Queene, weepe not for *Mortimer*,
> That scornes the world, and as a traueller,
> Goes to discouer countries yet vnknowne.   (2632–4)

Not Hotspur but Hamlet is adumbrated by Mortimer, when he sets out toward that undiscovered country from whose bourne no traveler returns. His augmented stature, outshadowing the other characters, largely determines the after-effect of the play. Ben Jonson apparently thought of expanding Marlowe's denouement into a neoclassical tragedy, *The Fall of Mortimer*; and though he left no more than a page or two, it constitutes another link between his work and Marlowe's, and projects a course for the hero-villains of Jonson's two completed tragedies. Michael Drayton was so impressed by Mortimer, "that some-what more then Man" (147), that he cast him as hero in his epic of Edward's reign, *The Barons' Wars*, which in its early version was entitled *Mortimeriados*. In addition to chanting — as Lucan had done — "a farre worse, then Civill Warre" (8), Drayton poetized the romance between Isabell and Mortimer with a pair of his Ovidian *Epistles*. It is noteworthy that Bertolt Brecht, in adapting *Edward II* to the modern German stage, vulgarizes Gaveston, whose music and poetry are reduced to drinking ale and playing whist, while refining and rationalizing Mortimer into a classical scholar turned politician. Marlowe may offer a cue for that interpretation in the soliloquy where Mortimer cites Ovid, and looks upon the Prince with the furrowed brow of a pedantic schoolmaster. Somewhere, conceivably during his short imprisonment in the Tower, Mortimer has picked up his sudden flair for disguises, equivocating letters, and the other ruses of Machiavellianism: his sentence of death for Edward has its counterpart in Ferdinand's condemnation of Antonio in *The Duchess of Malfi*. Edward, hesitating to commit Mortimer, acknowledged that "the people loue him well" (1036). Mortimer, in his Machiavellian phase, acknowledges:

"Feard am I more then lou'd" (2383). The sinister aspect of his character is shadowed in the accomplice he chooses for Edward's assassination. The assassin, Lightborne, naïvely and proudly boasting of his Italianate poisons and more ingenious professional tricks, is to Mortimer what the slave Ithamore was to Barabas. And Lightborne's name reveals the cloven hoof; for it had also belonged to one of the devils in the Chester cycle, and is neither more nor less than an Anglicization of "Lucifer."

In his grimly diabolical banter with Mortimer, Lightborne undertakes to murder the King by "a brauer way" than any of the tortures he has enumerated (2369). The horrendous details are decently obscured, both in the dialogue and in the business; but legend was painfully explicit in specifying how a red-hot spit had been plunged into Edward's intestines. The sight of the instrument would have been enough to raise an excruciating shudder in the audience; and subtler minds may have perceived, as does William Empson, an ironic parody of Edward's vice. It is when he beholds the frown of Lightborne that Edward knows the worst:

> I see my tragedie written in thy browes. (2522)

So, in the next scene, Isabell tells Mortimer: "Now . . . begins our tragedie" (2591). Edward's tragical history, like Tamburlaine's, is compounded of many tragedies. That of the Mortimers stood out among the stock narratives of unlucky statesmanship in the *Mirror for Magistrates*. Marlowe's Edward self-consciously catches the exemplary tone of that compilation:

> Stately and proud, in riches and in traine,
> Whilom I was powerfull and full of pompe,
> But what is he, whome rule and emperie
> Haue not in life or death made miserable? (1879–82)

The Earl of Leicester, in arresting him, garbs the humiliation in borrowed garments of Roman sententiousness:

> *Quem dies vidit veniens superbum,*
> *Hunc dies vidit fugiens iacentem.* (1920–1)

This was Seneca's formula for Thyestes, yet it applies to all tragic vicissitudes. Thus Jonson translates it, at the conclusion of *Sejanus*:

> For, whom the morning saw so great, and high,
> Thus low, and little, 'fore the 'euen doth lie. (V, 902–3)

Classical or medieval, the peripety is the same, the overturn from grandeur to misery. Edward, the slave of passion, diverges from the man of action, Tamburlaine, by suddenly moving away from the grandeurs of morning and lingering over the miseries of night. Should we conclude that Marlowe was moving back toward a more traditional concept of tragedy? "All liue to die," as Edward tells Spencer, "and rise to fall" (1979). All are corrupted by life, except for his son — who survives to exhibit, in Heywood's *Edward III*, the manly qualities his father has lacked. Marlowe's boyish Edward III, with the innocent wisdom of the stage-child, proclaims in three last words his "greefe and innocencie" (2670). Yet the process of corruption, as Marlowe implied in *The Jew of Malta*, has been a kind of experience purchased with grief and repaid by an awareness of the difference of things. The relative maturity of *Edward II* seems to mark some progression from innocence into experience. Lightborne's spit is an unspeakable counterpart for the scourge of the Scythian conqueror; and the moral advantage of masochism over sadism is, to say the least, a delicate question. But it marks a psychological advance, from terror to pity, when the protagonist experiences genuine agony; while, in philosophical terms, it replaces the values of Epicureanism with those of Stoicism.

Resignation is not the attitude that we intrinsically associate with Marlowe. The frailty of the body, the fallibility of the mind, and the transience of human glory come as highly reluctant admissions in his other tragedies. *Edward II* would prove, if it proved no more, Marlowe's ability to challenge his own assumptions. To see him reverse himself, to see his idiosyncrasies stamped upon a conventional formula, to see for once the would-be tyrant tyrannized over, is more than we might have expected.

> But what are kings, when regiment is gone,
> But perfect shadowes in a sun-shine day? (2012–3)

Shakespeare could hardly push that line of inquiry much farther. "The reluctant pangs of abdicating Royalty," Charles Lamb would argue, are often as poignantly rendered in *Edward II* as in *Richard II*; and Edward's death scene was as moving, to Lamb, as anything in ancient or modern drama. Shakespeare could balance his tragedy by handling the counterclaims of the opponents more sympathetically, envisioning the whole as a problem in statecraft, where

Marlowe saw little save individual rivalries. Richard's mistakes are due to lack of judgment, where Edward's are attributable to will; and in his willfulness he knows his mind, as Richard in his vacillation does not. The inconsistencies of the latter, his frivolity and his dignity, are more consistently portrayed; yet it is the former whose maladjustment seems more fundamental and whose suffering seems more intense. Richard's death, unlike his life, is an imitation of Christ, a passion play in which an earthly crown is superseded by a crown of thorns. Yet Shakespeare seems to be universalizing the plight that Marlowe had discerned and isolated; and Shakespeare's king is illuminated, like a gilded page from a medieval manuscript, by such lyrical trappings and masquerading embellishments as Marlowe had devised. Richard, descending symbolically into the base court, visualizes himself as Phaëthon. He plays his climactic scene, the deposition, even more histrionically than his predecessor. When he dashes the looking-glass to the floor, his gesture is a farewell to the *Mirror for Magistrates*. The reflection that has been conveyed to him is a reverberation, not from *Edward II*, but from *Doctor Faustus*:

> Was this Face, the Face,
> That euery day, vnder his House-hold Roofe,
> Did keepe ten thousand men?   (IV, i, 281–3)

When Marlowe's Edward finds brief sanctuary in the Abbey of Neath, for a fleeting moment of serenity he feels that he may have missed his real vocation, that he might better have lived in philosophical retreat, and that "this life contemplatiue is heauen" (1887). He exhorts his companions, and especially Baldock, to console themselves with Plato and Aristotle, counselors whom they have all too cynically laid aside for careers of action. The minor character Baldock, "that smoothe toongd scholler" (1845) who has urged the King not to behave like a schoolboy, is the representative of *libido sciendi* in this play, in so far as Edward and Mortimer represent *libido sentiendi* and *libido dominandi*. Baldock's gentry, as he puts it, derives "from Oxford, not from Heraldrie" (1046). Thence he has brought "a speciall gift to forme a verbe" (775) — the talent for putting words together, in Quintilian's phrase — and now he would like "to court it like a Gentleman" (752). Having graduated into the world as the tutor of Gaveston's future countess, he is prepared, when we meet him, to join the Spencers in their campaign for Edward's patronage. The elder Spencer, advising him to "cast the scholler off" along with his curate-like attire, reads him a Machiavellian lecture on worldly wisdom:

> You must be proud, bold, pleasant, resolute,
> And now and then, stab as occasion serues.   (762–3)

Interesting advice which a young Cambridge scholar, smooth-tongued and gifted at forming verbs, would take at his everlasting peril. Though prophecy doubtless went beyond Marlowe's intention, he may have deliberately added one or two strokes of self-caricature to this University Wit who comes to grief among the intrigues and politics of court. Since the historical Sir Robert Baldock had been Edward's Lord Chancellor, a man of affairs whose origin was by no means obscure and whose background was not specially academic, Marlowe must have gone out of his way to manifest the wry preoccupation he shared with Nashe and Greene and the other masters of arts who had rashly decided to practice the dubious trade of literature in the wicked city of London.

It is as if a painter, half in earnest and half in jest, had painted himself in the corner of some panoramic canvas. When we turn from *Edward II* to *The Massacre at Paris*, we note that Marlowe again has appended a signature in the secondary figure of Ramus. A recent discussion of that confused and confusing play, by P. H. Kocher, pertinently notices how Marlowe seems to delight in shedding the blood of preachers and scholars. Petrus Ramus, whose murder was for Protestants a martyrdom, could be considered the scholar's patron saint. His works, which so drastically simplified the relations between logic and rhetoric, and which attempted to devise a more pragmatic approach to both, had set off an intellectual revolution in the Cambridge of Marlowe's day. Although his endless dichotomies turned out to be as rigid as those scholastic predicaments which he strove to abolish, Ramus was the Reformation's strongest champion in questioning Aristotle and the Schoolmen. Marlowe's depiction shows him *"in his studie"* with his "bedfellow," Taleus, (376) who escapes. Since Ramus has dedicated his existence to learning, he has no gold and cannot ransom himself — a special twist of the frequent Marlovian plaint. The humbleness of his birth is contrasted with the pride of his reason, in his dialectical interchange with the Guise. The Guise resorts to the argument of force, and Ramus dies reasoning to the very last. Although the portrait is stiff and fragmentary, it should stay in our minds as an affirmation of that scholarly ideal from which Dr. Faustus so egregiously deviates. If Edward II fails to justify his own lofty calling, that may be in part because Marlowe owes his allegiance to an even loftier one. Consciously, he may be allegorizing his autobiography, as Keats maintained that Shakespeare did; he may be miscasting the artist as a king, like Thomas Mann in his twentieth-century novel of kingship, *Königliche Hoheit*. Art, which is notoriously protean, can assume innumerable shapes; yet, as we grapple with it, we come to apprehend the intelligence behind it; and where, if not in *Doctor Faustus*, are we able to overtake the artist within his elusive sphere, the intellect?

Chapter **V**

SCIENCE WITHOUT CONSCIENCE

Knowledge is power. The realization was Bacon's: *Nam et ipsa scientia potestas est.* But power corrupts, and Bacon — the Cambridge alumnus taking all knowledge for his province, the Lord Chancellor found guilty of corruption — demonstrated the incompatibility of the serpent and the dove. Hence the parable of Baldock in *Edward II*, the prodigal scholar corrupted by worldliness, was not uniquely applicable to Marlowe; given full scope, it could and did become an allegory for his century. Earlier in that century, Rabelais had voiced its self-conscious expansiveness in the famous letter purporting to have been written by the allegorical giant, Gargantua, to his even more gigantic son, Pantagruel. More than a father's thoughtful advice to a student, this was a medieval salute to the great instauration of humanism. Hailing the revival of the classics and the investigations into nature, it was charged with awareness of their potentialities for good — and likewise for evil. If the late invention of printing was an angelic inspiration, obviously gunpowder had been invented by diabolical suggestion. And Gargantua's eulogy is tempered with the warning that *science sans conscience* — science without conscience, or perhaps we should say "without consciousness" — is but the ruin of the soul (II, viii). There were lurking dangers, as well as enriching adventures, in this brave new world which was opening up before the European imagination. Yet we justifiably stress the excitement, the exploration, the experience, which no man has more fully personified than Leonardo da Vinci. The secret of power, for that powerful genius, was a desire for flight: *La potenza è solo un desiderio di fuga.* Along with his vision of a flying machine, his paintings and anatomical researches and projects of military engineering, his city planning and stage designing and endlessly fascinating notations, the artist-engineer momentarily considered the possibility of necromancy. That was a delusion, he duly noted; but if only it were possible, how much it could so easily obtain! Riches, conquest, ability to fly, everything, except escape from death.

Magic was originally the appurtenance of religion; and when religion cast it off, it subsisted in the outer darkness, along with appetites and curiosities which religion proscribed. Between magic and science, as we have more recently come to know it, the lines were not yet sharply drawn. Magicians, however, were rigorously distinguished on the basis of whether they practiced white or black magic: whether they sought to control the elements, through natural philosophy and supernatural wisdom, as Prospero does in *The Tempest*, or whether they trafficked with the devil and conjured up the dead, through witchcraft and particularly necromancy, as does Marlowe's ultimate protagonist. The legendary Faust was neither a creature of folklore, such as Pantagruel, nor a figure from history, such as Leonardo. His legend emerged from the flickering limbo between the admonitions of the Middle Ages and the aspirations of the Renaissance. More precisely, he was begotten by the Reformation out of the Teutonic north, like his fellow-unbeliever, the Wandering Jew, and quite unlike his Mediterranean contemporary, Don Juan, whose destiny ran so strangely parallel. That Faustus meant "well-omened" in Latin was a paradox which did not pass unobserved. The disreputable name and vagabond career of an actual Georg Faust can be traced from one German university to another, skeptically pursued by accusations of charlatanism and suspicions of pederasty. It is rumored that he enlivened the pedagogical technique of his classical lectures by the necromantic practice of bringing Homeric shades to life. Marlowe, to whom this feat had its perspicuous appeal, seems to class it with the so-called shadows of Cornelius Agrippa, and glories in having resurrected blind Homer to sing for his hero. More remotely Simon Magus, a charlatan hovering on the fringes of early Christianity, who was accompanied by a certain Helen and was killed in a desperate effort to fly, seems to have some bearing upon this story; and there was the Greek precedent of Empedocles, the philosopher who disappeared into Ætna. Dr. Faust lost his original Christian name and got another by being confounded with Johann Fust, one of the earliest printers and therefore the practitioner of an art still held by many to be ambiguous. The sinister repute of the prototype, thereby enhanced with an aura of Titanism, projected the shadowy image of a latter-day Prometheus, bearing gifts which were dangerous for mankind.

It is not clear how Faust gained his reputation as a god-defier, unless it be through his pretensions as a necromancer. He seems to have ended by mysteriously disappearing, leaving behind him a cloud of sensational rumors as to his "damnable life, and deserued death," his "Epicurish" habits and Atheistical blasphemies. These were gathered together a generation later, in 1587, and widely circulated by a pious printer, Johann Spies, through the solemnly edifying and crudely jocular redaction known as his *Faustbuch*. In 1592 it was published in the free English translation that Marlowe so closely depends upon for his play. The translator, who seems to have been more of a humanist than was the didactic Lutheran author of the chapbook, takes advantage of Faust's travels to expatiate upon Italian topography. Marlowe follows his guidance through the ruins of Rome, and the guide is responsible for such atmospheric details as the mention of Vergil's tomb. Moreover, he contributed an epithet which, though Marlowe makes no use of it, cannot have failed to affect his impression: at the University of Padua Faust registers as "the vnsatiable Speculator." The English *Faustbook* is at once a cautionary tale and a book of marvels, a jestbook and a theological tract. Its chapters, anecdotal and homilectic, are roughly grouped in three sections. The first deals, extensively and systematically, with the diabolical pact; the second, rather more discursively, with Faust's speculations and journeys; and the third, after a series of miscellaneous jests, with "his fearfull and pitiful ende." Here, amid much that was not germane to his purpose, was a vehicle for the highest and purest expression of Marlowe's *libido sciendi*, a speculative sublimation of Tamburlaine's or the Guise's insatiable thirst — a hero who, "taking to him the wings of an Eagle, thought to flie ouer the whole world, and to know the secrets of heauen and earth."

This desire for flight transcended the pomp and dalliance of those preceding plays which Marlowe all but repudiates at the outset of *The Tragicall History of Doctor Faustus*. Yet, although intellectual curiosity is now the activating force, it cannot finally be detached from the secondary motives that entrammel it, the will to power and the appetite for sensation. The interrelationship of thought and action is the major problem for Dr. Faustus, as it can become for Shakespeare's heroes. It is not just a historical coincidence that Hamlet and Faustus were both alumni of Martin Luther's university, Wittenberg; in other words, their consciences had been disciplined within the *feste Burg* of Protestantism. There, where Luther threw his inkstand at the devil, Faustus comes to terms with the adversary; yet, when Faustus laments his devil's bargain, he blames his alma mater: "O would I had neuer seene *Wertenberge*, neuer read booke" (1376). When he appears at court and is scoffed at by a courtier, he displays his professional pride by humbling the scoffer and bidding him thereafter "speake well of Scholers" (1100). The cry of the triumphant scholastic disputant, *sic probo*, must ring through a wider arena than the schools (197); the intellect must prove itself by mastering life at large. Scholarship is rewarded by no greater satisfactions for Faustus than sovereignty is for Edward and Tamburlaine, or conspiracy for Barabas and the Guise. What is worse, the notorious alternative to that straight and narrow path is the primrose path to the everlasting bonfire. The formal pattern of Marlovian drama tends to be increasingly traditional. Having created the tragedy of ambition with *Tamburlaine* and put his stamp on the tragedy of revenge with *The Jew of Malta* and tried his hand at the chronicle with *Edward II*, Marlowe reverts to the morality play with *Doctor Faustus*. But within the latter, the most general of forms, he elaborates the most personal of themes — an Atheist's tragedy, an Epicurean's testament, a mirror for University Wits.

The prologue, after its apology for not presenting matters of love and war, presents character in biographical synopsis and plot in ethical perspective. The universal hero of this morality will not be Everyman; he will be a particular private individual; and Marlowe highlights his attainment, as usual, by emphasizing the lowness of his birth. Nevertheless, the Muse intends to "vaunt his heauenly verse" upon this theme (6); and, passing over the unexpected gender of the personal pronoun, our attention is directed by the adjective to the vertical scale of the drama. Its coördinates will be nothing less than heaven and hell; while on the horizontal plane, at opposite sides of the stage, the conflict of conscience will be externalized by the debate between Good and Evil Angels; and, even as the heroes of the moralities traverse a circle of symbolic mansions, so Faustus will pay his respects to personifications of the World, the Flesh, and the Devil. As his academic career proceeds, it is metaphorically described. Literally, a scholar's name was registered in the Cambridge Grace-Book when he took a degree, and the quibble on the word "grace" serves to bring out its nontheological overtones:

So soone hee profites in Diuinitie,
The fruitfull plot of Scholerisme grac't,
That shortly he was grac't with Doctors name,

Excelling all, whose sweete delight disputes
In heauenly matters of *Theologie*,
Till swolne with cunning, of a selfe conceit,
His waxen wings did mount aboue his reach,
And melting heauens conspirde his ouerthrow.   (15–22)

The last three words, a Marlovian idiom for the counteraction of
antagonistic forces, recur in *Tamburlaine* (1455). In *Tamburlaine*
the emblem of tragic pride is Phaëthon, rashly attempting to drive
the fiery chariot of the sun. In *Doctor Faustus* it is Icarus, whose
"wings of waxe" had already figured as an omen portending the
tragedy of Dido (1651). In each instance it is a question of flying
too high, of falling from the loftiest height imaginable, of seeking
illumination and finding more heat than light. Faustus prefers, like
the Guise, to seek what flies beyond his reach; he is accused, in the
augmented version, of trying "to ouer-reach the Diuell" (1363).
After the prologue speaks of overreaching, the emphasis shifts from
the heavenly to the hellish — and the phrase "diuelish exercise" is
borrowed straight from the *Faustbook*. With this shift, the rising
verse subsides toward a dying fall, and the ethereal image of flight
gives way to grosser images of appetite. These were anticipated by
"swolne with cunning" and will be continued by allusions to *hubris*
in terms of overeating. "Negromancy" is given unwonted stress by
its overhanging monosyllable, and "blisse" reminds us that magic
is to Faustus what a crown was to Tamburlaine, gold to Barabas, or
companionship to Edward:

> For falling to a diuelish exercise,
> And glutted now with learnings golden gifts,
> He surffets vpon cursed Negromancy.
> Nothing so sweete as magicke is to him
> Which he preferres before his chiefest blisse,
> And this the man that in his study sits.   (23–28)

The speaker of these lines may well be Wagner, the famulus,
half-servant and half-disciple, since it is indicated that he reappears
to speak the later choruses. It is a long way from his moral earnest-
ness to the cynical tone of Machiavel introducing Barabas. But, as
with *The Jew of Malta*, this introduction is completed by drawing
aside the curtain to the inner stage — which, in Elizabethan theatrical usage, was appropriately called "the study." The protagonist is
then discovered in his literal study, the little room, the monkish cell

that comprises his library and laboratory. His profession is not usury but divinity, which subsumes all the others, permitting him to "leuell at the end of euery Art" (32). Thus his introductory soliloquy is no mere reckoning of accounts but an inventory of the Renaissance mind. Cornelius Agrippa, that disillusioned experimentalist, whose namesake plays an appropriate role in Marlowe's tragedy, had latterly made such a survey in his treatise *Of the Vanity and Uncertainty of Arts and Sciences*. Goethe's nineteenth-century Faust could do no better than bring up to date those *Fakultätswissenschaften*, those categories of learning which Marlowe now passes in review: *Philosophie, Juristerei, Medizin, Theologie.* Whatever the contemplative life can teach, his Dr. Faustus has learned. He has mastered the liberal arts, the learned professions, and the experimental sciences of his day. To be or not to be, *"on cai me on"* (40) — the existential dilemma seems to him insoluble; consequently, he is ready to take his leave of philosophy. Against Aristotle he quotes the axiom of Ramus that the end of logic is "to dispute well" (36); and, since rhetoric itself is a means toward some further end, it does not gratify Faustus' *libido sciendi*. As for jurisprudence and medicine, though they help man to exist, they do not justify his existence. The "bodies health" is scarcely a fulfillment of *libido sentiendi*; whereas *libido dominandi* requires more than a "case of paltry legacies" (58). Yet the Roman statute that Faustus cites at random does not seem to be wholly irrelevant; it has to do with the ways and means whereby a father may disinherit a son.

Saying farewell to the other disciplines, he turns again for a moment to theology, picks up Saint Jerome's Bible, reads from the Vulgate, and comments upon two texts:

Stipendium peccati mors est: ha, *Stipendium, &c.*
The reward of sinne is death: thats hard.
Si peccasse negamus, fallimur, & nulla est in nobis veritas
If we say that we haue no sinne,
We deceiue our selues, and theres no truth in vs. (67–71)

This latter text, quoted from the very epistle of Saint John (I, i, 8) that goes on to warn against worldly lust and vainglory, gives Faustus an ominous pause. Tentatively he balances it against the stern quotation from Saint Paul's epistle to the Romans (vi, 23). All men are sinners, ergo all men are mortal, he syllogizes with a

sophistical shrug: *"Che sera, sera"* (75). Such was Edward's sentiment, spoken in English rather than Italian, when he accepted his
fate: "That shalbe, shalbe" (1962). Faustus, whether in Calvinistic
or Epicurean fatalism, is anxious to say "Diuinitie, adieu," to embrace the "Metaphisickes of Magicians," and to replace the Scrip-
tures with "Negromantike bookes" (76-78) which, by the subversion of an adjective heretofore consecrated to religious objects, now
seem "heauenly." Faustus' references to his magical art, like Prospero's, sustain the additional ambiguity of referring us back to the
author's literary artistry, to the "lines" and "sceanes," the "letters
and characters" in which Marlowe himself set the end of scholarism.
As a scholar-poet, Marlowe had been taught that the aim of poetry
was profit and delight. Is it the scholar, the conjurer, or the artist
who can make good this boast?

> O what a world of profit and delight,
> Of power, of honor, of omnipotence
> Is promised to the studious Artizan?
> All things that mooue betweene the quiet poles
> Shalbe at my commaund, Emperours and Kings
> Are but obeyd in their seuerall prouinces:
> Nor can they raise the winde, or rend the cloudes:
> But his dominion that exceedes in this,
> Stretcheth as farre as doth the minde of man.
> A sound Magician is a mighty god.   (81-90)

The last line improves with the variant ending, more meaningful in
the context, "Demi-god." Marlowe's protagonists do not simply out-
Herod their fellow mortals; they act out their invidious self-compari-
sons with the gods; and, from Æneas to Faustus, they see themselves deified in one manner or another. Faustus' Evil Angel holds
out the hope that he will be "on earth as *Ioue* is in the skie" (104).
Ignoring his Good Angel and the threat of "Gods heauy wrath"
(100), Faustus readily amplifies the enticement, which far outdoes
all other Marlovian seductions. He envisages a hierarchy of spirits,
answering his queries and serving his whims:

> Ile haue them flye to *India* for gold,
> Ransacke the Ocean for orient pearle,
> And search all corners of the new found world
> For pleasant fruites and princely delicates.   (110-3)

The panorama extends across the western hemisphere, where they are subsequently pictured as Indians, obeying their Spanish masters and conveying

> from *America* the golden fleece,
> That yearely stuffes olde *Philips* treasury. (160–1)

But Marlowe's wandering fantasy comes home with an anticlimactic suggestion, which incidentally reveals the Canterbury boy who was sent to Corpus Christi on a scholarship:

> Ile haue them fill the publike schooles with silk,
> Wherewith the students shalbe brauely clad. (118–9)

Faustus has his own Rosencrantz and Guildenstern in the two adepts of the black art, Valdes and Cornelius. Abetted by their instructions, he repairs at midnight to a solitary grove, where he draws a magic circle and abjures the Trinity. Just as Sir Walter Ralegh's friends were alleged to have spelled the name of God backwards, so here the name of Jehovah is

> Forward and backward anagrammatiz'd. (243)

Blasphemy has its irreligious observances, and this is the dread ceremonial of the Black Mass. The play itself is almost macaronic in its frequent scholarly lapses into Latinity, and the incantation is deliberately heightened by what Faustus calls "heauenly words" (262) and the Clown will call "Dutch fustian" (431). Though the demon makes his due appearance, first as a dragon and then in the garb of a friar, he does not appear as the devil's plenipotentiary; he has responded to the conjuration, so he explains in scholastic terminology, because Faustus has jeopardized his soul. It is the first of Faustus' disappointments, and is immediately solaced by the delight that he takes in his personal relation with Mephostophilis. Again, even more emphatically than with Gaveston, the name itself is something to conjure with, all the more potent because it accounts for half a line of blank verse:

> Had I as many soules as there be starres,
> Ide giue them al for *Mephastophilis*. (338–9)

Marlowe's protagonists tend to isolate themselves; yet they also tend, as we have seen, to ally themselves with some deuteragonist. Edward had his evil genius in Gaveston, Barabas his demonic familiar in Ithamore; and Faustus has in Mephostophilis an alter ego who is both a demon and a Damon. The man has an extraordinary affection for the spirit, the spirit a mysterious attraction to the man. Mephostophilis should not be confused with Goethe's sardonic nay-sayer; neither is he an operatic villain nor a Satanic tempter. He proffers no tempting speeches and dangles no enticements; Faustus tempts himself, and succumbs to temptations which he alone has conjured up. What Mephostophilis really approximates, with his subtle insight and his profound sympathy, is the characterization of Porfiry, the examining magistrate in Dostoevsky's *Crime and Punishment*.

The dialogues between Faustus and Mephostophilis resemble those cat-and-mouse interrogations in which Porfiry teaches the would-be criminal, Raskolnikov, to accuse and convict himself. Faustus is especially curious about the prince of darkness, whose name once proclaimed him the bearer of light; who was once an angel "most dearely lou'd of God," as Mephostophilis points out, but was thrown from heaven for his "aspiring pride," the primordial tragic fault.

> And what are you that liue with *Lucifer*? (305)

Faustus asks. And Mephostophilis answers:

> Vnhappy spirits that fell with *Lucifer*,
> Conspir'd against our God with *Lucifer*,
> And are for euer damnd with *Lucifer*. (306–8)

The reiteration reminds us that Faustus' plight, or any other human predicament, is the outcome of that Miltonic struggle, that fall of the angels, that tragedy of tragedies which brought original sin and consequent suffering into the world. It is ironic, of course, that Faustus should be asking to be admitted into the company of the damned. But misery loves company, and Mephostophilis will warrant his own role by quoting the proverb in Latin. The special poignance of the relationship lies in his foreknowledge and his foresuffering. Once the sin is committed, he cannot but hold the sinner to his unholy covenant. Faustus, with a blithe humanistic pantheism, "confounds hell in *Elizium*" (295). He has no ear for Mephostophilis' heart-cry,

Why this is hel, nor am I out of it, (312)

nor for his painfully explicit amplification,

> Hell hath no limits, nor is circumscrib'd
> In one selfe place, for where we are is hell . . .
> All places shall be hell that is not heauen. (553-8)

Orcanes, the noble infidel in the second part of *Tamburlaine*, used a similar expression to affirm a belief in a god who is not circumscriptible. Nothing like this Marlovian conception is hinted among the fundamentalist tenets of the *Faustbook*, although Marlowe might have learned from Lucretius that during our lifetime we undergo what is fabled to happen afterwards in Acheron (III, 978-9). Faustus is quite as unconcerned with "heauen, and heauenly things" (452), when his Good Angel commends them to him; and when his Evil Angel bids him "thinke of honor and wealth" (453), he has no compunction in choosing the pomps of Satan. On condition that he be enabled to "liue in al voluptuousnesse" for twenty-four years (328), and that Mephostophilis obey his commands and reply to his inquiries, Faustus is willing to sign a legal deed empowering Mephostophilis and Lucifer "to fetch or carry the said Iohn Faustus body and soule, flesh, bloud, or goods, into their habitation wheresouer" (540-2). When his blood congeals, after he has stabbed his arm, he ignores the portent; and when it streams again, having been heated with coals, it warns him to escape while there is time: "*Homo, fuge*" (513). Instead, he affixes his bloody signature with a blasphemous mockery of the last words of Jesus, according to the gospel of Saint John (xix, 30): "*Consummatum est.*"

Mephostophilis does nothing to lure Faustus on; he suffers for him, he sympathizes with him, above all he understands him; and, through this understanding, we participate in the dramatic irony. Faustus persists in regarding his fiendish attendant as a sort of oriental slave of the lamp, and Mephostophilis ironically promises more than his temporary master has wit to ask. Some day, after one fashion or another, Faustus will be "as great as *Lucifer*" (484) — he will arrive at the kind of ambiguous greatness that Fielding would attribute to Jonathan Wild. In the interim he shrugs:

> Come, I thinke hell's a fable. (559)

SCIENCE WITHOUT CONSCIENCE 117

To which the suffering spirit replies with the bitterest of all his ironies:

I, thinke so still, till experience change thy minde. (560)

For Faustus, even more than for Edward or Barabas, the fruit of experience is disillusionment. As soon as the contract is signed and sealed, he is eager to resolve ambiguities, to satisfy the cosmic questions that teem in his brain. He is keenly aware that there are more things in heaven and earth than the trivium and the quadrivium; but his discussions with Mephostophilis scarcely proceed beyond the elementary data of natural history and the unquestioned assumptions of Ptolemaic astronomy. "Tush," Faustus cries impatiently, "these are fresh mens suppositions" (667). To the more searching inquiry, "Who made the world?" (677) his interlocutor must perforce be silent, since fiends are interdicted from naming God. When various books of occult and pseudo-scientific lore are provided, Faustus nervously thumbs through the black-letter pages, only to realize that he has exchanged his soul for little more than the quiddities of Wittenberg: "O thou art deceiued" (610). In his undeception he listens to the conflicting angels again, and again the Evil Angel outargues the Good. Faustus, at all events, is beginning to respect the grim silences of Mephostophilis. Now it becomes the latter's task to divert him, but each diversion turns out to be a snare and a delusion. Faustus, being "wanton and lasciuious, . . . cannot liue without a wife" (574). This demand is frustrated, as the *Faustbook* emphasizes, because marriage is a sacrament; whereas, for Mephostophilis, it is "a ceremoniall toy" (583). The best that Mephostophilis can provide is equivocally diverting: *"a diuell drest like a woman, with fier workes."*

There are more and more of these ghoulish antics, which always seem to end by intensifying the actual harshness of the situation. Faustus, prompted by the Good Angel for the nonce, inevitably breaks down and calls upon Christ. Thereupon — most terrifying shock of all — it is Lucifer who rises with Beelzebub, presumably through the trap from below the stage, to hold Faustus to the letter of their agreement. As a pastime and a confirmation of his unregenerate state, they witness together Lucifer's pageant of the Seven Deadly Sins, the *Walpurgisnacht* interlude at the midpoint of the play, a sight as pleasing to Faustus as Paradise was to Adam before the fall (717). Marlowe, interpolating this quaint procession of gargoyles, harked back to a more deeply rooted medieval tradition than the "hellish pastimes" of the *Faustbook* — to the earliest subject of the moralities, as well as the homilies of Chaucer and Langland. Marlowe's treatment, curiously enough, bears a closer resemblance to theirs than it does to the Renaissance triumph of Lucifera in *The Faerie Queene*. Pride is the inevitable leader, and the others follow as the night the day, parading the principal weaknesses of the flesh, brandishing their respective perquisites, and speaking their pieces in highly seasoned prose. Faustus must indeed be a hardened sinner to contemplate their grossness without revulsion. Though he has a greeting for each of them, it seems to be Gluttony that inspires his reaction: "O this feedes my soule" (781). This has been heralded when the prologue touched upon the theme of satiety, is resumed when Faustus is "glutted" with a foretaste of what lies ahead (106), and will be rounded out in the final scene where he diagnoses his illness as "a surffett of deadly sinne that hath damnd both body and soule" (1367). Perdition is the more awful for Mephostophilis because he has "tasted the eternal ioyes of heauen" (314). As for Faustus, he has candidly dedicated himself to carnal egoism:

> The god thou seruest is thine owne appetite. (443)

His quest for knowledge leads him to taste the fruit of the tree that shaded Adam and Eve, to savor the distinction between good and evil. From that point he abandons his disinterested pursuit — or, rather, he abandons himself to the distractions that Mephostophilis scatters along his ever more far-flung itinerary. His further adventures are calculated less to fulfill his boundless ambition than to palliate his disappointment, to make the most of a bad bargain.

The rest is hedonism. It is conveniently preluded by Wagner, as expository chorus, describing how Faustus, like Phaëthon and other reckless adventurers,

> Did mount himselfe to scale *Olympus* top,
> Being seated in a chariot burning bright. (795–6)

A characteristic accomplishment of the legendary Faust was aeromancy, the magical power of flight. Unlike his resurrections and pyrotechnics, this does not lend itself very effectively to theatrical presentation. Wagner narrates his aerial voyages "to prooue *Cosmography*" (798), and Faustus himself discusses geography with Mephostophilis, pausing significantly over that Venetian temple which "threats the starres with her aspiring toppe" (820), and ultimately alighting at papal Rome. There the slapstick banquet at the Vatican, where they snatch food and drink away from the Pope and the Cardinal of Lorraine, is at best a satirical comment upon the blind mouths of the clergy, and at worst a callow manifestation of Elizabethan Catholic-baiting. But the pith of the episode is the ceremony of anathema, which definitively places Faustus under the most solemn ban of the Church. The dirge of malediction, the curse with bell, book, and candle, "forward and backward" (888), is the religious counterpart of the sacrilegious rite he performed by anagrammatizing the name of God. He and Mephostophilis retort by beating the Friars and scattering firecrackers. The episode has been considerably augmented along these lines by Marlowe's presumptive collaborator, who introduces an antipope named Bruno — possibly in honor of Giordano Bruno — condemned to the stake and rescued by Faustus and Mephostophilis in the guise of cardinals. But it is a peculiarly Marlovian twist, an antireligious fascination with ceremonial, which animates Tamburlaine's burning of the Koran as well as Faustus' celebration of the Black Mass, and culminates in the ritual of excommunication. Faustus is pledged, as was Barabas, to pull down Christian churches. From the negative commitment of his Atheism he moves on to the positive exploit of his Epicureanism, when we next see him at the court of the Holy Roman Emperor. There we first behold him exercising his distinctive gift of sciomancy, and raising — in a more or less elaborated dumb show — the shades of Alexander and his paramour, evidently the fabulous Thaïs.

It must be admitted that Faustus is more impressive as an Atheist than as an Epicurean. We might have expected more for the price he is paying, after his terrible renunciation, than the jaunty hocus-pocus that produces grapes out of season for a pregnant duchess or defrauds a horse dealer and fobs him off with a leg-pulling practical joke. Such conjuring tricks may be mildly amusing, but are they worthy of the inspiration or worth the sacrifice? Certainly not; and we ought to feel some incongruity between the monologues and the gestures, between the seemingly unlimited

THE OVERREACHER

possibilities envisioned by Faustus' speeches and their all too concretely vulgar realization in the stage business. Putting ourselves in his position, we protest with Browning's *Paracelsus*, "Had we means / Answering to our mind!" We probably feel the incongruity more than the Elizabethans did, for a number of reasons: and first of all, because we have lost their habit of accepting the limitations of the stage as the conventions of the theater, of taking the word for the deed and the part for the whole. Suspending disbelief, in short, we ought to be more impressed than we usually are. Still, if we remain skeptical, we may remember that so was Marlowe; he is on record asserting that the prophets and saints of the Bible were so many jugglers. His refusal to believe in miracles may well have hindered him from making sorcery altogether credible in his plays — wherein, contrary to the custom of Shakespeare and his other contemporaries, there are no ghosts; except in *Doctor Faustus*, there are naturalistic explanations for seemingly supernatural interventions. This second consideration is neutralized by a third: whatever our doubts or Marlowe's, his audiences were convinced. His talent for lurid spectacle, supported by Henslowe's most elaborate properties, and by the intermittent discharge of squibs and crackers, undoubtedly graveled the groundlings. A supernatural atmosphere was devised and sustained with such effectiveness that a veritable body of legends grew up around the performance of the play, most of them involving a personal appearance of the devil himself, who is temporarily mistaken for one of the capering devils of the tiring house.

Large allowances should be made for the mangled and encrusted form in which *Doctor Faustus* has survived. Its very popularity seems to have subjected it to an inordinate amount of cutting and gagging and all the other indignities that dramatic texts are heir to. It was not published until 1604, more than a decade after Marlowe's death; this first quarto and later editions based on it seem to represent an unauthorized abridgment. The quarto of 1616 and others deriving from it seem to stem independently from a fuller and more authoritative manuscript, upon which editors are inclined to place increasing weight. Unfortunately, neither one — nor the combination of both — is satisfactory. The 1616 text contains about half again as much material, and preserves the play in clearer and firmer structure; yet much of that construction is filled in by an inferior hand,

and several important passages are omitted. These we know from the 1604 text, which is the one most frequently reprinted; and since it is so terse a condensation, it can be very handily performed; yet it is not devoid of extraneous matter, while some of its scenes are misplaced or unduly telescoped. The recent parallel edition of Sir Walter Greg does justice, at least, to the complexity of the problem. Moreover Sir Walter confirms, with his considerable authority, the tendency to push the dating ahead to the latest period in Marlowe's career. The argument for 1592, after the publication of the *Faustbook*, seems cogent — though it carries the surprising consequence of making *Doctor Faustus* the follower rather than the forerunner of Greene's *Friar Bacon and Friar Bungay*. Even more perplexing is the enigma of Marlowe's collaboration. Not that there seems to be much disagreement about the identity of his collaborator, Samuel Rowley. But why should Rowley's clumsy journeywork eke out the greatest masterwork the English theater had thus far seen? It seems unlikely, from what Kyd tells us, that Marlowe could have worked in harness with Rowley. Was his *Doctor Faustus*, then, a fragment like *Hero and Leander*? If so, was it left unfinished at his death, or had he dropped it somewhere along the wayside? All too understandably, he might have found his task an uncomfortable one. Was he inhibited from finishing it by some psychological complication, or by some more instrumental reason equally inscrutable at this date?

In spite of its uneven texture, we must view the play as a whole, since its total design is not less meaningful than its purple passages, and textual disintegration will not improve its fragmentary condition. Critics have questioned the authenticity of the comic scenes, on the grounds that Marlowe lacked a sense of humor — a premise which they support by begging the question, and denying his authorship whenever they are confronted with a humorous speech. Marlowe's laughter, to be sure, is not Shakespeare's; yet, as *The Jew of Malta* must have shown us, his wit has a salt of its own. Furthermore, Elizabethan tragedy delegates a conventional function to comedy, and *Doctor Faustus* need be no exception to that rule. Thus Wagner, the clever servant, mimics his master in chopping logic with the other students. He remarks, immediately after the scene in which Faustus has bargained with Mephostophilis, that the Clown "would giue his soule to the Diuel for a shoulder of mutton"

(359). Similarly, the hostlers, Rafe and Robin, burlesque the conjuration of Dr. Faustus; their scene, which is out of place in the 1604 text, should come after the scene in which Mephostophilis provides Faustus with conjuring books; for Robin, it appears, has just stolen one of those potent volumes; and Rafe, with its help, expects to seduce Nan Spit the kitchenmaid, even as Faustus' necromancy will capture the love of Helen of Troy. Before this comedy team joined Marlowe's dramatis personæ, Rafe and Robin had parts in Lyly's *Galatea*, where they played their pranks with alchemist's equipment; but there they had little connection with the main plot, while their roles are intrinsic — if not essential — to *Doctor Faustus*. And while the comic underplot reduces the main plot of Marlowe's drama to absurdity, the overplot is luminously adumbrated — sketched, as it were, in lightning against a black sky. It is the adumbration of Faustus' downfall, glimpsed in the aboriginal tragedy of the fallen archangel. Victor Hugo's formulation for western art, the intermixture of grotesque and sublime, could not adduce a more pertinent example.

How grandly all is planned! (*Wie gross ist alles angelegt!*) Goethe's appreciation of *Doctor Faustus*, as recorded by Crabb Robinson, must refer primarily to its conception. In its execution, it adheres somewhat too faithfully to the undramatic sequence of the *Faustbook*. The opening scenes are necessarily explicit in underlining the conditions of the pact; but, as a result, the play is half over before the document is ratified and Faustus can start out upon his adventures. Out of the 1,485 lines in the 1604 Quarto, 791 have gone by before he leaves Wittenberg for Rome. The 1616 Quarto augments the ensuing scenes and links them loosely together with allusions to the papal-imperial struggle, which Rowley apparently gathered from Foxe's *Book of Martyrs*. But both versions move anticlimactically from the Pope and the Emperor to the Duchess of Vanholt and the trivial incident of the grapes. This, in the text of 1604, concludes a scene which commences at the Emperor's court and includes midway the buffooneries of the Horse-Courser. Faustus is well advised to pause for an instant and meditate on the restless course of time. Such drastic telescoping seems to indicate an acting version constrained by the narrow resources of a touring company. It is divided into fourteen continuous scenes, whereas the text of 1616 is subdivided into twenty scenes which editors distribute among five acts. Viewed in outline, the plot is perfectly classical in its climactic ascent: the conjuration of Mephostophilis, the compact with Lucifer, the travels to Rome and elsewhere, the necromantic evocations, and the catastrophe. Faustus' rise is harder to triangulate than the careers of Marlowe's other heroes, because each worldly step is a spiritual lapse. Examined more technically, the play has a strong beginning and an even stronger end; but its middle section, whether we abridge it or bombast it out with Rowley's hack-work, is unquestionably weak. The structural weakness, however, corresponds to the anticlimax of the parable; it lays bare the gap between promise and fruition, between the bright hopes of the initial scene and the abysmal consequences of the last. "As the outline of the character is grand and daring," William Hazlitt has said, "the execution is abrupt and fearful."

At the request of the Emperor, Faustus has evoked no less a shade than Alexander the Great, archetype of *libido dominandi*. For the edification and pleasure of the scholars, when he returns to the university, he evokes the archetype of *libido sentiendi*. Among all the beautiful women who ever lived, they have agreed that Helen of Troy is peerless, "thè pride of natures workes," the "onely Paragon of excellence" (1268). Disputation is silenced when she makes her fugitive appearance in their incongruous quarters. Since the days when Marlowe studied the classics at Cambridge, Helen had been his cynosure of comparison — comparison with Zenocrate in *Tamburlaine* and even with Gaveston in *Edward II*. But metaphor is never enough for Marlowe; he must have the real thing, beauty in person; in *The Jew of Malta* policy was personified by Machiavelli himself; and the consummation of Faustus' desire — or the consolation, at any rate, for his regret — is to have Helen as his paramour. Mephostophilis produces her "in twinckling of an eie" (1327); and the glamor of the subsequent lines has obscured this interesting verbal coinage of Marlowe's, an apt phrase for a magician's assistant engaged in bringing off his employer's most spectacular trick. This, of all occasions, is the one to which language must rise; and, in so doing, it brilliantly redeems the shortcomings of previous episodes. The apostrophe to Helen stands out from its context, not because anthologists excerpt it, but because Marlowe carefully designed it to be a set piece, a purple passage, a supreme invitation

THE OVERREACHER

to love. Its lyrical formality, its practiced handling of stylistic and prosodic devices from his established repertory, set it off from the pithy prose, the sharp dialectic, the nervous colloquies and rhythmic variations of his maturing style. Characteristically, it does not offer any physical description of the heroine. It estimates, as Homer did, her impact. How should Faustus react to the sight that had stirred the elders of Troy to forget their arguments in admiration? Chapman would render their winged words in his *Iliad*:

> What man can blame
> The Greekes and Trojans to endure, for so Admir'd a Dame,
> So many miseries, and so long? In her sweet countenance shine
> Lookes like the Goddesses.   (III, 167–70)

That could be a marginal gloss for Marlowe's twenty lines, which constitute three fairly symmetrical strophes. The starting point for the first, the invocation, is the most rhetorical of questions. Though it is Marlowe's culminating hyperbole, it may not strike us with the fullest impact, precisely because it has struck so often before, because it has been echoed and reëchoed as one of the striking exaggerations of poetry — like the tower of ivory in the Song of Songs. The thousand ships are not exaggerated; they are specified by Ovid's matter-of-fact account of the Trojan War in the *Metamorphoses* (XII, 7); but here poetic audacity intervenes to transpose a lover's emotion into a large-scale naval operation. The topless towers are recurrent symbols for illimitable aspiration, and Marlowe habitually juxtaposes them to the all-consuming element of fire. Cavalierly he poses a moral issue, and the alternative is absolute: the destruction of a city, the calamities of war, the world well lost, all for love.

> Was this the face that lancht a thousand shippes?
> And burnt the toplesse Towres of *Ilium*?
> Sweete *Helen*, make me immortall with a kisse.   (1328–30)

The third line is an implicit stage direction, leading on to the enactment of a metaphysical conceit; whereupon Faustus claims that Helen's lips suck forth his soul, and then reclaims it with another kiss. Underneath their amorous byplay runs the disturbing hint that she may be a succuba; this may not be the only world that is at stake for him. When Dido wooed Æneas and spoke of becoming "immortall with a kisse" (1329), it seemed to be little more than a figure of speech. For Faustus immortality means vastly more than that, in one way if not in another, although he may actually get no closer to heaven than Helen's embrace. No wonder he changes his evaluation from otherworldly to mercenary terms:

> Here wil I dwel, for heauen be in these lips,
> And all is drosse that is not *Helena*.   (1333–4)

The second strophe is in the active mode of *Tamburlaine*, and the phrase "I wil" resounds through it. Since Helen is notoriously a *casus belli*, Faustus proposes to reënact the Trojan War through the sack of Wittenberg. He will be Paris as, in parody, Ithamore would be Jason, with Bellamira for his golden fleece. Faustus challenges the Greek heroes to a tournament, imagined as medieval tapestry rather than a classical frieze, a colorful but two-dimensional representation of the basic conflict between pagan and Christian values. In the third strophe the knight, returning to the lady he has championed, salutes her with a gallant array of invidious comparisons and mythological superlatives. He modulates from the threat to the persuasion, the more passive mode of *Edward II*. If he cannot visualize Helen distinctly, it is because she bedazzles him. Her fairness, outshining the starlight, surpasses the goddesses — or is it the gods?

> Brighter art thou then flaming *Iupiter*,
> When he appeard to haplesse *Semele*,
> More louely then the monarke of the skie
> In wanton *Arethusaes* azurde armes.   (1343–6)

It is not to these nymphs, but to Jupiter himself, that Helen is being compared. Strange as this may seem, it is not inconsistent with the prologue's allusion to a masculine muse. It throws some light back on the offer of Mephostophilis to procure the fairest of women for Faustus, be they as chaste as Penelope, as wise as the Queen of Sheba,

> or as beautiful
> As was bright *Lucifer* before his fall.   (589–90)

Helen, whatever she is, whoever she was, says nothing. Her part is purely visual, entirely mute. Faustus might almost be talking to himself, and when we notice how many of his speeches are addressed to himself, the play becomes a kind of interior monologue. Whatever satisfaction he obtains from Helen is bound to be illusory;

as a necromancer he knows in advance that the shadow is not substantial, that the apparition he has materialized will vanish sooner or later. The *Faustbook* reports that she bore him a child, which disappeared — along with its mother — on the day of Faustus' death. Was it a vision or a waking dream, or does the fair exterior disguise some hideous monster like Keats's Lamia? Lucian, in his *Dialogues of the Dead*, pictures Menippus descending into the underworld, inquiring after Helen, and being shown a skeleton. Yes, Hermes assures him, this was the skull that caused the Greeks to launch a thousand ships. And the refrain is the timeless *Ubi sunt?* Where are they now — Helen, Thaïs, Dido, Zenocrate? Marlowe cannot have been insensitive to the traditional mood so poignantly expressed by his sometime collaborator, Thomas Nashe:

> Brightnesse falls from the ayre,
> Queenes have died yong and faire,
> Dust hath closde Helens eye . . .

It is not for nothing that Faustus characterizes Helen by her face, with the connotation of skin-deep beauty as opposed to harsh truth. His rhetoric is an ornate façade, an esthetic surface masking an ethical reality. A third dimension is given to the speech by the entrance — after the first strophe — of a third character, who is indubitably real. This is the Old Man, whom the *Faustbook* identifies as a neighbor, the exemplary figure whom Marlowe employs as a spokesman for Christianity and a counterweight for the ideal of paganism. It is he who penetrates Faustus' conscience:

> Breake heart, drop bloud, and mingle it with teares.   (1277)

Faustus admits his sinfulness and might be moved to repent, were it not for the threatening Mephostophilis and the enticing Helen. When Faustus sweeps her off the stage, it is the Old Man who stays to pronounce the moral; and while Faustus enjoys her elusive favors, the Old Man is "sifted" and tried by devils; but his faith triumphs over Satan's pride, and he ascends to heaven while the fiends sink back into hell. The absence of this crucial speech is a reason for continuing to distrust the 1616 Quarto.

With every scene the pace of the drama accelerates, reaching a climax with the final monologue, which syncopates an hour into fifty-nine lines. This is much too fast, and we share the suspense with Faustus, whose contract expires at midnight; and yet, in a sense, it is slow enough to fathom — as it were — the thoughts of a drowning man. It is a soliloquy in the profoundest sense, since it isolates the speaker; at the end, as at the beginning, we find him alone in his study. Tragedy is an isolating experience. To each of us, as to Proust on the death of his grandmother, it conveys the realization that we are truly alone. When the time comes, each tragic protagonist must say, with Shakespeare's Juliet:

> My dismall Sceane, I needs must act alone.   (IV, iii, 19)

So with Faustus, whose fellow scholars rally him for becoming "ouer solitary" (1363). They must leave him to his solitude, just as the friends of Everyman desert him on his way to the grave. In contradistinction to the specious grandeur of Faustus' apostrophe to Helen, his last words are an inner revelation, the excruciated agony of a lost soul. It is now too late for vaunting or pleading; it is Marlowe's occasion to develop the less characteristic mode of lamentation; and he does so with the utmost resourcefulness, timing and complicating his flexible rhythms to catch the agitations of Faustus' tortured mind. It is hard to think of another single speech, even in Shakespeare, which demands more from the actor or offers him more. Edward Alleyn, in a surplice with a cross upon it, was famed for his portrayal of the part and may well have left some marks upon these lines. They begin, with a portentous sound effect, at the stroke of eleven:

> Ah Faustus,
> Now hast thou but one bare hower to liue,
> And then thou must be damnd perpetually.   (1419–21)

Time is the essence, and also the substance, of the soliloquy. Its underlying contrast between eternity and transience is heavily enforced, in this distich, by a slow succession of monosyllables leading up to the rapid adverb, with the hypermetrical syllable, "perpetually." Words of comparable significance — "ever," "still," "forever," "everlasting" — abound throughout. Where Edward implored the sun to gallop apace and hasten events, Faustus now bids the planetary system stand still. A humanist to the last, he recalls a line from Ovid's *Elegies*:

> *O lente, lente curite noctis equi.*   (1428)

The utterance falls ironically, but not inappropriately, from the lips of the scholar turned sensualist, the erstwhile lover of Helen of Troy. The difference is vast between his motive for wanting the dawn to be postponed and the classical lover's plea to Aurora. As Marlowe himself had rendered it:

Now in her tender armes I sweetly bide,
If euer, now well lies she by my side.
The aire is cold, and sleepe is sweetest now
And birdes send forth shrill notes from euery bough:
Whither runst thou, that men, and women loue not?
Hold in thy rosy horses that they moue not . . .
But heldst thou in thine armes some *Cephalus*,
Then wouldst thou cry, stay night and runne not thus.

(I, xiii, 5–40)

Such a miracle might be accomplished at the behest of the gods, as Jupiter boasted in *Dido*; but for Faustus, all too human, the spheres go on revolving. Soon it will be his turn to be tormented; and he is not armed, as the Old Man was, with faith. Suddenly he seems to witness an epiphany. 'See see," he exclaims, "where Christs blood streames in the firmament" (1432). The line echoes and answers Tamburlaine's final challenge, when he threatened to march against the powers of heaven and "set blacke streamers in the firmament." The change of colors is emblematic of two opposing attitudes toward death: massacre for the man of war, sacrifice for the man of peace. When Faustus excommunicated himself by signing the deed, his own blood was ominously reluctant to flow. He asked, "Why streames it not?" (498) and coals were brought to warm it — more omens. Blood, for the Guise, was the only fluid that could extinguish the flames of lawless ambition; but Faustus is denied the blood of Christ, the only thing that could save him, because of his own denial. "The heauy wrath of God" (1439), as the Good Angel admonished, is now on his head; and his diction grows scriptural, echoing the Prophets and the Apocalypse, as he vainly thinks of hiding from the "iretull browes" of Jehovah. The striking of the half-hour alerts him again to temporal considerations, both relative and absolute.

O no end is limited to damned soules.   (1458)

Damnation is an unlooked-for way of transcending limits and approaching infinity; it is immortality with a vengeance; and Faustus would rather be a soulless beast and look forward to oblivion. Marlowe elsewhere uses the trope of "water drops" when he reckons innumerable quantities. Here, with fire in the offing, they are a welcome mirage of dissolution; now, from the combining elements, a vapor ascends. If time oscillates between swiftness and slowness, space is measured by the span between heaven and hell. Although those two words are paired off against each other in this speech and through the play, somehow "hell" and its cognates occur fifty-eight times to forty-nine occurrences for "heaven" — the proportion is forty-five to twenty-seven in the shorter edition. Faustus is accorded a glimpse of paradise in the *Faustbook*; the 1616 Quarto directs the "throne," the Elizabethan god-in-the-machine, briefly to descend from the "heavens," the roof of the stage; while hell, which is also conveniently adjacent to the localities of the play, yawns in a discovery scene. The denouement is a foregone conclusion: "for vaine pleasure of 24. yeares hath Faustus lost eternall ioy and felicitie" (1396).

As the clock strikes twelve, with thunder and lightning, the leaping demons enter to carry him off; in terror he makes his last offer to burn his books, and his very last word is the shriek, "*Mephostophilis.*" He makes his definitive exit through the monstrous jaws of the hell-mouth. That popular but obsolete property, which Marlowe resurrected from the mysteries, symbolizes pain and punishment more terribly than the sordid details of Edward's murder and more pitifully than the crude melodrama of Barabas' caldron. There is one more scene in the 1616 version, where the scholars interchange proper moral sentiments; like the sextet at the end of *Don Giovanni*, it seems unduly sententious after what has just happened; and, with some justification, it is not printed in the Quarto of 1604. The Chorus, or Wagner, draws the arras across the inner stage, and the black curtain prevails over the smoking red grotesquerie. If the classical imagery of the epilogue is at odds with its medieval purport, this reflects the tension of the play. If the branch is cut, if Apollo's laurel is burnt, let it be an object lesson for those "forward wits" who are so enticed by "deepnesse." The celestial-infernal antithesis is conclusively asserted, and the workings of "heauenly power" are discerned in the "hellish fall" of Dr. Faustus. Thus the tragedy is framed by the fundamental dogmas of Christian morality. How far, then, should they be taken literally? How far do they merely furnish

Marlowe with expressionistic scenery? How far was he utilizing theology as a modern playwright might utilize psychology? Faustus has maintained that hell is a fable, and Mephostophilis has declared — in an unexpected burst of humanistic fervor — that man is more excellent than heaven. Dr. Faustus' worst mistake has been to confound hell with Elysium. Between the classic shades and the quenchless flames, even in *Tamburlaine*, Marlowe had discriminated. If heaven was placed in hell, or hell in heaven, the inversion had to be reversed; and the reversal is all the more decisive in *Doctor Faustus* because it comes as a recognition, and because the movement of Marlowe's imagination — at its uppermost — turns and takes a plunge into the abyss.

Unless, with the credulous members of his audience, we regard his fireworks as sparks of hellfire, we must assume that Marlowe's Inferno is a genuine but unlocalized phenomenon. In the same spirit, Paracelsus repeatedly averred that there is a heaven in each of us, and Milton's Satan announces: "My self am Hell" (IV, 75). There is a god infused through the universe, so it was affirmed in *Tamburlaine*; and there is a hell which has no limits, Faustus is informed by Mephostophilis. Every man, according to his lights and through his own endeavors, has a chance to know both; and Milton is not being paradoxical when Satan announces in *Paradise Lost*:

> The mind is its own place, and in it self
> Can make a Heav'n of Hell, a Hell of Heav'n.　　　　(I, 254-5)

The Seven Deadly Sins, the Good and Evil Angels, Mephostophilis himself, upon this level, may be regarded as materializations like Helen of Troy. "Hell striues with grace" in a *psychomachia*, a spiritual battle within the breast of Faustus (1302). Pointedly the Old Man rebukes him for excluding "the grace of heauen" from his soul (1349). It is plainly lacking, but has he excluded it? Before his blood was dry on the parchment, he was thoroughly remorseful; and his remorse, increasing over his pleasure, gradually deepens into the hopeless despair of his concluding soliloquy.

> Contrition, prayer, repentance: what of them?　　　　(448)

he has wondered; he has resolved to renounce his magic, and been distracted by his Evil Angel. Later, when his Good Angel all but persuades him to repent, he tries; but his heart is so hardened that he can scarcely utter such words as "saluation, faith, or heauen" (630). Yet he does so, with no little eloquence; and, by uttering the name of God, he prays — albeit no more effectually than Claudius in *Hamlet*. As between the "Neuer too late" of the Good Angel and the "Too late" of the Evil Angel, the latter prevails with a Manichæan fatality (691). Christian doctrine vouchsafes mercy to repentant sinners:

Tush, Christ did call the thiefe vpon the Crosse. (1147)

Even "the Serpent that tempted *Eue* may be sau'd" (1371). Then why not Faustus? Having become a spirit in form and substance, has he ceased to be a man? Why, when the Old Man all but converts him, should Faustus accept the dagger of Mephostophilis? Why, when he calls upon Christ, is it Lucifer who emerges? George Santayana, acting as devil's advocate, and felicitously stating the case for Faustus as a martyr to the ideals of the Renaissance, would argue that he "is damned by accident or by predestination; he is brow-beaten by the devil and forbidden to repent when he has really repented." The pedestrian counterargument would be based on the *Faustbook*'s account of Faustus, "neuer falling to repentance truly" but "in all his opinions doubtfull, without faith or hope." Luther, followed by such English theologians as Richard Hooker, in his revolt against Catholicism had made contrition so difficult that at times it seemed virtually unattainable. What was worse for Faustus, he was no ordinary sinner; he was, like Marlowe himself, that impenitent and willful miscreant whom Elizabethan preachers termed a scorner. Far from denying sin or its wages, death, his course of action was premised on their inevitability: *Che sera, sera*. This led him, not to fatalism, but to an extreme act of the will — namely, the commission of an unpardonable sin, a sin against the Holy Ghost. Casuistry could have found theological loopholes, had a penitent Faustus been conceivable. But that would have presupposed an orthodox Marlowe.

As a measure of his heterodoxy, it has proved suggestive to compare *Doctor Faustus* with *El Mágico Prodigioso*, the sacramental drama of Calderón, grounded upon the analogous legend of Saint Cyprian. There the magician repents, forswears his magic, is converted to Christianity, and undergoes martyrdom — to be reunited in heaven with his lady, who also dies a Christian martyr. Death is a happy ending in the next world, after the uncertainties and horrors of life here below. Tragedy is intercepted by eschatology. Extremes meet, when we glance away from that simple and reassuring cosmos toward the chaos of modernity, and to the magistral exploration of it that Goethe achieved in his *Faust*. Goethe's Faust is a man of affirmations, bedeviled by a spirit of denial, whom he overreaches in the end by what — to sterner moralists — might well seem a legalistic ruse. He is free to stray so long as he strives; the forfeit need only be paid when he is satisfied with the passing moment. Though he is momentarily tempted to express such satisfaction, it is not occasioned by the present but by the prospect of a better world in the future. Hence his soul remains his own, on condition that he persist in his strivings toward the infinite, aided and comforted by eternal womanhood. Tragedy is here defeated by optimism. Enlightenment and humanitarianism absolve and regenerate Faust, just as salvation cancels out sin in that unworldly world of the Middle Ages which is still reflected by Calderón. Balancing precariously between those two worlds, Marlowe achieves his tragic equilibrium: the conviction of sin without the belief in salvation. That is sheer damnation; but damnation is man's unmitigated lot; this is hell, nor are we out of it. Such a pessimistic view is woefully incomplete; but tragedy is an intensive rather than a comprehensive inquiry, which concentrates upon the problem of evil and the nature of suffering. When Marlowe swerved from his predilection for the good things of life, he concentrated upon the evils with unflinching — not to say unbearable — intensity.

Doctor Faustus does not have the coherence of Calderón's ethos or the stature of Goethe's protagonist; yet, contrasted with the English play, the Spanish seems naïve and the German sentimental. We need not push these contrasts invidiously, given the differences in time and place, in poetic language and dramatic convention. Given the unchallengeable greatness of Goethe's achievement, it is noteworthy that certain readers have preferred Marlowe's treatment of the legend — notably Scott and Coleridge, Lamb and Hazlitt, all of them conceivably biased by their cultural leanings, and by their unfamiliarity with the second part of *Faust*. The first part, the romantic and domestic drama of Gretchen, admittedly belongs to

Goethe's little world; it may have been in emulation of Marlowe that Goethe went on to investigate the macrocosm. It may well be that Faustus has less in common with Faust than with Euphorion, the hybrid offspring of Faust and Goethe's Helena, who meets a premature death by attempting to fly. It may well be, in spite of Marlowe's narrower range and less philosophical outlook, that he grasped the core of his subject more objectively and with a keener awareness of its implications; that, because his background was nearer to obscurantism than to enlightenment, he appreciated the hazards and pangs of free-thinking. A later epoch than Goethe's, with less faith in progress or hope for individualism, may feel itself in closer accord with the earlier poet. It cannot dream about flying, with Leonardo, since the dream has not only come true but turned into a nightmare. It can add very little, except for amen, to the admonition of Rabelais that science is ruinous without conscience. It cannot but discern its culture-hero in the ancient myth of Icarus, in Cervantes' twice-told tale of the curious impertinent, above all in Marlowe's tragedy of the scientific libertine who gained control over nature while losing control of himself.

"The reason Milton wrote in fetters when he wrote of Angels & God, and at liberty when of Devils & Hell, is because he was a true Poet and of the Devil's party without knowing it." Blake's problematic note to *The Marriage of Heaven and Hell*, like most paradoxes, stresses a neglected facet of a complicated truth at the expense of what is more obvious. Marlowe, much more obviously than Milton, is committed to this kind of poetic diabolism; and, conversely, Marlowe can write with genuine yearning of paradise lost. No doubt he yearns all the more avidly with Faustus, but with Faustus he condemns himself; the Good Angel and the Old Man are at liberty, while Mephostophilis is in perpetual fetters. Yet, it is just at this point that Marlowe abandons his preoccupation with unfettered soaring, and seems to submit himself to ideas of durance, torment, and constraint. If he is imaginatively identified with any character, it is no longer Faustus; it is Mephostophilis, who suffers with Faustus like a second self yet also plays the cosmic ironist, wise in his guilty knowledge and powerful in his defeated rebellion. Through his agency Marlowe succeeds in setting the parable of intelligence and experience within a Christian framework, even while hinting that the framework is arbitrary and occasionally glancing beyond it.

Such is the attitude of ambivalent supplication that Hart Crane rephrases in his poem "For the Marriage of Faustus and Helen":

> Distinctly praise the years, whose volatile
> Blamed bleeding hands extend and thresh the height
> The imagination spans beyond despair,
> Outpacing bargain, vocable, and prayer.

Such is the way in which Goethe's Faust eluded his devil's bargain, and it applies to Marlowe if not to Faustus. If hell is destruction, it follows that heaven is creation; and perhaps the highest form of creation is that engendered out of the very forces of destruction, the imagination spanning beyond despair. Perhaps we may say of Marlowe what the Florentines said of Dante: this man has been in hell. As we broadly interpret that concept, many men have been there; but few have mastered their terrors and returned to communicate that mastery.

Chapter **VI**

THE DEAD SHEPHERD

Whatever comes after that climax, when the protagonist goes hurtling down to the everlasting bonfire, is bound to seem an artistic and moral anticlimax. Fortunately such evidence as we have, confirming such a reaction, allows us to view *Doctor Faustus* as Marlowe's final work. Even his flair for outdoing his previous efforts would have been hard pressed to cap that ultimate *tour de force*. The fact that he did not complete his masterpiece himself, for one reason or another, suggests that he may not necessarily have expected to continue as a playwright. His early death is so intrinsic a part of his career, indeed of his vocation, that it seems peculiarly idle to conjecture about what else he might have written. What is noteworthy, under the circumstances, is that he managed to stay alive for twenty-nine years, and to write seven plays plus a certain amount of nondramatic poetry. Nature imitated art so ruthlessly that Marlowe's life became an Atheist's tragedy; and *Doctor Faustus* could be retrospectively viewed, not merely as a literary testament, but as a kind of deathbed recantation. After such knowledge, what forgiveness? The gesture is a plausible one among writers, and its very failure to fit Marlowe's other writings can be adduced as a token of plausibility — just as some critics measure the piety of Baudelaire and Rimbaud by their blasphemies. But it scarcely accords with the complexities of *Doctor Faustus* itself, which is so much more than a work of edification attesting Huck Finn's precept that "Overreaching Don't Pay." Faustus, miserable sinner that he is, never reforms or sees the light; instead, he carries his curiosity along with him into the next world. "Vgly hell gape not," he cries in the penultimate line, "come not *Lucifer*" (1476). And even here William Empson points out a possible ambivalence, conveyed by strongly emphasizing the vocatives and by not accenting the negatives. This may be going too far, but it goes in Marlowe's consistent direction — the direction of Tamburlaine pausing only to immolate the Koran, of Mortimer setting forth like a traveler to discover countries yet unknown.

From that progression *Hero and Leander* stands somewhat apart; it does not necessarily come at the end. Though it is fragmentary, we need not infer that Marlowe was deeply immersed in it when he died. Though the material connects it with his early immersion in Ovid, it is much more highly polished than his academic exercises. Since his productive span was so short and his habits were

THE OVERREACHER

so irregular, he may have been working at it intermittently over several years. *Desunt nonnulla*: something is clearly missing when it breaks off, but not very much of the narrative he has been paraphrasing. Notwithstanding, George Chapman's continuation is twice again as long, and is subdivided into four Sestiads because the scene is laid in the town of Sestos — much as Chapman's Homer consists of Iliads — and also because the total poem now contains six parts. Marlowe's fragment has been unevenly broken into a first Sestiad of 484 lines and a second of 334. This is already more than twice the length of the Greek original, and Marlowe's treatment is correspondingly free. His author, Musæus, a late Alexandrian, was commonly confused with a mythical namesake, famed as the oldest of poets and mentioned as such by Faustus. Poets of the Renaissance — Bernardo Tasso, Boscán, and Marot, as well as Marlowe — assumed that, by adapting the elegant *epyllion* of Musæus into their respective languages, they were communing with the spirit of poetry at its elemental source. Readers like Swinburne, accepting that assumption, charmed themselves into believing that *Hero and Leander* was a spontaneous draught from the purest springs of Hellenism. Later readers are likely to be more struck by its artful elaboration, and by that same intermixture of pagan and Gothic components which distinguishes the apostrophe to Helen. Marot's version is simpler and more conventional, more of a ballad or a romance. Douglas Bush aptly illuminates the workmanship and the inspiration of Marlowe's poem by suggesting that it bears a closer resemblance to a Cellini saltcellar than to a Grecian urn.

It is sensuous and passionate, if not simple — and was Milton, who gave us that definition, simple? Not only does Leander play "the Orator" but his approach to Hero is that of "a bold sharpe Sophister" (I, 340, 197). Sophistically, he disclaims all sophistry:

> My words shall be as spotlesse as my youth,
> Full of simplicitie and naked truth.   (I, 207–8)

The contrast, as it develops, lies between the sophistication of his words and the naïveté of his actual love-making. Marlowe's two Sestiads, contrasting the proposal with the consummation, pair off innocence with experience. The artless youth of Abydos has fully mastered the rhetoric of Petrus Ramus; he is as sure as Dr. Faustus that the aim of logic is to convince one's hearers; and, in his magisterial disputation against chastity, he summons the quiddities of scholasticism to the support of *libido sentiendi*. "The rites," he opines,

> In which Loues beauteous Empresse most delites,
> Are banquets, Dorick musicke, midnight-reuell,
> Plaies, maskes, and all that stern age counteth euill.　　(I, 299–302)

This is not, nor could it be, unabashed hedonism. The tension between the indulgence and the repression of such pleasures is not simply the ageless debate between ardent youth and crabbed age; it is a struggle between the Christian conscience, be it medieval or Puritan, and natural instincts reaffirmed by the classical Renaissance. In the struggle, Marlowe's position may have been extreme; but so was his consciousness of the traditional forces arrayed against him. He knew that he could never attain the freshness of empiricism without undercutting the encrustations of dogma. He knew, too, that the initiation his poem celebrates is a more authentic rite than any other; and it amused him to picture Venus, not Diana, presiding over Elizabethan revels presented under the guise of religious observances. The warmth of his subject is mitigated by the continual interplay of his paradoxes and epigrams; the sensuousness of the lovers is cooled by the sententiousness of the poet, who speaks for once in his own voice rather than through dramatic mouthpieces. His couplets are not always closed, not quite heroic, prosodically speaking; and, when they occasionally run over, the effect is deliberate and sweeping. The tone is mock-heroic; as a narrator, Marlowe is more like Chaucer than like Spenser; and his comingled ironies and sympathies resemble those of *Troilus and Criseyde*.

The test of Marlowe's success at presenting what Chapman would have called a banquet of sense is the latter's sequel. He announces the change as soon as he takes up the story: "Loues edge is taken off . . ." (III, 5). That is not entirely Chapman's fault; Marlowe has already skimmed off the sweetness and left him to take care of the bitter residue. Chapman, by way of postponing it, surrounds his lovers with metaphysical conceits, allegorical graces, and impersonal personifications. In his reliance upon the goddess of ceremony and his concentration upon the marriage ritual, he formally veils those sensual appetites for which Marlowe has been stating the case. His imagination is conceptual, where Marlowe's was more immediately perceptual. In celebrating the senses, Marlowe exercises them; above all others, he exercises the faculty of vision. His surfaces are richly overlaid with such decorations as Hero's tears, which Cupid changes into a string of pearls. But the eyesight is involved more organically; for Marlowe was not less prepossessed by looks than he was by words; and the motivating impulse of the poem is love at first sight. "What we behold," Leander affirms, "is censur'd by our eies" (I, 174). The opening description of the lovers is primarily visual, with both of them; but, with Hero, it also appeals to smell and sound; while, with Leander, the appeal is to touch and taste — to both the tactile senses. Hero the fair is envisaged as a majolica shepherdess, wreathed in artificial flowers, and ingeniously shod in birdlike buskins which chirp as she walks. Although "*Venus* in her naked glory" decorates her garments, she herself is elaborately appareled (I, 12). Amorous Leander, on the other hand, is fondly described in terms of his physique, his physical attractiveness to goddesses and gods alike, and the possibility of mistaking him for "a maid in mans attire" (I, 83). By implication he is likened to Ganymede:

Ioue might haue sipt out *Nectar* from his hand. (I, 62)

In contradistinction to Leander, Hero does not appear unclothed until the end of Marlowe's fragment, and there she is vicariously described in terms of her lover's evaluation:

Whence his admiring eyes more pleasure tooke
Than *Dis*, on heapes of gold fixing his looke. (II, 325-6)

Boy wins girl, girl loses boy — we are prepared for surprises when the Marlovian fancy plays upon that elementary theme. We are not surprised that this boy and girl are paragons of their sexes, courted and envied by the immortals whose "headdie ryots, incest, rapes," and pictured metamorphoses bedeck the temple where Hero worships Venus (I, 144). Jupiter's courtship of Ganymede, which inaugurated *The Tragedy of Dido*, has its insistent parallel in Neptune's courtship of Leander, whom he mistakes for Ganymede. This has no justification in Musæus, beyond the incidental statement that Leander prayed to Neptune before swimming the Hellespont. The invitation to love that Marlowe embroiders, out of that passing mention, is not less voluptuous than the lovers' encounters. The sea-god, caressing the swimmer's body, begins a tale which is suggestive of Gaveston's masques for Edward, and which is significantly broken off. Rosemond Tuve, in her cogent analysis of the rhetorical structure of the poem, cautions us against reading this passage too literally, and reminds us that the Elizabethans could have taken the myth as a metaphor. Such a reading would relieve a delicate situation and sublimate it again from the metaphorical to the literal plane, visualizing Leander caressed by the waves and Neptune as the ocean he personifies. "The water is an Element" — when it bears Æneas from Dido — "no Nimph" (1353). The classic phrase *sub Jove* refers to the sky, to the animistic idea behind Jove; and Marlowe's conception of "flaming Iupiter," similarly, could have been an ethereal one; coupled with the image of Arethusa's azured arms, for which there is no mythological authority, it need imply no more than Olympian radiance embracing the stream personified by the nymph. The embrace of Narcissus, which dissolves into water and leaves the lover tragically alone with himself, portends the fate of Marlowe's protagonist, when Leander's charms are invidiously compared with

<blockquote>
                    his
That leapt into the water for a kis
Of his owne shadow, and despising many,
Died ere he could enioy the loue of any.   (I, 73–6)
</blockquote>

But such metaphors are elaborated by Marlowe into a mythology of his own. He had a Greek precedent in Poseidon's abduction of Pelops, the charioteer and culture-hero, who is compared to Ganymede in Pindar's first Olympian ode. Other accounts of that famous dynasty, and of the curse that descended through Atreus, tell how Pelops was served up to the gods as a sacrifice by his father, Tantalus. Only his shoulder was eaten, and it was replaced by an ivory one, which is now surpassed — Marlowe tells us — by the whiteness of Leander's skin. It was the crime of Tantalus to have stolen nectar and ambrosia, and his punishment in Hades made his name a notorious byword for overreaching. The father steals the food of the gods; the son, handsome enough to be cupbearer to the gods, is all but devoured by them. The generations of men yearn for forbidden delights; for their talents, which they plunder from heaven, they are duly punished. These dark hints are confirmed by the Latin motto on the title page of *Hero and Leander,* as first published with Chapman's sequel in 1598: *Ut nectar, ingenium.* Marlowe's allegorical machinery links the intrusion of Neptune with the still longer excursion that seems to fall between the first and second Sestiads. This has been dismissed as irrelevant, as if Marlowe were like Boscán, who conflated his *Leandro y Hero* with Vergilian digressions on beekeeping. But the relevance of the tale of Mercury is indicated by the epigraph about genius and by the initial description of Leander; for Hermes, in order to win a coy shepherdess, had filched a cup of nectar; whereupon Jove

> waxt more furious
> Than for the fire filcht by *Prometheus.* (I, 437–8)

Yet Hermes, through the intervention of Cupid, gains the upper hand over Jove; the Fates, infatuated with him, perform his behest; momentarily he banishes the gods, brings the Titans back to Olympus, and restores the golden age. But, since he does not return the love of the Fates, the revolution is short; Jupiter's reign of lust and war is all too soon resumed; and Mercury, that volatile fellow, that patron of thieves and scholars, would be imprisoned in hell,

> but that Learning, in despight of Fate,
> Will mount aloft, and enter heauen gate. (I, 465–6)

The Fates revenge themselves with their well-known decree that learning shall always be accompanied by poverty. And Marlowe in person, half ruefully, half ironically, voices the plaint of the malcontent scholar-poet that found its theatrical spokesmen in Baldock and Ramus. Thus it will ever be; the boors will inherit the earth;

> And fruitfull wits that in aspiring are,
> Shall discontent run into regions farre. (I, 477–8)

Marlowe was given to asking the question "Why?" and answering with fabled explanations — why Cupid is blind, why half the world is black. The interlude of Mercury is an etiological fable which, while explaining the poet's uneasy position, sketches his Utopia and hints at a much larger problem: the strained relations between the human and the divine. Hermes was the bearer of unhappy tidings in *The Tragedy of Dido.* Here he determines the denouement by turning the Fates against Cupid, so that love will be thwarted by destiny and Hero will end by losing Leander to Neptune. An inept sequel by Henry Petowe, which is equally untrue to Marlowe and to Musæus, and which raises any estimate of Chapman's additions, unites the lovers in a happy ending. With Marlowe the very brightness of the auspices foretells disaster:

> As if another *Phaeton* had got
> The guidance of the sunnes rich chariot. (I, 101–2)

The alternation of light and shade follows the Ovidian paradox that "darke night is *Cupids* day" (I, 191). The poem breaks off with the car of daybreak arriving to separate the lovers, and with the carriage of night crashing down to hell. Looking back to the introductory portrait of Hero, we should have perceived in it an omen; for, at the feet of the Venus embroidered upon her sleeves, lies the prostrate Adonis. The lovers meet at the festival of Adonis, the dying god whose cult was so recurrent a manifestation of tragedy. But their tragedy, though fated, is averted by Marlowe's own — or, at any rate, by whatever led him to abandon his manuscript. It can be maintained that the break is inevitable — if not a part of the author's design, like the hiatus that terminates Swift's *Battle of the Books*. Marlowe does not need the torch that Musæus provides, since he does not come to the fatal night when it is extinguished. He does bring Hero and Leander together in a secluded tower by the shore, and their union is likened to the conjunction of Venus and Mars. It is a resolution of the antithesis, which runs through Marlowe's work, between creative and destructive energies. The strife, by its very striving, is metamorphosed into its opposite, which is love:

> She trembling stroue, this strife of hers (like that
> Which made the world) another world begat
> Of vnknowne ioy. (II, 291–3)

This is as near as Marlowe comes to describing sensations which have invited and eluded all the pens that ever poets held. While the enjambments flex the lines with their climactic and onomatopoetic rhythm, the parenthesis shifts its ground to the primal mystery of generation, anticipating Donne's sudden zigzags from sex to philosophy. Behind the lyric profusion of the poem is shadowed an allegory: a naturalistic parable of the mind and the world, of the straits that divide human beings from each other, of taking the plunge and gaining the prize, of desire fulfilled and nature claiming her due, of towering exaltation and treacherous depths. The conclusion it never reaches is the starting point of *Lycidas* and *The Waste Land*, death by water.

Try as we do to focus our attention upon the poem itself, we are constantly made aware of the personality behind it, and never more forcibly than at the page where his pen seems to be lifted for the last time. *Hero and Leander* survived him with a special aura of pathos, as if Marlowe had been composing an elegy upon himself: the cut branch that might have grown straight, the prodigal who was such a prodigy. Posthumously, Robert Greene went on bidding for scandalous success; George Peele, who was to die soon afterward, had little doubt that Marlowe was now employed in writing "passions for the souls below"; while Gabriel Harvey, shaking his head, conceded the loss of a "Gargantua minde." Since Marlowe died two decades before Ben Jonson demanded that readers accept printed plays as literary works, *Hero and Leander* was the virtual basis of his reputation as a writer. Happily for that reputation, which was bedeviled in so many other ways, his poem was enthusiastically accepted as the ripest specimen of the erotic genre that included Shakespeare's *Venus and Adonis*. Shakespeare, who was imitating Marlowe here, as in his early drama, makes a graceful acknowledgment in *As You Like It*, when the shepherdess comments and quotes:

> Dead Shepheard, now I find thy saw of might,
> Who euer lov'd, that lou'd not at first sight?   (III, v, 81-2)

Though poetry cannot communicate the incommunicable, it finds its warrant and its reward in the corroboration of those who experience and recognize the feelings it seeks to convey. The dead poet lives in the lovers who pay him such tribute. Shakespeare reverts from the Marlovian couplet to the more humorous vein of *The Jew of Malta*, with the cruel epitaph of Touchstone's jest: "When a mans verses cannot be vnderstood, nor a mans good wit seconded with the forward childe, vnderstanding: it strikes a man more dead than a great reckoning in a little roome" (III, iii, 12–15). It is interesting that Shakespeare should offer these testimonials in one of his most Shakespearean comedies, since his debt to his forerunner is evident in every one of the genres that Marlowe practiced: tragedy, history, lyric and narrative verse. Even Marlowe's latent comic vein would affect the more satirical playwrights; and in so far as Elizabethan comedy was romantic, its language could not fail to be influenced by *Hero and Leander*. After the romantics had echoed it, the satirists burlesqued it; Nashe retold it to establish the etiology of his red herrings, and Jonson reduced it to puppetry on the Bankside — since by the time of *Bartholomew Fair*, it had become "too learned, and poeticall for our audience" (V, iii, 110).

John Lyly had been the innovator in comedy, as Marlowe was in tragedy. When Lyly switched from Euphuistic prose to blank verse in his latest play, *The Woman in the Moon*, his passionate shepherds could but adopt the Marlovian speech of persuasion:

> I'le giue thee streames whose pibble shalbe pearle . . .   (V, i, 104)

Robert Greene had balked at the adoption of blank verse as the idiom of tragedy. Yet Greene was never the man to resist a fashion; and, with the triumph of *Tamburlaine*, he tried to outbrave the Marlovian speech of intimidation.

> I clap vp *Fortune* in a cage of gold,

boasts *Alphonsus* (1481); but the royal canopy of Aragon makes a feeble showing after the Scythian chariot drawn by kings. *Selimus*, the most abjectly imitative of these camp-following tragedies of ambition, verbally reckons with "millions of Diadems" (1620). But the imitation multiplies the compliment to Marlowe's originality, and the multiplication quickly attains the point of diminishing returns. Marlowe had endowed the purposes of Elizabethan drama with words and gestures, both persuasive and intimidating, which were repeated until they exhausted their impact. After a decade of Tamburlaine and his followers, their speeches were tagged as "fustian" — the sort of cheap material that wears badly, and that looks better on the stage than anywhere else. Fustian had its inveterate admirers, but they too were disreputable, notably Ancient Pistol in the second part of *Henry IV*. Even Pistol's befuddled echo rings hollow, and redounds to the disadvantage of Tamburlaine's pomp:

> These be good Humors indeede. Shall Pack-Horses,
> And hollow-pamper'd Iades of Asia,
> Which cannot goe but thirtie miles a day,

Compare with *Cæsar*, and with Caniballs,
And Troian Greekes? . . .
                    Shall we fall foule for Toyes?   (II, iv, 177–83)

By the turn of the century, *Tamburlaine* was synonymous with that
brash theatricality which the English theater had now outgrown.
The role that Alleyn had created was truly a part to tear a cat in, to
split the ears of the groundlings and make Hamlet grit his teeth;
while Hamlet's creator, Burbage, and other more sophisticated
actors, soon to be patronized by King James I, developed with the
developing Shakespearean repertory at the new Globe Theater.
Meanwhile Shakespeare had rounded out the cycle of histories with
Henry V, which coincided chronologically with the highest point in
the fortunes of the Earl of Essex. The last few years of Elizabeth's
reign heralded the Stuarts with a waning of political hopes and a
tightening of economic opportunities. Literature reversed its heroic
trend; satire flourished; poets waxed introspective; tragic heroes
were, typically, disinherited princes rather than self-enthroning
conquerors.

Attempts have been made to enlarge the restricted canon of
Marlowe's plays by ascribing to him the authorship of several
Shakespearean histories, with presumptive revision and collaboration in varying degrees from the other University Wits and from
the upstart crow himself. The most recent and rigorous bibliographi-
cal studies, however, render unto Shakespeare the substantial integrity of his text. To think of him rather as an emulator than as a
collaborator is sounder in every respect, and enables us to watch
him assimilating and bettering his instructions. It was enough for
Marlowe, with his other achievements, to have written *Edward II*.
Shakespeare's journeywork is full of unassimilated Marlowe, and
smells no less of the classics than it would if he too had gone to the
university. But it was Shakespeare's mastery of the English chronicle
that gave the drama a local habitation and gradually eliminated its
artificial coloring.

Not *Amurath*, an *Amurath* succeeds,
But *Harry, Harry*,

in the second part of *Henry IV* (V, ii, 48–9). Hotspur, in the first
part, is not so much a Marlovian character as a characterization of
the Marlovian attitude in all its intransigence, truculence, and

grandiloquence. But Hotspur is the champion of a losing cause; and for his practical rival, Prince Henry, the sweetness of a crown is hedged with cares and responsibilities. For Macbeth it is much more complex; and ambition is revenged by conscience, long before Macduff has whetted his sword. Yet, whenever Shakespeare's heroes stand with their backs to the wall defying the world, they betray a wild trick of their Marlovian ancestors: Othello in his valedictory, Coriolanus at the gates of Rome, Antony flinging the absolute alternative: "Let Rome in Tyber melt . . ." (I, i, 33). Hyperbole presupposes exalted occasions; if the time is unpropitious, the result is bathos — or, at any rate, belittlement. When Marlowe's tropes were pirated for *The Taming of a Shrew*, making the domestication of Kate sound like the tenth labor of Hercules, they covered the short distance between the sublime and the ridiculous. When Thomas Nashe deliberately squinted through the wrong end of the telescope, he improvised a hyperbolic prose which was hailed as the English counterpart of Aretino's invective. Somehow the fine madness, the *furor poeticus*, was becoming a stranger and remoter phenomenon. Such pedestrian forms as domestic drama asked for a less elevated tone: *Arden of Feversham* was least convincing in its "Ouidlike" embellishments of middle-class adultery (I, i, 60). Such a play as Dekker's *Old Fortunatus* marks a transition by skillfully alternating between a Marlovian sphere of wish-fulfillment and the prosaic realism of every day.

The daring-dash-and-grandiosity, to sum up Marlowe's style in a Goethean phrase, was no longer attuned to the epoch. Shakespeare had glanced in passing at the new spirit, the increasingly social and psychological observation of playwrights, when he permitted Pistol to speak of humours. This was the slogan for Jonsonian comedy; and Jonson's *Discoveries* would look back, with neoclassical asperity, at "the *Tamerlanes*, and *Tamer-Chams* of the late Age, which had nothing in them but the *scenicall* strutting, and furious vociferation, to warrant them to the ignorant gapers" (777–9). But, even with Ben Jonson, the gap is wide between critical theory and theatrical practice; and in the theater, as T. S. Eliot has shown, "Jonson is the legitimate heir of Marlowe." That patrimony was equivocal, like the will that defrauds the heirs in *Volpone* while enticements are dangling under their very noses. Jonson unquestionably inherited Marlowe's rhetoric of enticement; but, whereas most of Marlowe's characters take the proffered jewels and delicacies at their face value, Jonson's cheaters employ them as Barabas did — to ensnare and delude. Jonson never lets us forget how selfishly and how unnaturally they deviate from the norms of morality, as when Volpone promises Celia:

> . . . could we get the phœnix
> (Though nature lost her kind) shee were our dish.   (III, vii, 204–5)

The luxuries of *Volpone*, though tainted, are perfectly tangible; those of *The Alchemist* do not really exist, but are conjured up by such puissant and mighty talk as that of Sir Epicure Mammon; and the alchemy itself is no magical art but a coney-catching swindle devised by Subtle, "the FAUSTUS, / That . . . cures / Plague, piles, and poxe" (IV, vi, 46–8). Here again, poetry and life are at odds; what is concrete with Marlowe is insubstantial with Jonson; the imaginative fabric is exploited to mask a sordid scene. Jonson's locale is ordinarily what Marlowe's was fitfully at Malta and Paris, the city and especially the underworld. In the Rome of *Sejanus*, neutralized by the pressures of opportunism, "Mens fortune there is vertue" (III, 740). As he loses his public, Jonson escapes from the commercial sharpness of his subject matter — from Volpone's "fine delusive sleights" (I, ii, 95) — into the illusory realm of the court masque: for example, in *Love's Triumph through Callipolis*. His unfinished pastoral, *The Sad Shepherd*, is not less poignant than *Hero and Leander* as a record of discontinuity, with its nostalgia for Elizabethan May-games and its protest against the rampant Puritanism that would soon be closing the playhouses. The sad shepherd and the dead shepherd — *Arcades ambo*.

The succession is more explicit with George Chapman, whom Marlowe had known through Sir Walter Ralegh's circle. A laying on of hands takes place in the third Sestiad of *Hero and Leander*, when Chapman invokes the "most strangely-intellectuall fire" of Marlowe's muse (III, 183). If that incandescence does not inform Chapman's Sestiads, it is breathed by some of the protagonists that he went on to portray. Most of his tragedies are located on the terrain of contemporary French politics that Marlowe had signalized in *The Massacre at Paris*. But Chapman's heroes have less scope than their predecessors, for they are contemporaries of Jacobean courtiers rather than of Elizabethan adventurers; they are not conquerors followed by kings but followers of kings. Bussy d'Ambois displays his prowess and policy in duels and amours; as a soldier of fortune, he is deservedly its victim; and fortune, for Chapman, is the sternest necessity. Virtue, in its eternal opposition, is by no means the Machiavellian *virtù;* it is once more the Stoic and Christian concept. Thus the wheel of Marlovian ethics comes full circle, precisely as it did for Mortimer. Bussy, the corrupted man of action, is balanced by his contemplative brother, Clermont d'Ambois, the "Senecal man" who rises above the world through his contempt for it, the Hamlet-like revenger who hesitates and — having done his duty — commits suicide. Marlowe's heroes might have lived by the maxim of *Bussy d'Ambois:*

> Who to himselfe is law, no law doth neede,
> Offends no Law, and is a King indeede.   (II, i, 203–4)

But kingship is no longer a problem of expansion and domination; it becomes, as its sphere contracts, a problem of self-control. The individual manifests his will, not by actively controlling his fortunes, but by exerting the more passive virtues of resignation and fortitude in the face of events beyond his control. In *The Conspiracy of Byron* the protagonist combines the prowess of Tamburlaine with the policy of the Guise, and his stormy eloquence would do credit to either or both:

> There is no danger to a man, that knowes
> What life and death is: there's not any law,
> Exceeds his knowledge.   (III, iii, 140–2)

But in the sequel, *The Tragedy of Byron,* self-assertion is confounded by royal authority. True knowledge is self-knowledge, Byron finally realizes, just as the higher law is an inner law. "Talk of knowledge," he concludes resignedly. "It serues for inward vse" (V, iv, 50–1).

Marlowe's influence, through the later Jacobean and Caroline drama, is sporadic and diffused. Yet, in some measure, every dramatist felt it directly or indirectly. The popularity of *The Jew of Malta* prompted many revivals, and stimulated the newer writers then coming to grips with the tragedy of revenge. Among them, John Marston reveals the closest affinities, stylistic and temperamental, though the decade between the two may spell the difference between his eccentricity and Marlowe's centrality. John Webster, who yields only to Shakespeare and Marlowe among the English tragic dramatists, owes most to Shakespeare; to Marlowe he owes very little in detail, but something perhaps in the posture of his characters, his splendid sinners and grim ironists, and the palatial ruins in which they dwell. Cyril Tourneur may have found an exemplar, if not a model, for his *Atheist's Tragedy* in Marlowe. A generation after his death, unexpectedly but appropriately, Marlowe's rhetorical intonation flavors the speeches of the mortgage-holding villain, Sir Giles Overreach, in Philip Massinger's melodramatic comedy, *A New Way to Pay Old Debts*. Marlowe might have been, but was not, forgotten by the new school of courtly playwrights centering on John Fletcher. Fletcher's collaborator, Francis Beaumont, satirizing the middle class in *The Knight of the Burning Pestle*, has his merchant sack an apprentice by sending him out "to discover / New masters yet unknown" (I, ii, 7). When the title character rants, in *Philaster*,

> Place me, some god, upon a *Piramis*,
> Higher than hills of earth, and lend a voice
> Loud as your thunder to me,   (IV, iv, 91–3)

it might almost be said that his prayer is forthwith answered, and he is filled with Marlovian afflatus. Indeed it could be said that, through the continuing vogue of Beaumont and Fletcher, Marlowe's astounding terms were transmitted to the Almanzors and Drawcansirs of the Restoration heroic play. Fletcher's well-made plays were skillfully contrived to please the ladies, and his versification was as different from Marlowe's as it could be while remaining within the bounds of blank verse. But when Fletcher tried his experiment in pastoral tragicomedy, *The Faithful Shepherdess*, reminiscence from Marlowe was inescapable. When the river-god woos the nymph, he is predestined to fall into the familiar melody of "The Passionate Shepherd to His Love":

> And if thou wilt go with me,
> Leaving mortal companie,
> In the cool streams shalt thou lye,
> Free from harm as well as I.   (III, i, 408–11)

This is the measure that Keats employs to evoke the "souls of poets dead and gone" who frequented the Mermaid Tavern. It is not quite the meter of "The Passionate Shepherd"; it is that which Shakespeare uses for fairies' spells and witches' incantations; and it differs from Marlowe's iambic tetrameter by dropping the first foot and thereby shifting to a trochaic beat. Milton demonstrates the trochaic rhythm in *L'Allegro*:

> These delights if thou canst give,
> Mirth with thee, I mean to live. (151–2)

Which is syncopated against the iambic couplet of *Il Penseroso*:

> These pleasures *Melancholy* give,
> And I with thee will choose to live. (175–6)

Although both couplets reverberate to Marlowe's bucolic refrain, Milton characteristically proposes a choice. The esthetic choice becomes ethical in *Comus* — the perfect foil for *Doctor Faustus* — and is sharpened and deepened by Milton's succeeding poems. Mephostophilis has adumbrated some of the darker aspects of *Paradise Lost*; and Pandemonium is a Marlovian apocalypse; but there is likewise Eden, and Milton out-Marlowes Marlowe when he blazons it forth in comparisons and superlatives. When Milton's dramatis personæ transcend their classical prototypes, as they invariably do, it is not vainglory but an act of piety. The very notion of a Christian epic is founded upon the conviction that this argument is

> Not less but more Heroic than the wrauth
> Of stern *Achilles*. (IX, 14–5)

But, of course, it is Milton's humanistic commitment that makes such choices difficult, weighty, and tense; that makes his great renunciation of Greece, in *Paradise Regained*, a secular crucifixion. The Marlovian dialectic of temptation is given monumental treatment by Milton, who — for better or worse — resists where Marlowe succumbs. Yet we have noted a prophetic strain in Marlowe, a Hebraism which sometimes comes to the surface as concretely as Milton's Hellenic feeling. It may be more pertinent to envision each of them wrestling with his particular angel than to relegate either to the devil's party. *Samson Agonistes* is a belated epilogue to Elizabethan tragedy, completing the cycle initiated by *Tamburlaine*, as well as a Puritan commentary upon the Restoration. The shackled agonist is a divine avenger, who starts from humbled pride and proceeds toward moral victory. The pedestal that self-consciously raises his prowess to this isolated stature is more Æschylean than Marlovian. Milton's personal spokesman could not be Marlowe's; it is their common medium that registers the largest indebtedness and the nearest kinship. How Milton reanimated blank verse, by variously drawing out the sense, hardly needs to be illustrated. How he extended the geographical and astronomical flight of Marlowe's imagery is salient enough in Satan's interplanetary journey, or the hemispheric vistas that Michael exhibits to Adam.

During the eighteenth century Marlowe, the embodiment of all the proscribed excesses, practically ceased to occupy a place in English literature. Seldom reprinted, little discussed, and never performed, his works dropped into the limbo of subliterature, from which the gradual forays of antiquarianism and the enthusiasm of certain romanticists were to rescue him in the nineteenth century. Since unique books have unusual fates, which are often interconnected, we are not as amazed as we otherwise might be at the return of *Doctor Faustus* to Germany, its survival through a puppet show, and its resurgence via Lessing in Goethe. In England, Marlowe's later fame has been that of a poet's poet. His tutelage must have aided Keats, in *Endymion,* to cultivate "ravishments more keen / Than Hermes' pipe" (II, 875–6). But the shock of recognition is a stimulus only when it encounters reciprocal talent. When Robert Bridges cites Marlowe in *The Testament of Beauty*, the touchstone shows up the tired flaccidity of his own verse and the tame eclecticism of his thought. Marlowe, despite his premature eclipse, was fortunate in working within an exciting context of fertile idioms and usable notions, which fellow-poets could bandy back and forth with enhancements and innovations at every stage. A slight but significant instance is his "Passionate Shepherd." This lyric was itself the distillation of a mood which thematically recurs, as we have frequently seen. It was also a provocation to rejoinders and sequels on the part of Marlowe's friends and successors, who are perspicuously mirrored in their responses. Robert Herrick, in "To Phyllis, to Love and Live with Him," welcomed the occasion to revel in those rustic amenities which he obviously enjoyed so much more than Marlowe. John Donne, in "The Bait," turned the pastoral into a piscatory, where — with the expected twist of Donne's unexpectedness — the fisherman is caught by the fish.

But the truest counterpart was Ralegh's answer, printed with "The Passionate Shepherd" in *England's Helicon*, "The Nymph's Reply to the Shepherd." Marlowe's poem was sung when his works went unread; Sir Hugh Evans sang it to keep up his waning courage in *The Merry Wives of Windsor*; in *The Compleat Angler* Izaak Walton hears it from a milkmaid, and hears the rejoinder from the milkmaid's mother. The mirth and melancholy of the two songs are proper to the ages of the singers; the nymph replies with sobering commonplaces which are no less Elizabethan than the ebullient promises of the shepherd; time passes, beauty fades, and men are false.

> If all the world and loue were young,
> And truth in euery Sheepheards tongue,
> These pretty pleasures might me moue,
> To liue with thee, and be thy loue.

The debate was not confined to Ralegh and Marlowe. It was a strongly marked tendency of Italian literature during the Cinquecento, which — according to Francesco de Sanctis — oscillated between idyll and carnival, between a bucolic and a satirical outlook. It was exemplified in Thomas Nashe's "Scholler-like Shepheard," Robert Greene, who longed for the countryside from the stews of London, oscillating between Arcadian romances and pamphlets exposing the chicaneries of coney-catchers. It was a phase of that primitivistic longing for ease and happiness and simplicity which is a sentimental revelation of crowded cities, complicated lives, and mellow civilizations. In the Christmas play, *The Return from Parnassus*, the Cambridge scholars end by becoming shepherds, having run through the other trades and thrived by none; but, alas, their sheepcote is the Isle of Dogs, a garbage-dump in the middle of the Thames. Such was the end of scholarism for Marlowe: after the seductions of the metropolis, the cohabitation of learning and poverty. It is easy to understand why Thomas Dekker, who spent so much of his life in a debtor's prison, dramatized the fable of Fortunatus and his wishing-purse. Essentially Marlowe did likewise, somewhat more subtly, when — for a few pounds from Philip Henslowe — he imagined Barabas counting his gold. That was stage money, and the magic of Faustus was sleight of hand; but the art that conjured with them was genuine, the power of the studious artisan to create a world of profit and delight, the evocative power of the mighty line and the hyperbolic image.

Any man was free to wish for such powers as life had not granted him: to be a magician, a merchant-prince, a king. To be a poet was not so much to make one's own wishes come true as to grant a vicarious realization — to play Mephostophilis, as it were — to the wishes of other men. All of us are gratified and soothed by the appealing wish-dream of the passionate shepherd. Would it were true, we say with the skeptical nymph. But Sir Walter Ralegh was not the first, and Sigmund Freud is not the last, to observe that the pleasure principle must be tempered by the sense of reality. That sense is not instinctive; it has to be learned; and, proverbially, there is only one teacher. *Experientia docet.* "And your experience makes you sad," says Rosalind to the melancholy Jaques in *As You Like It* (IV, i, 27). Whatever Marlowe's experience may have been, it changed his mind, as Faustus was warned by Mephostophilis; it must have been purchased with grief, as was Abigall's experience. Marlowe must have felt a hell of grief, like Edward, like Mephostophilis himself; and, unlike Faustus, he ran no risk of confounding hell with Elysium. The nightmare of the hell-mouth is at least as real as the daydream of Helen of Troy.

> Yet both exist side by side in the human intellect; as it were, the battle with its fury and its bloody swords, together with the harp-playing, the drinking from golden cups, and the kisses of fair women in the tents. And it is in these two forms that all poetry has been composed, lyric beauty and epic power. Which is the greater? [This is Liàm O'Flaherty, as it happens, writing of Joseph Conrad.] To me the battle and the blood, the terrible Genghiz, with his camel herds, his hosts of horsemen and his jewelled concubines, the storming of Troy, the war for the great bull of Cuailgne, all the terrible madnesses of men and women crashing their bodies and their minds against the boundary walls of human knowledge.

Fantasy may be an escape from anxieties; and Marlowe may dally in that golden world where, as Sir Philip Sidney well understood, poetry improves upon nature. There, if not elsewhere, the words "live" and "love" are synonymous. "Live with me" is also Tamburlaine's suit to Zenocrate, who is persuaded to live and die with him;

while Edward poses for himself the alternative of either living or dying with Gaveston. The scholarly career from which Faustus strays, guided by fallen angels who live with Lucifer, was to "liue and die in *Aristotles* workes" (33). But that would have been a cloistered state of unworldly isolation; whereas the individual is dependent upon a society; and the individualistic Barabas can neither live with others nor without them. Loving only himself, trusting neither Christians nor Turks, he vainly undertakes to "live with" both; and the island of Malta is an embattled citadel of self-interest — even as the gulf between two individuals is crossed when Leander swims from Abydos to Sestos.

The heroine of *Hero and Leander*, whose name increases a pre-existing confusion, diverges somewhat from the heroines of Marlowe's plays: the embalmed Zenocrate, the evanescent Helen, the rejected Dido, the neglected Isabell, the unfaithful Duchess of Guise. Hero's foredoomed love is happily consummated, where Abigall enters a convent and dies a virgin; while the characteristic Olympia, in the Second Part of *Tamburlaine*, is wooed but not won; she tricks her unwary suitor into cutting her throat. The passionate shepherd's lyric is a monologue, and the nymph's response — if we heed it — is a rejection. Moving from Venus to Mars, from love to strife, Marlowe effected his militant entrance into the theater; leaving the meadows of pastoralism for the fields of conflict, he armed himself with the Machiavellian dictum that it is better to be feared than loved. Since drama is the most social of the arts, and mono-drama is a contradiction in terms, he resolved it through the dramatization of masterful personalities overpowered by contradictory circumstances — the immovable object, the irresistible force. Love and majesty do not agree with each other; affection, seemingly thwarted, gives way to aggression; yet Marlowe's threatening oratory is disarmingly prone to lapse into amorous cajolery. Unloved, the Marlovian protagonist desiderates a companion, a minion, a deuteragonist; and here the exception that proves the rule is the Uranian Eros of Edward and Gaveston. More ideally, with Faustus and Mephostophilis, the second self becomes a projection of the ego, a *daimon*. "One is no number" for Leander and Hero (I, 255), but Marlowe's dramatic heroes stand alone in their singularity and single-mindedness. Conscious at every moment of their identity, they are supremely self-conscious at the moment of death. From what we know of Marlowe's own character, we may fairly suppose that he threw a good deal of himself into these monomaniac exponents of the first person: egoists, exhibitionists, infidels, outsiders.

As Marlowe progresses from Tamburlaine and Barabas to Edward and Faustus, the mask seems to fit more closely; the viewpoint is more sympathetic, and fear is mellowed by pity. After his imaginary flights through the realms of higher policy, he comes back with Faustus to the scholar's study. He has pursued ambition, the wish to outsoar one's fellow men, as well as revenge, the animus against them. Between the active voice of Tamburlaine and the passive voice of Edward, between the scourge of sadism and the self-torture of masochism, Barabas is the equivocating figure who unwittingly contrives his own punishment. The triumph symbolized by the chariot is easy and unrealistic; but there is poetic justice in the caldron; and Marlowe's deepened concern with suffering propounds its final symbol in the hell-mouth. Among the reiterated images that carry his peculiar impetus through his various writings, probably the most typical recurrence is the constellation of "topless towers" and "quenchless fires." Both of these complementary phrases impose concreteness on the idea of infinity: unlimited construction, ambition, pride; unlimited destruction, purgation, suffering. The underlying antagonism between civilization and nature has its *locus classicus* in Faustus' vision of the Trojan holocaust, and again in the frescoes that adorn Hero's temple:

> Loue kindling fire, to burne such townes as *Troy*.   (I, 153)

Fire is so standard a trope for love that Racine's lovers speak casually of *nos feux*. Doubtless its primitive symbolism was phallic. However, the taming of fire was the crucial step toward human culture, as prefigured in the myth of Prometheus, the fire-bringer. Freud finds an analogy for this in the curbing of the sexual instinct, and asserts that the findings of psychoanalysis "testify to the close connection between the ideas of ambition, fire, and urethral erotism." In *The Tragedy of Dido*, where the fiery imagery culminates in an actual funeral pyre, the Promethean theft is associated with all-consuming and unrequited passion, when the Queen begs Æneas to "quench these flames." But in *The Massacre at Paris* it is the ambitious thoughts of the Guise which are flames, and they can only be quenched with blood; and it is the same with Tamburlaine's thirst for sovereignty. Red was, at all events, Marlowe's favorite color.

Tamburlaine, who burned the town where Zenocrate died, who shed so much blood freely and callously, felt no pain when he stabbed himself as a lesson to his sons. When Faustus stabbed himself as a preliminary to signing the devil's contract, his blood did not flow. This was an unheeded omen of his damnation, when the drop of Christ's blood that would save his soul is denied him; and it seems to betoken what is conspicuously lacking in Marlowe's heroes, the motives of altruism and self-sacrifice. For that lack, for their egoism, they suffer; Apollo's laurel bough is immolated, and fireworks prefigure hellfire — not the refining flames of Dante's purgatory. With mothlike fascination, Marlowe keeps returning to the blaze that prefigures — even more than love or ambition — sin purged by sacrifice. No wonder Chapman eulogizes Marlowe's intellectual fire, while Drayton affirms that "his raptures were / All air and fire." Air, the sky, the combining element, is no less important for Marlowe, hypersensitive as he was to brightness and altitude. The sun, the first cause of both heat and light, beats continually upon his metaphors. It is the fiery chariot of Phaëthon, swinging from the upsurge of triumph into the peripety of suffering. It is the vehicle that sweeps Goethe's Faust through the ether into new spheres of pure activity:

> *Ein Feuerwagen schwebt auf leichten Schwingen*
> *An mich heran! Ich fühle mich bereit,*
> *Auf neuer Bahn den Äther zu durchbringen,*
> *Zu neuen Sphären reiner Tätigkeit.* (702–5)

There could be no more luminous image for the audacity of a mind which, as Lamb declared of Marlowe, "delighted to dally with interdicted subjects." Marlowe was playing with fire, after all, in no innocuously figurative sense; men were burned at the stake, in his day, for lesser heresies than those he is recorded as professing. Moreover, if he practiced the homosexuality he seems to have preached and preoccupied himself with, that was another crime punishable by burning. If it was not the unpardonable sin of Faustus, if it was not the Olympian theft of Mercury, it was the vice avenged by Edward's flaming spit. Mario Praz, a leading expert on problems of literary pathology, has diagnosed Marlowe's obsession as a

"Ganymede complex." What other critics have designated as his thirst for the impossible, Professor Praz would interpret as a sublimation of Marlowe's attitude toward sex.

Such interpretations are relevant, but marginal, to the understanding of Marlowe's creative processes. His preoccupation with beautiful youths is an idyllic mood, which he is repeatedly forsaking for more ambitious and realistic themes. It would be more appropriate to borrow a phrase which Dr. Henry A. Murray has introduced into clinical psychology, and to classify Marlowe's case as an "Icarus complex." The disposition to isolate one's self on a higher plane, while attracting the admiration of others, is not an infrequent pattern of motivation, although competitiveness and exhibitionism — even when channelized into the theater — rarely lead to such corruscating results. If individuals of this type are attracted less to the opposite sex than to their own, it is chiefly because they are animated by self-love; therein they are akin to another prototype; they are narcissists. In their autistic fantasies they fly, and their chief anxiety is the dread of falling. Since Icarus was the archetype of the overreacher, Marlowe was by temperament a tragedian. This is explicitly acknowledged when the prologue attributes Faustus' downfall to waxen wings which mount beyond his reach, or when Dido calls after Æneas:

Ile frame me wings of waxe like *Icarus*,
And ore his ships will soare vnto the Sunne,
That they may melt and I fall in his armes:
Or els Ile make a prayer vnto the waues,
That I may swim to him like *Tritons* neece:
O *Anna*, fetch *Orions* Harpe,
That I may tice a Dolphin to the shoare,
And ride vpon his backe vnto my loue.   (1651–8)

It was not fire but water, the quenching element, that killed Icarus; unscorched by the sun, he was drowned in the sea; Neptune prevailed over him, as over Leander — of whom we are reminded by Dido, sea-changed into a Nereid. The dolphin reminds us, not of Queen Elizabeth serenaded, nor of Antony's dolphin-like sensuality, but of Arion's musical enchantments and of the poet's powers over nature. The demonic familiars of Faustus are conceived in the shape of lions or horsemen or giants, and sometimes of women or unwed maids,

Shadowing more beautie in their ayrie browes,
Then has the white breasts of the queene of Loue.   (157-8)

This is a highly revealing preference. The brows of the spirits, who seem as sexless as angels, are preferred to the breasts of Venus. It might be inferred that Marlowe's sensibilities were less intrigued by sexual than by intellectual beauty — the beauty of Lucifer in his radiant pride. Venus' brows are invidiously compared with Tamburlaine's crest, and Zenocrate's brows shadow triumphs and trophies — in other words, her eyes, which reflect his actions. His own "frowning browes and fiery lookes," on the other hand, are a foretaste of death (252); and so is the frown of the Guise. So Edward sees his tragedy written in Lightborne's brows; and the wrath of God appears to Faustus in the ireful brows, the watchful eyes, the face of an estranged and angry father. That parallels the struggle, embodied in Helen and the Old Man, between beauty and truth. Dido offered Æneas as many soldiers as there were drops in the ocean. Faustus' last thoughts leap from combustion to liquefaction, with his yearning to lose his identity, to change his soul into "little water drops" (1472).

Icarus is a rebellious son, like Phaëthon, for whom the sun is a father-image; and Marlowe is capable of punning upon this association. Both sons are iconoclasts, unfilial rebels against the cosmic order. Hence Thomas Heywood mentions them, together with the Titans, as awful examples of "vaine Curiosity" in his *Hierarchy of the Blessed Angels*:

Either like bold aspiring *Phaeton*,
To aime at the bright Chariot of the Sun?
Or with his waxen wings, as *Icarus* did,
Attempt what God and Nature haue forbid?
What is this lesse, than when the Gyants stroue
To mutiny and menace war 'gainst *Ioue*.

The caveat against intellectualism was potent even in the seventeenth century. Pascal, that ascetic scientist, revived the warnings of Saint John and Saint Augustine against the lusts of the mind, the flesh, and the will — rivers of fire which bounded the wasteland of worldliness. It has been convenient for us to borrow Pascal's terminology, in characterizing the triad of basic urges that Marlowe so impenitently expressed. We have watched his genius devising poetic modes for each of them: the lyric plea for *libido sentiendi*, the epic vaunt for *libido dominandi*, and the tragic lament for *libido sciendi*. The most damnable appetite of all, which subsumed all the others because it wholly possessed the ego, was what Pascal's Jansenist masters termed *libido excellendi*. What could characterize Marlowe more succinctly, or better sum up his Icarian desire for flight? For the Jansenists, the urge to excel was the very temptation that had spoken through the serpent to Adam and Eve: "And yee shall bee as Gods, knowing good and euill" (Genesis, iii, 5). The subtle tempter, Mephostophilis, argues that man is more excellent than heaven. In their pursuit of excellence Marlowe's protagonists are goaded, like Captain Ahab, by the devilish tantalization of the gods. In effect, they partake of ambrosia; they violate divine authority; and the jealousy of the gods is visited upon their prideful heads. Theirs is the archetypal dilemma of *Prometheus Bound*. Tragedy, which ends by accepting the universe, cannot begin without challenging it; and Marlowe sounded this challenge for England as Æschylus did for Greece. If Marlowe seems the more iconoclastic, it is because the idols had accumulated; it was not a question of smashing rejection or chastened submission; a man could not come to his own terms with the cosmos except by risking charges of impiety.

"Tragedy is only possible to a mind which is for the moment agnostic or Manichæan," as I. A. Richards has acutely remarked. "The least touch of any theology which has a compensating heaven to offer the tragic hero is fatal." This applies with especial pertinence to *Doctor Faustus*, where the god-in-the-machine refuses to descend and the Evil Angel is a better theologian than the Good. Some would hold that tragedy, like so many other perspectives, is a substitute for religion; yet religion itself is a substitute for precise knowledge of the human condition; and the tragic view, as a branch of knowledge, faces existence without recourse to supernatural assumptions. "What certifies Olympus and reconciles the gods?" asks Goethe, in the prologue to *Faust*, and answers: "The might of man as revealed by the poet" (156–7). Tragedy is the ripened growth of a humanistic, as distinguished from a theological, culture. The tragic dramatist is not a high priest, but rather what Nietzsche would term a dragon-slayer, disposing of the illusions while enlarging the sympathies of his fellow men. Had Marlowe survived for a few years more and absorbed the new philosophy, Marjorie

Nicolson surmises, it might have inspired an optimistic body of poetry and counterbalanced the pessimism of Donne. That engaging surmise may be warranted by Marlowe's imaginative response to the old-fashioned science he knew, though it does not take account of either the formal intention or the ethical purport of his tragedies. Since man is born to trouble as the sparks fly upward, one may well be more interested in the sparks than in the trouble. But *Doctor Faustus* is, to say the least, not an expression of scientific optimism. Less room is left for chance, nemesis closes in further, with every successive work. Leander, predestined to be a victim, ironically pleads for the inevitable:

> It lies not in our power to loue, or hate,
> For will in vs is ouer-rul'd by fate.   (I, 167–8)

The Play-King in *Hamlet* puts it less peremptorily:

> Our Willes and Fates do so contrary run,
> That our Deuices still are ouerthrowne.   (III, ii, 221–2)

Heretofore virtue and fortune have been Marlowe's names for character and plot in the universal drama. If fortune was providence, virtue was acceptance; if fortune was luck, virtue was drive; in any event, the dramatic confrontation is between circumstance and the individual, the personality and the situation he confronts. Now, it would seem, an inexorable fatality looms behind a capricious fortune, limiting the range of man's potentialities, and humbling his virtue by weakening his free will. "Our erected wit maketh vs know what perfection is," wrote Sidney, "and yet our infected will keepeth vs from reaching vnto it." Will, overreaching itself, encounters the limitation superimposed by fate. But wit, the intellect, climbing toward the infinite, is not so readily circumscribed. It is forever striving to refute the geographers, to prove cosmography, to resolve ambiguities. If it cannot probe unsearchable mysteries, it can push to the outside limits of the known; and there it can speculate, as Hamlet did, on "thoughts beyond the reaches of our Soules" (I, iv, 56). Every man is limited by conditions, as if — like Faustus — he had signed a contract; but his recognition of those realities which frame his life is, in its way, a victory over them; and the incongruity between them and his ideals of perfection is the wisdom of Mephostophilis, irony. Mephostophilis, in the last analysis, transcends Marlowe's heroes because he transcends the ego; he likewise retains his detachment from the inscrutable forces he is condemned to serve. As agent he bears his burden of complicity, as ironic commentator he frees himself. We cannot act without incurring guilt, we cannot think without transcending ourselves. The vista that Mephostophilis opens to us is a grasp of all that is not within the self, the encroachments and complications and contingencies that men oversimplify when they imprecate the bitch-goddess, Fortuna. Often she seems more intelligent than they. "Seemeth she not to be a right artist?" inquired Montaigne. But, as he keenly realized, it is their intelligence that discerns a pattern in her fortuitous ironies. It is their art that limns those circumstantial artistries which, as Hardy insists, repeat themselves timelessly. Tragedy is a ritual which initiates men into reality, and irony is the perspective of tragedy.

While science, capitalism, imperialism were at the beginning of their modern development, Marlovian tragedy was able to project the inordinate courses they would pursue, through Marlowe's insight into the wayward individualist and into the life that is lived — as he would put it — "without control." Living in a day when controls were external and ubiquitous and high-handed, he boldly asserted the values of freedom. Subsequently, this became much easier; and, with facility, came devaluation. Faustianism has become the veritable ideology of liberal man, the principal myth of western civilization, as Oswald Spengler pointed out in predicting the decline of the historical epoch that arose with the Renaissance. Faust, in the twentieth century, is not the man he was in the nineteenth: he is the decadent esthete of Thomas Mann or the intellectual snob of Paul Valéry. While the art of the drama has been mechanized and amplified, the scope and audience of the serious artist have diminished. If he has a hero, it is not the dynamic Faust but Flaubert's Saint Anthony, the resigned protagonist who secludes himself, yet is haunted by the desires he has resisted. If he takes a watchword from Goethe, uncharacteristically, it is renunciation. If he favors a figure of speech, it is understatement, *meiosis* rather than *hyperbole*. If he is a poet he takes his leave of hyperbole, with Mallarmé's *Prose pour des Esseintes*. It is only through mystical correspondences that he can link the symbolic world of poetry with the actual world of experience — the two worlds that Marlowe brought so much closer together. In the Middle Ages the distinction between them had been carefully upheld: literature coexisted with life on parallel planes that never quite touched. The movement toward naturalism, broadly speaking, was that gradual abandonment of the metaphysical plane for the literal which F. M. Cornford has called "infiguration," calling attention to Marlowe as one of its innovators. If this is so, Marlowe enjoyed his strategic position because his background was still sustained by the mythical and the universal, even while he was engaged in bringing the factual and the personal into the foreground.

We look back toward him from an austere vantage-point, from which the naturalistic impulse seems almost to have run its expansive course. Our writers, perhaps with good reason, do not glory in our world. Yet one of them, James Joyce, has suggested a happy ending to the tale of Icarus. The son, by trying his wings, learns to fly; growing up, he becomes the father, Dædalus; and mankind is richer by virtue of his craftsmanship. Knowledge may be power, and power may corrupt, yet beauty preserves — we are so much older than Marlowe, and so little wiser. T. S. Eliot authorizes us to believe that Marlowe had the most thoughtful and philosophical mind among the Elizabethan dramatists, albeit — Mr. Eliot adds — "immature." We know what Mr. Eliot means by maturity, since he has referred to Congreve in elsewhere defining it; and though it is not as common as it should be, it is not so rare as the gift of early ripeness we cherish in Marlowe. Young enough to retain the fresh perceptions of youth, old enough to have lived through its self-deceptions, he had in him — as Drayton perceived — "those braue translunary things / That the first poets had." With him we not only taste the alluring fruit; we walk in the sunlit innocence of the garden; and, plunging back farther into primordial darkness, we seem to witness the blinding flash of creation. It is Lucretius who gives us our best summation, when he eulogizes his master Epicurus:

> His vigorous and active Mind was hurl'd
> Beyond the flaming limits of *this* World
> Into the mighty Space, and there did see
> How things begin, what can, what cannot be;
> How all must die, all yield to fatal force,
> What steddy limits bound their natural course;
> He saw all this and brought it back to us.

This is quoted from the seventeenth-century translation of Thomas Creech, but some of the Latin phrases seem nearer to the letter and to the spirit of Marlowe's English — the *vivida vis animi* of his heroes, the *flammantia mœnia mundi* against which they hurl themselves, and the *finita potestas* that overwhelms them. Conversely, in Marlowe's phraseology, Lucretius was indeed a forward wit, divinely discontent, fruitful in aspiring, running to regions far. If Marlowe learned the lyric mode from Ovid and the epic mode from Lucan, it may well have been Lucretius who schooled him in tragic discernment of the nature of things. For Lucretius, too, life was grand and grave and harsh, and death was premature. Neither poet took the middle way; poetry takes the way of fine excess. Excess tempts youth to stray from the *via media*, the *mediocritas*, the mean between extremes that Bacon recommends. But in his parables, *De Sapientia Veterum* (XXVII), the prosaic Bacon concedes that age goes astray through defect; and whereas defect crawls upon the earth like a serpent, excess makes itself at home in the skies like a bird. The course of Icarus, defying the laws of gravity and common sense, was obviously uncertain and unsafe; yet even Bacon was compelled to admire it, because its youthful swiftness kindled a certain magnanimity.

APPENDICES

A. Emblem

(See title page)

The woodcut of Icarus is reproduced from page 28 of *A Choice of Emblems* by Geoffrey Whitney (London, 1586). The page is headed *In Astrologos,* and the emblem is applied to those who scrutinize the heavens too curiously. Both the heading and the design itself, like so many of Whitney's emblems, are taken from continental editions of Alciat. In place of Alciat's briefer Latin verses, Whitney points the moral in these two stanzas:

Heare, ICARVS with mountinge vp alofte,
Came headlonge downe, and fell into the Sea:
His waxed winges, the sonne did make so softe,
They melted straighte, and feathers fell awaie:
    So, whilste he flewe, and of no dowbte did care,
    He moou'de his armes, but loe, the same were bare.

Let suche beware, which paste theire reache doe mounte,
Whoe seeke the thinges, to mortall men deny'de,
And searche the Heauens, and all the starres accoumpte,
And tell therebie, what after shall betyde:
    With blusshinge nowe, theire weakenesse rightlie weye,
    Least as they clime, they fall to theire decaye.

Naïve as this may be, it reveals the extent to which Marlowe drew upon common language, as well as common lore, for his archetypal image of the tragic overreacher. Whitney also cites a line from Martial, which parallels Bacon's cautious interpretation of the legend, as well as two distichs from Ovid which bracket Icarus with Phaëthon. The same associations, as they affected Shakespeare, are discussed by E. A. Armstrong in *Shakespeare's Imagination* (London, 1946), pp. 36–7.

B. Blank Verse

(See pp. 10–15 above)

The prosodic developments sketched in Chapter I can be more fully illustrated here. Certain passages in *The Tragedy of Dido* are not merely dramatic paraphrases; they are direct translations from Vergil's *Æneid*. It is therefore possible, by comparing them with the corresponding lines from Surrey's translation, to specify what is peculiarly Marlovian in the formation of blank verse. A link between Surrey and Marlowe, from the year 1561, is supplied by the Vergilian echo from *Gorboduc*. A later echo from *The Tragedy of Selimus*, an anonymous imitation of *Tamburlaine*, shows how the Marlovian style has taken possession of the Vergilian image.

Vergil, Æneid, IV, 265–76

Continuo invadit: "tu nunc Karthaginis altae
fundamenta locas pulchramque uxorius urbem
exstruis? heu! regni rerumque oblite tuarum!
ipse deum tibi me claro demittit Olympo
regnator, cælum et terras qui numine torquet;
ipse hæc ferre iubet celeris mandata per auras.
quid struis? aut qua spe Libycis teris otia terris?
si te nulla movet tantarum gloria rerum
nec super ipse tua moliris laude laborem,
Ascanium surgentem et spes heredis Iuli
respice, cui regnum Italiæ Romanaque tellus
debentur."

The Earl of Surrey's Translation, IV, 341–56

Thus he encounters him: "Oh careles wight,
Both of thy realme, and of thine own affaires;
A wifebound man now dost thou reare the walles
Of high Cartage, to build a goodly town?
From the bright skies the ruler of the gods
Sent me to thee, that with his beck commaundes
Both heuen and earth; in hast he gaue me charge,
Through the light aire this message thee to say:
What framest thou? or on what hope thy time
In idlenes dost wast in Affrick land?
Of so great things if nought the fame thee stirr,
Ne list by trauaile honour to pursue,
Ascanius yet, that waxeth fast, behold,
And the hope of Iulus seede, thine heir,
To whom the realme of Italy belonges,
And soile of Rome."

The Tragedy of Dido, lines 1435–47

Why cosin, stand you building Cities here,
And beautifying the Empire of this Queene,
While *Italy* is cleane out of thy minde?
To, too forgetfull of thine owne affayres,
Why wilt thou so betray thy sonnes good hap?
The king of Gods sent me from highest heauen,
To sound this angrie message in thine eares.
Vaine man, what Monarky expectst thou here?
Or with what thought sleepst thou in *Libia* shoare?
If that all glorie hath forsaken thee,
And thou despise the praise of such attempts:
Yet thinke vpon *Ascanius* prophesie,
And yong *Iulus* more then thousand yeares. . .

Vergil, *Æneid*, IV, 365–384

"Nec tibi diva parens, generis nec Dardanus auctor,
perfide, sed duris genuit te cautibus horrens
Caucasus, Hyrcanæque admorunt ubera tigres. . .
nusquam tuta fides. eiectum litore, egentem
excepi et regni demens in parte locavi;
amissam classem, socios a morte reduxi. . .
i, sequere Italiam ventis, pete regna per undas.
spero equidem mediis, si quid pia numina possunt,
supplicia hausurum scopulis et nomine Dido
sæpe vocaturum. . . ."

The Earl of Surrey's Translation, IV, 477–504

"Faithlesse! forsworn! ne goddesse was thy dam,
Nor Dardanus beginner of thy race,
But of hard rockes mount Caucase monstruous
Bred thee, and teates of tyger gaue thee suck. . .
Did I not him, thrown vp vpon my shore,
In neede receiue, and fonded eke inuest
Of halfe my realme, his nauie lost, repair;
From death's daunger his fellowes eke defend? . . .
To Italie passe on by helpe of windes,
And through the floods go searche thy kingdom new.
If ruthfull gods haue any power, I trust
Amid the rocks thy guerdon thou shalt finde,
When thou shalt clepe full oft on Didos name. . . ."

Gorboduc, IV, i, 71–76

Ruthelesse, vnkinde, monster of natures worke,
Thou neuer suckt the milke of womans brest,
But from thy birth the cruell Tigers teates
Haue nursed thee, nor yet of fleshe and bloud
Formde is thy hart, but of hard iron wrought,
And wilde and desert woods bredde thee to life.

The Tragedy of Dido, lines 1564–81

Thy mother was no Goddesse periurd man,
Nor *Dardanus* the author of thy stocke:
But thou art sprung from *Scythian Caucasus*,
And Tygers of *Hircania* gaue thee sucke . . .
Wast thou not wrackt vpon this *Libian* shoare,
And cam'st to *Dido* like a Fisher swaine?
Repairde not I thy ships, made thee a King,
And all thy needie followers Noblemen? . . .
Goe, goe and spare not, seeke out *Italy*,
I hope that that which loue forbids me doe,

The Rockes and Sea-gulfes will performe at large,
And thou shalt perish in the billowes waies,
To whom poore *Dido* doth bequeath reuenge.

The Tragedy of Selimus, lines 1234–8

Thou art not false groome son to *Baiazet*,
He would relent to heare a woman weepe,
But thou wast borne in desart *Caucasus*,
And the Hircanian tygres gaue thee sucke,
Knowing thou wert a monster like themselues.

C. The Verse-Sentence

(See pp. 13, 38, 40, 125–30 above)

These calligrammatic rearrangements may serve to clarify the interrelationship between the metrical and the grammatical structure of Marlowe's lines. Continuity is indicated on the horizontal plane, while the vertical is used for parallel constructions and further complications. The only blank verse that would appear as we normally print it, according to this method of rearrangement, would be a passage in which each line was a single and simple sentence. Thus we can see at a glance how the rhetorical period is extended, and how it doubles back upon itself. Verse-sentences are more frequent in *Tamburlaine*, where units of speech are longer and more formal, than in the increasingly succinct and variegated patterns of Marlowe's other plays; but even in *Doctor Faustus*, as the examples indicate, Marlowe's augmented repertory of expressive devices does not exclude deliberate formality.

Our soules,
   whose faculties can comprehend
        The wondrous Architecture of the world:
          And measure euery wandring plannets course,
Still climing after knowledge infinite,
And alwaies moouing
        as the restles Spheares,
Wils vs to weare our selues
     and neuer rest,
       Vntill we reach the ripest fruit of all,
          That perfect blisse
          and sole felicitie,
          The sweet fruition of an earthly crowne. (*Tamburlaine*, 872–80)

If all the pens
    that euer poets held,
       Had fed the feeling of their maisters thoughts,
And euery sweetnes
    that inspir'd their harts,
       Their minds,
       and muses on admyred theames:
If all the heauenly Quintessence
    they still
       From their immortall flowers of Poesy,
         Wherein
         As in a myrrour
         we perceiue

If these had made one Poems period
And all combin'd in Beauties worthinesse,
       Yet should ther houer in their restlesse heads,
          The highest reaches of a humaine wit.

One thought,
one grace,
    one woonder at the least,
        Which into words no vertue can digest.

(*Tamburlaine*, 1942–54)

I wil be *Paris*,
    and for loue of thee,
        Insteede of *Troy* shal *Wertenberge* be sackt,

And I wil combate with weake *Menelaus*,
    And weare thy colours on my plumed Crest:

Yea I wil wound *Achillis* in the heele,
    And then returne to *Helen* for a kisse.

O thou art fairer then the euening aire,
    Clad in the beauty of a thousand starres,

Brighter art thou then flaming *Iupiter*,
    When he appeard to haplesse *Semele*,

More louely then the monarke of the skie
    In wanton *Arethusaes* azurde armes,

And none but thou shalt be my paramour.

(*Doctor Faustus*, 1335–47)

You starres
    that raignd at my natiuitie,
    Whose influence hath alotted death
        and hel,

Now draw vp Faustus
    like a foggy mist,
        Into the intrailes of yon labring cloude,

That
    when you vomite foorth into the ayre,
        My limbes may issue from your smoaky mouthes,

So that my soule may but ascend to heauen.

(*Doctor Faustus*, 1443–9)

D. Libido

(See pp. 27, 33, 36, 39, 40, 61, 66, 68, 84, 86, 103, 110, 113, 124, 140, 160, 161 above)

Under the heading "Of Epicures and Atheists" in Thomas Beard's *Theatre of Gods Iudgments* (1597), Marlowe is not untypically described as "suffering his lust to haue the full raines." (See Tucker Brooke, *Life*, p. 113.) However, the application to him of the terms *libido sentiendi, libido sciendi,* and *libido dominandi* may require a few words of further explanation and historical cross-reference. The triple conception, which is so deeply rooted in early Christian asceticism, goes back to the first epistle of Saint John (ii, 16), with its absolute distinction between love of the world and love of the Father, and more especially its warnings against lust of the flesh (or *voluptas*), lust of the eyes (or *curiositas*), and pride of life (or *vana gloria*). This was a crucial formulation for Saint Augustine, himself a great formulator of the tensions between paganism and Christianity; under these three categories he scrutinizes his own spiritual condition in the tenth book of his *Confessions*; and, since his Pelagian opponents sought to justify the natural impulses, he was bound to express strong views on *concupiscentia* in his treatise *De vera religione*. The ascetic attitude is implicit, at all events, in medieval doctrine; and, perhaps for that reason, the anti-libidinous triplex does not seem to have been very explicitly formulated during the Middle Ages. To some extent it was hypostatized into the idea of the Seven Deadly Sins: the handmaids of Fortune are Concupiscencia-carnis and Couetyse-of-eyes in the B-text of *Piers Plowman* (XI). Of course the Renaissance, in its secular, classical, and experimental aspects, cultivated those very sources of feeling which had been traditionally outlawed. Any naturalistic world-view tends to rehabilitate them, and the modern tendency has been to recognize them frankly as constants of human motivation. But secularism and worldliness, in their turn, have provoked ascetic and puritanical reactions — such as that which, within the French Catholic church of the seventeenth century, took the form of Jansenism. During western Europe's most fruitful epoch of material and intellectual achievement, some of its most thoughtful minds were attracted to a movement founded upon the consciousness of man's depravity and grounded upon a revival of Saint Augustine's teachings. In his commentary on these teachings, the *Augustinus* (Paris, 1641), it was Cornelius Jansenius who enunciated the phrases *libido sentiendi* and *libido sciendi* (II, 136–8). To such desires, which lead toward sins of the flesh and the eyes,

Jansen would add a third — the worst of all — which corresponds to Augustine's *ambitio sæculi*:

Sed est & tertia libido maximè omnium imperiosa atque perniciosa, duabusque præcedentibus libidinibus quò spiritualior, mentique propinquior & intimior, eò tenaciùs adhæret, tanquam quæ non suburbia mentis, sed ipsam arcem occupauit. Hæc est illa spiritibus damnatis propria cupiditas quâ timeri et amari ab hominibus, in se, donisque Dei gloriari, dominari aliis, & sibi placere lubet: quæ vno verbo *libido excellendi* appellari potest. Hæc oppugnatu et expugnatu difficillima est, & vltima; quia uisceribus animi profundiùs impressa illo diabolico telo: *Eritis sicut Dii*.

Having started from the threefold admonition of Saint John, the passage concludes by quoting the guileful argument of the serpent in Genesis (iii, 5), the most dangerous of temptations to overweening intellectual pride. *Vous serez comme des dieux* — this is likewise the epigraph to the French version by Arnauld d'Andilly of Jansen's *Discours de la réformation de l'homme intérieur* (Paris, 1659), which goes on to warn against the fruit of the tree, and particularly against those three passions which are the source of all the vices: "*la volupté de la chair, la curiosité de sçavoir, et l'orgueil*" (p. 25). Jansen's most brilliant disciple, Pascal, put it somewhat otherwise — "*la chair, l'esprit, la volonté*" — thereby identifying pride and will. As his final description of that last category, he contributed the phrase *libido dominandi* (*Pensées*, ed. Léon Brunschvicg, Paris, 1921, II, 369–73):

"Tout ce qui est au monde est concupiscence de la chair, ou concupiscence des yeux, ou orgeuil de la vie: *libido sentiendi, libido sciendi, libido dominandi*." Malheureuse la terre de malédiction que ces trois fleuves de feu embrasent plutôt qu'ils n'arrosent! Heureux ceux qui, étant sur ces fleuves, non pas plongés, non pas entraînés, mais immobiles. . .

Yet, amid the waters of Babylon, the exiles mourn for the porches of Jerusalem; in the midst of this world, they long for a better one; so Pascal continues a meditation inspired by Augustine's paraphrase of the psalm of exile. And if the Bible-reading physicist, Pascal, believed that too much light was dazzling, more professional theologians could be more suspicious and hostile toward "*le désir d'expérimenter*" — as was Bossuet in his *Traité de la concupiscence* (*Oeuvres*, Versailles, 1816, X, 365). Obscurantism is by no means a thing of the past, though the Jansenist terms are no longer in common use; certain twentieth-century critics of romantic literature, notably Irving Babbitt and Julien Benda, have applied them rather cavalierly to the whole current of modernism in thought and art. Meanwhile, science itself has undertaken to adjudicate the claims of the so-called *libido*; and the principal cleavage between the two leading schools of psychoanalysis occurs precisely in this area. For both Freud and Jung it is the concept of a motivating force; but Vienna and Zürich differ on how specifically it is sexual drive and how generally it is psychic energy. C. G. Jung's *Wandlungen und Symbole der Libido* (Leipzig, 1925) touches on some imaginative consequences of the notion, and is at once less rigid and less rigorous than Freud's incidental discussions.

APPENDICES

E. Virtue and Fortune

(See pp. 25-7, 30-5, 41, 48, 52, 85, 99, 149, 150, 162, 163 above)

A semantic study of these two terms, in relation to the concepts they denote, would soon become a history of ethics in the one case and of metaphysics in the other. We could concentrate upon the antithesis between fortune and virtue, limit our period to the Renaissance and our documentation to Elizabethan drama, indeed to Shakespeare, and fail to exhaust the subject in a monograph again as long as the foregoing volume. However, since Marlovian tragedy moves between those opposite poles, we have had frequent occasion to invoke them; and here, perhaps, the invocation should be supplemented by a scattering of examples which may serve to place Marlowe's usage in a wider perspective. The question, "Which contributed more to the Romans in the conquest of their Empire, either their vertue, or their fortune," was by no means a new one when Machiavelli raised it in his *Discourses upon the First Decade of Titus Livius* (trans. Edward Dacres, London, 1636, p. 252). Plutarch had raised it in the form of a debate between the personified goddesses; unfortunately for Virtue, the fragment breaks off before she has stated her argument; but, elsewhere among the *Moralia*, Plutarch makes it clear that he is on her side; and, when he applies the same question to the conquests of Alexander the Great, he awards her the palm. Plutarch interprets Roman history in the light of Greek philosophy, and behind his eclecticism lie centuries of speculation and controversy over the roles of τύχη and ἀρετή — words which also play their respective parts in Greek tragedy. Taking issue with the Epicureans for their emphasis on chance, "shewing that it taketh away all distinction of good and euill," Plutarch takes a position quite compatible with Christian morality, as his translator, Philemon Holland, emphasizes: "He prooueth that prudence and wisdom ouer-ruleth this blind Fortune" (*Morals*, London, 1603, p. 229). Plutarch's *Lives* offer many occasions for extolling Roman virtue in its public or military aspect, and for using the Latin word *virtus*, which Sir Thomas North translates by "valiantness." One suspects Plutarch — and, for that matter, the Roman historians — of over-protestation, inasmuch as the Romans built a temple to Fortuna, and her cult was obviously more popular than the more austere cultivation of a more abstract virtue. The fatalism of military culture was similarly reflected in the Anglo-Saxon reliance on Wyrd. The vicissitudes of one conception during the Middle Ages have been comprehensively studied by H. R. Patch in *The Goddess Fortuna in Mediaeval Litera-*

ture (Cambridge: Harvard University Press, 1927). The emergence of the term *virtù*, with its moral and scientific implications for the Renaissance, is suggestively discussed by Leonardo Olschki in *Machiavelli the Scientist* (Berkeley, 1945). Machiavelli's famous alternative, posed in the opening chapter of the second book of his *Discorsi*, leads him into an even more controversial question: whether Christianity, because of its otherworldly orientation, is less conducive to heroic action than paganism. *Il Principe* begins and ends by balancing the claims and counterclaims of *fortuna* and *virtù*; the seventh chapter insists that the Prince's virtue should equal his fortune, while the twenty-fifth judiciously considers *Quanto possa la Fortuna nelle cose umane, et in che modo se li abbia a resistere.* As a poet, in his *Capitolo della Fortuna*, Machiavelli shows an almost superstitious respect for the omnipotence of the goddess in human affairs. That poets disagree about her, that Homer ignores her while Vergil stands in awe of her, was pointed out by Petrarch, who concluded the second dialogue of his *Secretum* by promising to write on this matter himself — a promise he presumably fulfilled in *De remediis utriusque fortunæ.* Boccaccio was paying his respects to her in writing his tragic narratives, *De casibus virorum et feminarum illustrium.* So long as tragedy stresses the falls of princes, Dame Fortune remains its presiding spirit, as in Sackville's Induction to the *Mirror for Magistrates*:

> Loe here (quoth Sorowe) Prynces of renowne,
> That whilom sat on top of Fortunes wheele
> Nowe layed ful lowe, like wretches whurled downe,
> Euen with one frowne, that stayed but with a smyle.   (526–9)

The traditional attitude assumes, not only that fortune is more powerful than all other worldly powers, but that she is particularly hostile to virtue. It is she, as Ronsard describes her in his *Discours contre Fortune,*

> *A qui le vice agrée et la vertu desplaist.*

And it is she who usually gets the upper hand, as Spenser concedes in *The Faerie Queene*:

> Fortune, the foe of famous cheuisaunce
> Seldome (said *Guyon*) yields to vertue aide,
> But in her waye throwes mischiefe and mischaunce,
> Whereby her course is stopt, and passage staid.   (II, ix, 8)

One of the commonest emblems, reproduced by Whitney (*Choice of Emblems*, p. 70), depicts *Fortuna Virtutem Superans*. But the struggle would not always be one-sided. Paracelsus, that Faustian intellect, in his *Liber de bona et mala fortuna*, scoffs at the notion of fortune's wheel as a lazy man's excuse for not improving his luck by his own endeavors. Benvenuto Cellini recalls that his father, having contrived a revolving mirror for the Medici, engraved upon it:

Rota sum: semper, quoquo me verto, stat Virtus.

An opportune compromise is Bacon's suggestion "that the wheeles of [a man's] Minde, keepe way, with the wheeles of his *Fortune.*" In his essay "Of Fortune," Bacon inclines toward a Machiavellian view: "But chiefly, the Mould of a Mans *Fortune*, is in his own hands." This, in his final revision of 1625, he supports with a quotation — as it happens — from Sallust: *"Faber quisque Fortunæ suæ."* Such sentiments were encouragements to a rising middle class, whose virtues — for well over a century, and with increasing advantage — had been compared to those of the aristocracy. Toward the end of the fifteenth century, the dialectic between virtue and nobility became the characteristic theme of the first English secular play, Henry Medwall's interlude of *Fulgens and Lucres*, where the virtuous plebeian wins out over the fortunate patrician. Yet the allegorical commonplaces survive into Elizabethan drama, as a passing glance at the repertory reveals: for example, *The Rare Triumphs of Love and Fortune.* The machinery of Kyd's *Soliman and Perseda* is controlled by personifications of Love, Fortune, and Death, with the triumph of the last easily predictable. Dekker's *Old Fortunatus* is our dramatic *locus classicus*; for it is framed within a series of dumb shows, presided over by Fortune and Virtue in turn; and, though Fortune smiles at the outset, it is Virtue who smiles at the ending. Greene, who so stridently echoed Marlowe's challenges to Fortune, actually named his son "Fortunatus." The decline of Greene's fortunes, accentuating his *hubris*, gave Gabriel Harvey the opportunity to speak of "Infortunatus Greene." Fortune in person, possibly symbolized by a wooden effigy, lent its name to London's largest playhouse, built by Philip Henslowe in 1600. The Cambridge scholars who fared so ill in London, and above all in the theater, express their disgust in the second part of *The Return from Parnassus*:

> So merry fortune's wont from ragges to take
> Some ragged grome, and him a gallant make.　　(1931-2)

APPENDICES　　　　　　　　　　　　　　　　　　181

This was a gibe at Edward Alleyn, grown prosperous through creating Marlovian title-roles and appearing as leading man of the Henslowe company. When the gentlemen-scholars go on to lament,

The world and fortune's playd on vs too long.

they may also be glancing at Shakespeare's playhouse, the Globe. Shakespeare characteristically seems to prefer the antithesis of Fortune and Nature, which he develops in *King John* (III, i, 52–61), and to move away from the sphere of fortune toward that of nature, as Rosalind accuses Celia of doing in *As You Like It* (I, ii, 42). Sir Thomas More, in his meters for the so-called *Book of Fortune*, which seems to have been a kind of fortune-telling game, had already played upon that polarity. Fortune, in Shakespearean context, seems artificial and somewhat old-fashioned, as described by the poet in *Timon of Athens* or by Fluellen — responding to Ancient Pistol — in *Henry V*: "Fortune is an excellent Morall" (III, vi, 40). Yet it is destined to figure importantly in the Roman plays; it figures not merely in Hamlet's ribald banter with Rosencrantz and Guildenstern, but in the Player's curse that voices Hamlet's feelings so movingly; while, in *King Lear*, the imagery of Fortune's wheel reinforces Shakespeare's most searching inquiry into the ways of blind necessity — or is it providential design? The wheel's full circle might be said to outline the pattern of Chapman's tragedies, which revolve from the opening words of *Bussy d'Ambois* — the recognition that the world is ruled by "Fortune not Reason" — toward the Stoic comments on Queen Elizabeth's court in *The Conspiracy of Byron*:

> . . . you haue layde
> A brave foundation, by the hande of virtue:
> Put not the roofe to fortune.   (IV, i, 177–9)

Fortune again was predominant in Jonson's *Sejanus*; the catastrophe is based on a satire of Juvenal which is almost medieval in its stress upon mutability; the peripety, when the statue of the goddess so emphatically refuses to be propitiated, is almost Marlovian. It crashes down; but virtue is in the ascendant; and Jonson's poetic justice exalts the latter at the expense of the former. The mistake of his Machiavellian characters has been to equate the two. This is precisely the equation demonstrated by the later, ampler, and more cynical human comedy of Balzac, whose Vautrin has the habit of declaring: "*La fortune c'est la vertu.*" By this time, the attempts of science to determine causation have all but dissipated the old awe of fortune, and the paradox scarcely outlasted the Marquis de Sade's subtitle for his *Justine: Les Infortunes de la vertu*. Meanwhile, *virtù* had become synonymous with *bric-à-brac*, and *virtuoso* with *dilettante*. Yet, as a framework for understanding character and plot in the tragedies of the Renaissance, virtue and fortune continue to be more relevant than many of the neo-Aristotelian or pseudo-Hegelian terms that have supplanted them. Their relevance to Spanish and Italian drama is respectively suggested by A. F. G. Bell, "Notes on the Spanish Renaissance," *Revue hispanique*, LXXX (1930), no. 178, especially pp. 618–24, and A. H. Gilbert, "Fortune in the Tragedies of Giraldi Cinthio," *Renaissance Studies in Honor of Hardin Craig* (Palo Alto, 1941), pp. 32–43. Hardin Craig has historically sketched the ethos of Elizabethan tragedy in "The Shackling of Accidents," *Philological Quarterly*, XIX (1940), no. 1, pp. 1–19, and S. C. Chew has related literature and iconology in "Time and Fortune," *English Literary History*, VI (1939), no. 2, notably — for our purposes — p. 101.

F. Colors

(See pp. 49, 129, 130, 158 above)

BLACK — *Dido* 1064, 1533; *Tamburlaine* 1431, 1563, 1999, 2048, 2096, 2388, 2596, 2714, 2969, 3201, 3971, 4002, 4210, 4441; *Edward II* 544, 753; *The Massacre at Paris* 1114; *Doctor Faustus* 991, 1007; *Hero and Leander* I, 50. COAL-BLACK — *Tamburlaine* 943, 1790, 1853, 2711.

WHITE — *Dido* 621, 1382; *Tamburlaine* 285, 1249, 1422, 1423, 1555, 2096, 2594, 4101; *The Jew of Malta* 815; *Edward II* 544; *The Massacre at Paris* 236, 237; *Doctor Faustus* 158; *Hero and Leander* I, 30, 65, 66; II, 242. MILK-WHITE — *Dido* 202, 615; *Tamburlaine* 85, 294, 1259, 1849, 2757, 4111; *Hero and Leander* I, 298.

RED — *Tamburlaine* 1427, 1497, 1498, 2096, 4525; *Hero and Leander* II, 89. CRIMSON — *Tamburlaine* 2537, 3298. SCARLET — *Tamburlaine* 1427, 1899, 2306, 2359, 3466. VERMILLION — *Tamburlaine* 1561, 4198; *Hero and Leander* I, 395. PURPLE — *Dido* 206, 614, 1041; *Tamburlaine* 1448, 2242, 2649, 4365; *Hero and Leander* I, 10; II, 88, 106.

BLUE — *Hero and Leander* I, 15. BLUISH — *Dido* 497. AZURE — *Hero and Leander* II, 165, 274. AZURED — *Dido* 101; *Doctor Faustus* 1346.

GREEN — *Dido* 612; *Tamburlaine* 4100; *The Jew of Malta* 1811; *The Massacre at Paris* 726; *Hero and Leander* I, 11.

YELLOW — *Dido* 1377; *Hero and Leander* I, 347.

BROWN — *Dido* 1376; *Edward II* 1343.

GRAY — *Dido* 102; *The Jew of Malta* 1833.

This gathering of line-references is less significant in itself than it is in relation to the whole of the spectrum, and to the shades that are either weakly represented or totally ignored in Marlowe's work. The translations, for obvious reasons, have not been canvassed. Not only is the contrast with Shakespeare striking, but it may well offer a criterion for absolving Marlowe from collaboration in the disputed chronicles or the apocryphal tragedies, where the representation of colors is much more normal. Within the Marlovian canon there also seem to be striking disparities between *Dido*, *Hero and Leander*, and especially *Tamburlaine*, on the one hand, and on the other the virtual color-blindness of *The Jew of Malta*, *Edward II*, *The Massacre at Paris*, and *Doctor Faustus* — although the latter may be

APPENDICES

somewhat slighted by this reckoning, which is based on the shorter text. The lack is compensated, to some extent, by an emphasis on colorful substances, as well as on terms conveying bedazzlement or obscurity. Here the figures merely denote the incidence:

AMBER — *Tamburlaine* (1).

IVORY — *Dido* (1); *Tamburlaine* (6); *Hero and Leander* (2).

CRYSTAL — *Dido* (3); *Tamburlaine* (8); *Hero and Leander* (1).

GOLD — *Dido* (4); *Tamburlaine* (28); *The Jew of Malta* (33); *Edward II* (8); *The Massacre at Paris* (5); *Doctor Faustus* (5); *Hero and Leander* (5). GOLDEN — *Dido* (14); *Tamburlaine* (13); *The Jew of Malta* (4); *Edward II* (3); *The Massacre at Paris* (1); *Doctor Faustus* (3); *Hero and Leander* (9).

BLOOD — *Dido* (9); *Tamburlaine* (51); *The Jew of Malta* (6); *Edward II* (22); *The Massacre at Paris* (9); *Doctor Faustus* (15); *Hero and Leander* (4). BLOODY — *Dido* (1); *Tamburlaine* (17); *Edward II* (5); *The Massacre at Paris* (8).

FIRE (with compounds) — *Dido* (15); *Tamburlaine* (34); *The Jew of Malta* (12); *Edward II* (5); *The Massacre at Paris* (5); *Doctor Faustus* (2); *Hero and Leander* (9). FIERY — *Tamburlaine* (17); *The Jew of Malta* (4); *Doctor Faustus* (2); *Hero and Leander* (1).

FLAME (with cognates) — *Dido* (4); *Tamburlaine* (12); *The Massacre at Paris* (1); *Doctor Faustus* (1); *Hero and Leander* (1).

BRIGHT (with cognates) — *Dido* (4); *Tamburlaine* (15); *The Jew of Malta* (2); *Edward II* (3); *Doctor Faustus* (5); *Hero and Leander* (4).

DARK (with cognates) — *Dido* (4); *Tamburlaine* (8); *The Jew of Malta* (3); *Edward II* (2); *Hero and Leander* (5).

G. Title Roles

(*See pp. 42, 62, 82, 84, 86, 87, 127 above*)

	LINES		PERCENTAGE
	PART	PLAY	
Dido	525	1736	30
Tamburlaine (I)	758	2316	33
Tamburlaine (II)	879	2330	38
Barabas	1190	2410	49
Edward	719	2670	27
The Guise	314	1263	25
Dr. Faustus (1604)	698	1485	47
Dr. Faustus (1616)	812	2131	38

These figures become more meaningful when compared with the practice of other playwrights. Here the Shakespearean extreme is *Hamlet*, where the title role — largely because of the seven soliloquies — takes up almost 38 per cent of the lines in the play. If the part of Macbeth is proportionately almost as long, it is because so much of that play has apparently been cut (compare the two versions of *Doctor Faustus*). The norm, for Shakespeare's protagonists, is a part which averages no more than a quarter of the total; at the opposite extreme is *Julius Cæsar*, where the title character is almost a minor role.

H. Speeches

(*See pp. 44, 72, 97, 121, 122 above*)

	TOTAL LINES	CUES	AVERAGE LENGTH IN LINES
Dido	1736	350	5.2
Tamburlaine I	2316	390	5.9
Tamburlaine II	2330	368	6.3
Jew of Malta	2410	854	2.8
Edward II	2670	948	2.8
Massacre at Paris	1263	354	3.6
Doctor Faustus (1604)	1485	428	3.5
Doctor Faustus (1616)	2131	595	3.6

Hamlet, in this respect, comes close to the Shakespearean norm, with an average of about 3.2 lines per single speech.

I. Plots

(*See pp. 25, 26, 30, 33–5, 56–60, 76, 86, 101–3 above*)

The following diagrams indicate, in rough outline, how Marlowe altered the structure of tragedy. The medieval conception, which emphasized royal downfall, is still predominant in *Richard II*. *Tamburlaine* not only shifts the emphasis from the passive acceptance of fortune to the active exercise of virtue, but elevates its unique protagonist to the point where his only victorious rival is death. More typically the ambitious hero, like Macbeth, must suffer the human consequences of his actions; the usurper, in his turn, is cut down by the revenger; and the motive of ambition is counterbalanced by the motive of revenge, which comes to the fore in *The Spanish Tragedy*. As the plots cross and turn and repeat each other, it becomes harder to distinguish these motives; heroes rise at the expense of their predecessors and fall to the advantage of their successors, as in the cycle of plays that revolves around the friends and enemies of Julius Cæsar. The ups and downs of *The Jew of Malta* are episodes in the battle of wits between Barabas and the Governor. *Edward II*, for all its complications, finally reverts to the traditional pattern.

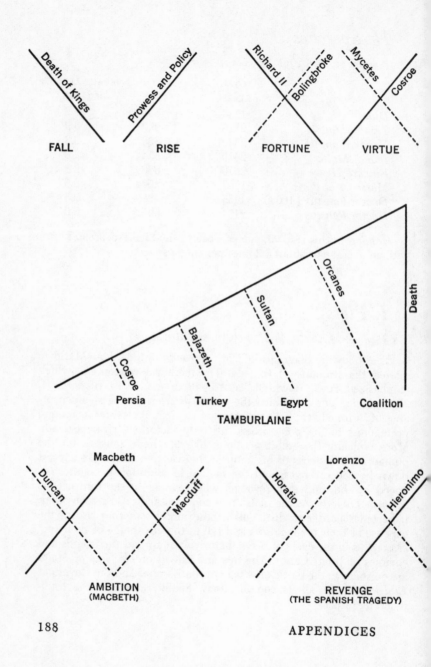

FALL   RISE   FORTUNE   VIRTUE

Death of kings / Prowess and Policy / Richard II / Bolingbroke / Mycetes / Cosroe

TAMBURLAINE

Cosroe / Bajazeth / Sultan / Orcanes / Death

Persia   Turkey   Egypt   Coalition

Duncan / Macbeth / Macduff

AMBITION
(MACBETH)

Horatio / Lorenzo / Hieronimo

REVENGE
(THE SPANISH TRAGEDY)

APPENDICES

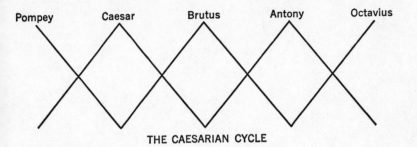

THE CAESARIAN CYCLE

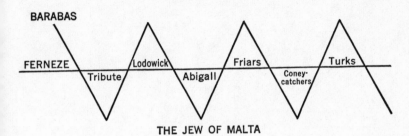

THE JEW OF MALTA

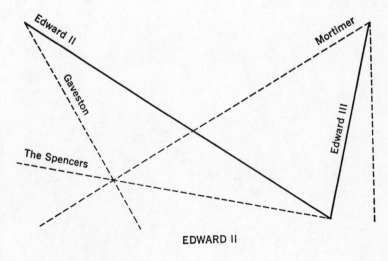

EDWARD II

APPENDICES

Authorities

I. THE END OF SCHOLARISM

Francis Bacon, "Of Atheism," in *A Harmony of the Essays,* ed. Edward Arber (London, 1871), p. 337.

Howard Baker, *Induction to Tragedy* (University, Louisiana, 1939), especially chapter II, "The Formation of the Heroic Medium."

C. F. Tucker Brooke, *The Life of Marlowe and The Tragedy of Dido* (London, 1930), biographical documentation cited here from appendices, pp. 83–114.

C. F. Tucker Brooke, "Marlowe's Versification and Style," *Studies in Philology,* XIX (1922), no. 2, pp. 186–205.

W. H. Clemen, *Shakespeares Bilder* (Bonn, 1936), p. 334.

T. S. Eliot, "Christopher Marlowe," in *Selected Essays* (New York, 1932), p. 104.

Willard Farnham, *The Mediaeval Heritage of Elizabethan Tragedy* (Berkeley, 1936), especially chapter X, "The Establishment of Tragedy upon the Elizabethan Stage."

R. S. Forsythe, *"The Passionate Shepherd* and English Poetry," *Publications of the Modern Language Association of America,* XL (1925), no. 3, pp. 692–742.

Abraham Fraunce, *The Arcadian Rhetorike,* ed. Ethel Seaton (Oxford, 1950), p. 18.

Gabriel Harvey, *Letter-Book,* ed. E. J. L. Scott (London, 1884), pp. 110–1.

Gabriel Harvey, *Marginalia,* ed. G. H. Moore Smith (Stratford, 1913), pp. 147, 200.

Philemon Holland (trans.), *The Morals of Plutarch* (London, 1603), p. 538.

Leigh Hunt (ed.), *Imagination and Fancy* (London, 1845), p. 97.

P. H. Kocher, *Christopher Marlowe: A Study of His Thought, Learning, and Character* (Chapel Hill, 1946), especially pp. 33–68, on the alleged atheism.

Thomas Nashe, *Works,* ed. R. B. McKerrow (London, 1904–08), on *Dido,* IV, 294; preface to *Menaphon,* III, 311, 312, 316.

George Puttenham, *The Arte of English Poesie,* ed. G. D. Willcock and Alice Walker (Cambridge, England, 1936), pp. 154, 191.

Ezra Pound, *Pavannes and Divisions* (New York, 1918), p. 196.

H. E. Rollins (ed.), *England's Helicon* (Cambridge: Harvard University Press, 1935), II, 186–9, textual commentary on "The Passionate Shepherd."

Caroline Spurgeon, *Shakespeare's Imagery* (New York, 1936), p. 13.

Richard Vogt, *Das Adjektiv bei Christopher Marlowe* (Berlin, 1908), pp. 16–18.

Francis Bacon, "Of Masques and Triumphs," in *A Harmony of the Essays*, p. 540.

R. W. Battenhouse, *Marlowe's Tamburlaine: A Study in Renaissance Moral Philosophy* (Nashville, 1941).

A. H. Bullen (ed.), *The Works of Christopher Marlowe* (London, 1885), III, xix.

F. I. Carpenter, *Metaphor and Simile in the Minor Elizabethan Drama* (Chicago, 1895), pp. 38, 48.

W. J. Courthope, *A History of English Poetry* (London, 1904), II, 405.

Havelock Ellis (ed.), *The Mermaid Series: Christopher Marlowe* (London, 1887), p. xxxv.

U. M. Ellis-Fermor, *Christopher Marlowe* (London, 1927), p. 50, observations on color.

U. M. Ellis-Fermor (ed.), *Tamburlaine the Great* (London, 1930), especially the introduction.

P. H. Kocher, *Christopher Marlowe*, pp. 70–8, 188, on political and social views.

W. J. Lawrence, *The Elizabethan Playhouse: Second Series* (Stratford, 1913), p. 20.

Jules Lemaître, *Impressions du théâtre* (Paris, 1891), V, 83.

Louis Le Roy, *The Variety of Things*, trans. R. A. (London, 1594), pp. 108^v, 119^v.

Michel de Montaigne, *Essays*, trans. John Florio (London, 1893), I, 147.

John Nichols, *The Progresses and Public Processions of Queen Elizabeth* (London, 1823), II, 565, text of the poem *Elizabetha Triumphans* by James Aske.

Sir Walter Ralegh, *The History of the World* (London, 1614), sigs. D^v, D2.

Sir Philip Sidney, "An Apology for Poetry," in *Elizabethan Critical Essays*, ed. G. G. Smith (Oxford, 1904), I, 161.

Ethel Seaton, "Marlowe's Map," in *Essays and Studies by Members of the English Association* (Oxford, 1924), X, 13–35.

Hallett Smith, "*Tamburlaine* and the Renaissance," *University of Colorado Studies*, B, II (1945), no. 4, pp. 126–31, on the influence of Le Roy.

A. J. Toynbee, *A Study of History* (Oxford, 1939), IV, 495.

Lorenzo Valla, *On the Donation of Constantine*, ed. C. B. Coleman (New Haven, 1922), p. 31.

III. MORE OF THE SERPENT

Francis Bacon, *A Harmony of the Essays*, pp. 502, 210, on revenge, beauty.

H. S. Bennett (ed.), *The Jew of Malta and The Massacre at Paris* (London, 1931).

F. T. Bowers, *Elizabethan Revenge Tragedy* (Princeton, 1940).

J. L. Cardozo, *The Contemporary Jew in Elizabethan Drama* (Amsterdam, 1925).

E. K. Chambers, *William Shakespeare* (Oxford, 1930), II, 199, quotation from John Weever.

Hardin Craig (ed.), *Machiavelli's "The Prince": An Elizabethan Translation* (Chapel Hill, 1944), p. 72.

T. S. Eliot, *Selected Essays*, p. 105.

Gabriel Harvey, *Marginalia*, p. 108.

Leo Kirschbaum, "Some Light on *The Jew of Malta*," *Modern Language Quarterly*, VII (1946), no. 1, p. 55, an argument for integrity based on the relationship to *Titus Andronicus*.

James Russell Lowell, *The Old English Dramatists* (Boston, 1893), p. 41.

Thomas Newton (ed.), *Seneca His Tenne Tragedies* (London, 1927), I, 61.

Mario Praz, "Machiavelli and the Elizabethans," *Proceedings of the British Academy*, XIII (1928), 49–94; subsumes and modifies previous studies.

Jean-Paul Sartre, *Le Diable et le Bon Dieu* (Paris, 1951), p. 252.

E. E. Stoll, "Shylock," in *Shakespeare Studies* (New York, 1927), pp. 255–336.

Geoffrey Whitney, *A Choice of Emblems* (London, 1586), p. 216.

G. P. Baker, "Dramatic Technique in Marlowe," *Essays and Studies* (Oxford, 1913), IV, 179–82, remarks on Marlowe's treatment of historical material.

H. S. Bennett (ed.), *The Jew of Malta and The Massacre at Paris.*

Bertolt Brecht, *Leben Eduards II von England* (Potsdam, 1924), written in collaboration with Lion Feuchtwanger.

W. D. Briggs (ed.), *Marlowe's "Edward II"* (London, 1914), with introductory sketch on the development of the chronicle play.

C. F. Tucker Brooke, *Life of Marlowe,* pp. 48, 99, 107.

H. B. Charlton and R. D. Waller (eds.), *Edward II* (London, 1933).

John Donne, "Ignatius His Conclave," in *Complete Poetry and Selected Prose,* ed. John Hayward (London, 1929), p. 372.

William Empson, "Two Proper Crimes," *The Nation,* CLXIII (1946), no. 16, pp. 444–5, review of Kocher's *Christopher Marlowe.*

Thomas Heywood, *An Apology for Actors* (London, 1612), sig. F3.

Raphael Holinshed, *Chronicles of England, Scotland, and Ireland* (London, 1807), II, 587, 547.

P. H. Kocher, "François Hotman and Marlowe's *Massacre at Paris,*" *Publications of the Modern Language Association,* LVI (1941), no. 2, p. 365.

Charles Lamb, *Specimens of the English Dramatic Poets* (London, 1835), I, 31.

L. J. Mills, "The Meaning of *Edward II,*" *Modern Philology,* XXXII (1934), no. 1, pp. 11–32, emphasizing the theme of friendship.

Francis Bacon, *Meditationes Sacræ*, in *A Harmony of Essays*, p. 128.

F. S. Boas (ed.), *The Tragical History of Dr. Faustus* (London, 1932).

W. W. Greg, "The Damnation of Faustus," *Modern Language Review*, XLI (1946), no. 29, pp. 97–107.

W. W. Greg (ed.), *Marlowe's "Dr. Faustus": 1604–16* (Oxford, 1950).

William Hazlitt, *Works*, ed. A. R. Waller and Arnold Glover (London, 1902–03), *Lectures on the Age of Elizabeth*, V, 203, reference to Goethe and Coleridge, VII, 313.

W. S. Heckscher, "Was this the face . . . ?" *Journal of the Warburg Institute*, I (1937), no. 4, p. 295, raising the question of Lucian's possible influence, a point anticipated by W. D. Briggs in his edition of *Edward II*, p. 150.

Otto Heller, *Faust and Faustus* (Saint Louis, 1931), one of the few attempts to establish connections between Marlowe and Goethe.

Leo Kirschbaum, "Marlowe's *Faustus*: A Reconsideration," *Review of English Studies*, XIX (1943), no. 75, pp. 225–41.

J. G. Lockhart, *Life of Sir Walter Scott* (Boston, 1901), III, 281.

L. M. Oliver, "Rowley, Foxe, and the *Faustus* Additions," *Modern Language Notes*, LX (1945), no. 6, pp. 391–4.

P. M. Palmer and R. P. More (eds.), *Sources of the Faust Tradition* (New York, 1936), pp. 230, 176, 194, 137, 223, 151, 152.

Henry Crabb Robinson, *On Books and Their Writers*, ed. E. J. Morley (London, 1938), I, 369, 425, on Goethe's opinion of Marlowe, and also Lamb's opinion of Goethe.

George Santayana, *Three Philosophical Poets* (Cambridge: Harvard University Press, 1910), pp. 146–50.

Percy Simpson, "Marlowe's *Tragical History of Dr. Faustus*," *Essays and Studies* (Oxford, 1929), XIV, 20–34, on corruption of the text.

Leonardo da Vinci, *Codice Atlantico* (Milan, 1902), fol. 302, p. 1057.

Leonardo da Vinci, *Notebooks*, ed. Edward MacCurdy (London, 1938), I, 86–8.

VI. THE DEAD SHEPHERD

J. W. Ashton, "The Fall of Icarus," in *Renaissance Studies in Honor of Hardin Craig* (Palo Alto, 1941), pp. 152–9.

C. F. Tucker Brooke, "The Reputation of Christopher Marlowe," *Transactions of the Connecticut Academy of Arts and Sciences*, XXV (1922), quotations from Peele and Drayton, pp. 358–9.

Douglas Bush, *Mythology and the Renaissance Tradition in English Poetry* (Minneapolis, 1932), p. 130.

Léonce Chabalier, *Héro et Léandre et sa fortune en Angleterre* (Paris, 1911).

F. M. Cornford, *Thucydides Mythistoricus* (London, 1907), p. 132.

Thomas Creech (trans.), *T. Lucretius Carus: His Six Books of Moral Philosophy* (London, 1700), p. 4.

T. S. Eliot, *Selected Essays*, pp. 133, 113, incidental remarks from essays on Ben Jonson and Shakespeare's Senecanism.

William Empson, *Seven Types of Ambiguity* (New York, 1931), p. 261.

Sigmund Freud, *Civilization and Its Discontents*, trans. Joan Rivière (London, 1930), p. 51.

Thomas Heywood, *The Hierarchy of the Blessed Angels* (London, 1635), p. 147.

M. H. Jellinek, *Die Sage von Hero und Leander in der Dichtung* (Berlin, 1890).

Charles Lamb, *Specimens of the English Dramatic Poets*, I, 45.

L. C. Martin (ed.), *Marlowe's Poems* (London, 1931).

Michel de Montaigne, *Essays*, I, 237.

M. H. Nicolson, *The Breaking of the Circle* (Evanston, 1950), pp. 149–51.

Liàm O'Flaherty, *Joseph Conrad: An Appreciation* (London, 1930), pp. 7–8.

Mario Praz, "Christopher Marlowe," *English Studies*, XIII (1931), no. 6, pp. 209–23.

I. A. Richards, *Principles of Literary Criticism* (London, 1925), p. 246.

H. E. Rollins (ed.), *England's Helicon*, text of Ralegh's poem, I, 185–6.

Sir Philip Sidney, in *Elizabethan Critical Essays*, I, 157.

Rosemond Tuve, *Elizabethan and Metaphysical Imagery* (Chicago, 1947), pp. 157–61, 252–80.

INDEX